Mysticism

and

Religion

Robert S. Ellwood, Jr.

School of Religion
University of Southern California

PRENTICE-HALL, INC., Englewood Cliffs, New Jersey 07632

Library of Congress Cataloging in Publication Data

ELLWOOD, ROBERT S   (date)
   Mysticism and religion.

   Includes bibliographical references and index.
   1. Mysticism—Comparative studies.   I. Title.
BL625.E44   291.4'2   79–15395
ISBN 0–13–608810–4
ISBN 0–13–608802–3 pbk.

Editorial/Production supervision and design by Judy Brown
Cover design by Bill Agee
Manufacturing buyer: John Hall

Quotation on page 80 from *The Way of the Sufi* by Idries Shah. Copyright © 1968 by Idries Shah. Reprinted by permission of the publishers, E. P. Dutton, and A. P. Watt Limited. Quotation on page 95 from Thomas Merton, *Seeds of Contemplation.* Copyright 1949 by Our Lady of Gethsemani Monastery. Reprinted by permission of New Directions Publishing Corporation and Anthony Clarke Books. Quotation on pages 98–99 from The New English Bible. © The Delegates of the Oxford University Press and the Syndics of the Cambridge University Press 1961, 1970. Reprinted by permission. Quotation on pages 113–15 from Sermon 28 "Blessed are the poor" in *Meister Eckhart: A Modern Translation* by Raymond B. Blakney. Copyright, 1941 by Harper & Row, Publishers, Inc. By permission of the publisher. Quotation on pages 162–65 from *Roll, Jordan Roll: The World the Slaves Made,* by Eugene D. Genovese. Copyright © 1972, 1974 by Eugene D. Genovese. Reprinted by permission of Pantheon Books, a Division of Random House, Inc.

PRENTICE-HALL INTERNATIONAL, INC., *London*
PRENTICE-HALL OF AUSTRALIA PTY. LIMITED, *Sydney*
PRENTICE-HALL OF CANADA, LTD., *Toronto*
PRENTICE-HALL OF INDIA PRIVATE LIMITED, *New Delhi*
PRENTICE-HALL OF JAPAN, INC., *Tokyo*
PRENTICE-HALL OF SOUTHEAST ASIA PTE. LTD., *Singapore*
WHITEHALL BOOKS LIMITED, *Wellington, New Zealand*

Contents

2

Mysticism: Religious Encounter with Ultimate Reality

3

A History of Mysticism

4

The Structure
of Mystical Experience

5

Mysticism and
Religious Thought

6

Mysticism, Worship, and Technique

7

Mysticism and the Sociology of Religion

8
The Mystic Path

9
Postscript: Mysticism and the Future of Religion

For Sherry and Shelly

Preface

Many books on mysticism have been written. Some are accounts of personal experiences, and some are doctrinal treatises or technical manuals outlining the meaning or method of mystical experience within a particular spiritual tradition. Some write of mysticism as though it were identical with occultism and psychical phenomena. Of those books treating mysticism in an objective and scholarly manner, some are literary, most interested in those mystics who were also great masters of poetry or prose; others are philosophic, concerned with the ideas of those accounted mystics; and still others are psychological, focusing on the mental dynamics of mystical experience. Some modern works, such as Margharita Laski's splendid *Ecstasy*, strive to combine all three perspectives.

Many approaches to mysticism deal with it chiefly as an aspect of religion. Others, like Laski and R. C. Zaehner in *Mysticism Sacred and Profane*, distinguish carefully between religious and secular mysticism —the later being nature mysticism, aesthetic experience, love and child-birth experiences, self-transformation processes, and the like which can be shown to parallel the processes of religious mystical experience, but do not employ religious language.

These vast oceans of literature about mysticism, however, have not succeeded in satisfactorily resolving certain fundamental problems. We find little agreement on how the word *mysticism* is most usefully defined, on what experiences we may regard as mystical, and on what discipline we should use for interpretation: psychological, philosophical, theological, or historical. Assuming that a certain psychologically definable experience of ecstasy (self-interpreted as union with all that is) were accepted universally as the mystical experience, opinion would still range from viewing it as the supreme good of human life, to picturing it as a dangerous hallucination likely to lead to fanaticism. Assessment of the relation of mysticism to society and the history of religion is comparably in a state of disarray.

The present book will not solve these problems. It is hoped, however, that some will find useful two tasks it does undertake: to provide an overview of major issues and positions in the study of mysticism, and to attempt a closer integration of mysticism studies with religious studies than has often been achieved so far. Regarding the latter point, my opinion is that, whatever the ultimate nature of mystical experience, religiously interpreted mysticism is inseparable from the rest of religion. All that is observable about mysticism interfaces with the ideologies, practices, and sociologies of its total religious environment. To isolate the mysticism of a religion from this matrix is to make its ecology as unnatural as that of zoo animals taken away from the field. Those studies of mysticism that fail to take seriously the total spiritual and social environment, while sometimes of technical value if well done within a narrow scope, often end up conveying too ethereal and precious a view of mystical experience to be wholly valid for its meaning in life.

In order to emphasize the interaction of mysticism and religion, we shall concentrate on religious mysticism in this book and will use as a working definition of mysticism one that includes religious interpretation of the experience. This is not to impugn the validity of those studies showing a parallel between religious mystical experience and certain secular ecstatic experiences. Often these experiences and religious mysticism are equally intense and transformative for the individual and follow similar processes. But my approach in this connection is fundamentally historical and functional, and it does appear that religiously interpreted ecstasies play a different role in history and society, as well as appearing to be of a different order to the individual. In this respect, then, these experiences *are* different. For it must always be emphasized that the interpretation of an experience is *part* of the experience as it functions in both individual and social psychology. For the sake of clarity, then, I will use the term *mysticism,* which originally and generally has religious—or at least transcendent—connotations, for religiously interpreted intense experiences, and the term *ecstasy* as a more generic word for both religious and secular experiences of that sort.

In this way I hope to stress that religious mysticism is essentially and inseparably a part of religion in the ecology of any religious culture; it is structurally shaped by it while helping impel its psycho-social dynamics. Mysticism is not something from another dubiously religious order that certain adepts tack on to the cultural religion. Rather, just as there is no clear distinction between *mystical experience* and *religious experience,* only differentials of certain tendencies and styles of interpretation; so there is really no clear distinction between *religious experience* and *religion.* Religion, like any social construction, does not really exist except in the experience of those who participate in it. We can really only speak of individuals sometimes heightening that experience with emotionalism, or a clarity beyond emotion, and at certain times directing religious attention toward subjectivity more than social relations.

In this light, I would like to make particularly clear what this book is and is not about, in order to avoid misunderstandings of those accustomed to other perspectives on the subject. I am not so much concerned with mysticism in an abstract and philosophical sense; instead I am concerned with mysticism as experience and interpretation in interaction with religion. My definition is:

> Mystical experience is experience in a religious context which is immediately or subsequently interpreted by the experiencer as encounter with ultimate divine reality in a direct nonrational way which engenders a deep sense of unity, and of living during the experience on a level of being other than the ordinary.

This definition will be discussed later. It is designed particularly to isolate experiences among people of all sorts of personality and sophistication who tend toward the illuminative and unitive states of classical mysticism, and who interpret their experiences as direct encounter with the ultimate religious reality. This definition is a fairly wide-sweeping net and has led to the inclusion of some material that may be surprising to some readers (such as that from ceremonial magic rites and antebellum slave religion).

I do not claim these experiences are the same as the experiences of such classic mystics as Saint Teresa or Ramakrishna. In our discussion of the mystic path in chapter 6, it becomes evident where these experiences might be placed in the classic schema by those who wish to do so. However, since these experiences to the seeker "feel like" what is generally called mystical experience (in other words, direct encounter with the ultimate divine reality), they have as much right as any to participation in a discussion of mysticism and religion.

There is a purist view of mysticism and a type of mysticism studies that seems to want to limit the subject matter to a rather small circle of elect souls, mostly Hindu, Buddhist, Sufi, and Catholic. These elect have described experiences of a calm and sublime unitive sort, determined a fairly clear if difficult path leading toward them, and established a world view based on these experiences. Most of these persons had a good social background—however much they freely gave up for the quest— a good education, and an ability to write (or good biographers). It is certainly not my intention to denigrate these great individuals who have been the subject of many conventional studies in mysticism, nor do I wish to cast aspersions on the value of the scholarly work about them to which I, like so many others, am deeply indebted.

Nonetheless, for the purposes of this book, I do not apologize for adding shamans, slaves, occultists, and evangelical converts. Certainly the experience of an illiterate slave is not the same as that of a monk of steady spiritual discipline schooled in mystical theology. Yet somehow it does not sit well to reject the slave's experience as not meaningful to understanding the phenomena of mysticism. After all, the slave's moan or jubilation comes out of the same depths as the monk's meditation. It is equally a conjunction of religious concepts, practice, and sociology of which is interpreted as direct experience of the divine. Whether the parameters of mysticism are rightly drawn here the reader must judge.

However, in the present book all this is brought together on the grounds that mysticism cannot be delimited on philosophical *a priori* grounds, but only in terms that come out of the experience itself, that is, the experiencer's self-interpretation of it. On that ground—as an experience that seems a direct nonrational contact with the divine—the shaman, evocational magician, evangelical convert, and contemplative are all equal. From it we can go on to speak phenomenologically about structures, types, and paradigms that appear within this assemblage, and that—especially as they illuminate the frontiers between mystician and its religious environment—is what this volume tries to do.

I hope this study will provoke in some readers further reflection on these matters to carry the discussion beyond where I have left it. I hope also these pages will impart to many a sense of the richness and variety of human mystical experience. The hours spent in preparing this book were exhilarating as only time spent near some of the deepest and freshest wellsprings of joy and vision can be. If on these pages a trace of that gladness still shimmers, those hours will have been well spent.

R.S.E.

Some Approaches to Mysticism

A Nation of Mystics?

In January 1975 the distinguished sociologist of religion Andrew Greeley reported the results of a survey he had conducted among Americans concerning "mystical experience." His findings indicated that four out of ten Americans have had, or believe they have had, such an experience. He went on to comment that psychological testing suggested a high correlation between having had a mystical experience and good mental health.[1]

The 1977–1978 Gallup poll on religion in America gives a comparable, though somewhat lower, figure. In response to the question, "Would you say that you have ever had a religious or mystical experience—that is, a moment of sudden religious insight or awakening?" 31 percent responded "yes." Of this group ten percent (one third of those saying "yes") said it was an otherworldly union with a divine being, carrying with it a conviction of the forgiveness of sins and salvation. For five percent it was a dramatic spiritual awakening to nature, and another five percent said it was an experience related to healing. For four percent the experience involved visions, voices, and dreams, and for two percent it was "turning to God in crisis." Another five percent said they couldn't describe it.[2]

Not all these experiences may be mystical by a strict definition. Yet however it is defined, it does not appear that mysticism is a rare and exotic experience limited to monasteries or to a few favored souls. Rather, it is common to ordinary streets and houses, a part of ordinary life if not of everyday life.

What is mysticism and the mystical experience? How does it differ from other religious experiences? If we start with the annals of religious experience that involve contact with transcendent realities, the bazaar of alternative gods and universes they offer is richly stocked.

Sometimes the experience is of blinding light, sometimes of an infinite dark that seems more profound than any light. Sometimes the deity deigns to take on ordinary human form or communicates in voices and visions. Sometimes the experiencer uses the language of ascent, as though being lifted up to a high heaven; sometimes it is descent, as though plunging to the core of something. Then sometimes the extraordinary reality comes to him or her as a fire within or a supernal fire that seems to blaze under the cool surfaces of plants, rocks, and people. Sometimes the experience is ineffably calm, sometimes a bubbling like laughter, sometimes profound rhythmic surges of inexpressible rapture.

Religious experiencers use many metaphors as they struggle to communicate what has come over them. Not only do they use the language of divine light and darkness, but also liquid language—flowing, melting, waving. Also, mystics use pilgrimage language making the contemplative process an inward journey to a secret treasure or erotic language comparing divine passion to the ravishments of human love. Some have even used the language of intoxication. Nonetheless many of them generally know these are only words.

Their experience is not merely one of strong sensation, because they also know why they have been brought to this state. Their experience has that quality William James called, in the passage at the end of this chapter, *noetic*—an experience of both feeling and knowing. Through these raptures one feels he or she is learning something or fully realizing something already known. For James, this is one of the distinctive marks of what is called mysticism.

What then is the mystical experience really like, and what does it mean? We shall begin in this chapter with a study of some concrete cases of possible mystical experience and then look at a number of definitions of mysticism. In the following chapter, we shall endeavor to create and interpret a definition of our own.

The first narrative is an experience of Zen Buddhist *kensho* or enlightenment by an American schoolteacher of German-Jewish background. After a tumultuous life, which included escape from Nazi brutality, she attended with her husband a Zen *sesshin* or period of intensive training.

Zen is a school of Buddhism that emphasizes meditation, called *zazen*, as a means toward Buddhist enlightenment. The use of *koan*, riddles or seemingly meaningless expressions, is also common, especially in dialogue or *dokusan* between a student and a *roshi* or Zen master. Holding these *koan* in mind can stop the activity of the "monkey mind" or stream of consciousness and allow one to realize who he or she is when ordinary thought ceases. To escape from the traps made by ego and simply be one with the Void of the universe is really the meaning of Buddhist enlightenment. The *koan* this writer was given was *Mu*, which means *Nothingness* in Japanese—but it is Nothingness with a positive meaning ultimately, for in it is absolute freedom.

Mrs. A. M., An American schoolteacher, age 38   /   Of Jewish and Gentile parentage, I was born in Germany, where I led the idyllic childhood of an elf in Grimm's fairy tales. My father, a Jew, earned the respect of everyone in our sleepy medieval town, not only for his learning as a doctor of laws but also for his unlimited generosity. My mother, of Lutheran German background, was loved by rich and poor alike for her understanding, her charity, and her joy of life. Completely sheltered from financial and other worries, I grew up in childish innocence.

The words "God" and "religion" were never discussed in my family, as my parents thought it best to leave the choice of Judaism or Christianity to us children when the time was ripe. My early exposure to the Old and New Testaments came in the class in religion at school, where the Lutheran translation of the Bible made a profound impression on me.

Hitler rose to power and everything changed. My childhood dreams blew up in smoke and I was faced with the stark reality of persecution. Brick by brick the Nazis knocked the security from the wall surrounding my ego. The love and respect we had enjoyed disappeared and we knew only loneliness and anxiety.

Friendless, I withdrew into myself and spent most of my time reading. Voraciously I went through my father's vast library, looking for stories of romantic hue, of *Weltschmerz*, in which I imagined myself the heroine.

The climax of persecution for my family came on the infamous ninth of November, 1938, when our home along with other Jewish houses was destroyed by hordes of drunken storm troopers, my father brutally beaten and dragged off to a concentration camp. My mother was in Berlin at the time, and my sister and I were left in desolation, shivering in the attic of our once so beautiful home. In my soul's despair I uttered the first real prayer of my life: "God help us!"

Penniless but with pioneer spirit my family landed by boat in San Pedro, California, on January 24, 1939. Miraculously we had escaped from the clutches of the Nazis and, thanks to the affidavits of my mother's sisters in Los Angeles, now embarked hopefully on a new life.

I pinched pennies for four years and was able to attend the University of California at Los Angeles, Eventually I obtained my master's degree in education and became a full-fledged language teacher.

Now married, on September 3, 1955, my first child, a beautiful blue-eyed girl, was born. With the little money we had and with my husband's GI rights we purchased a tract house near both our schools.

Between home and school my life moved on an even keel. In 1957 my son was born and in 1960 my second daughter. My leisure time I spent reading books on philosophy and religion. The story of Yogananda of India impressed me deeply. Later I became even more profoundly interested in the wisdom of the Orient through a series of lectures I heard on the philosophy of East and West. Zen literature followed, and finally my husband and I formulated a definite plan to visit Japan and India "after our children are a little more mature," in order to seek enlightenment ourselves.

In the meantime one of my teacher friends interested me in joining a group in depth psychology. Somewhat familiar with the Freudian unconscious, I now became acquainted with Jung's viewpoint regarding the possibility of full inner development between the ages of thirty-five and forty. I practiced meeting life's challenges minute by minute, with some success. The only thing, however, which kept me from greater achievement was the lack of a purpose greater than myself. "What am I living for?" I asked myself again and again. I had all material advantages: good health, professional success, a lovely family, leisure time, no financial worries, yet I could find no deep inner satisfaction.

When my husband suggested a vacation in Hawaii in the summer of 1962, I said: "Why not?" In spite of the fact that we were roaming about the beach at Waikiki with three children and two surfboards, both of us were actually looking for something more spiritual. Fortunately my husband discovered a zazen group which was meeting at a private residence in Honolulu. "Why wait till we visit Japan?" we decided. "Let's get accustomed to sitting now. We probably need years of conditioning anyway."

Much to our delight we found that a roshi, an enlightened sage from Japan, was stopping in Hawaii to lead a sesshin before embarking on a tour through the United States. This group of serious zazen participants was small and they welcomed us to join. A little embarrassed by our ignorance of Buddhism, my husband and I took turns at home every other evening with the children while each of us went to do zazen and learn about Buddhism for two weeks prior to the sesshin. The pain of the half-lotus posture chagrined me, because I had been athletic all my life and imagined I could do this comfortably with no training. "Am I ready for this?" I questioned myself. "I came to Hawaii for relaxation, not meditation." A neurotic fatigue crept through my whole body and I can't remember when I have ever been so tired.

Before the sesshin formally opened, Yasutani-roshi's preliminary lectures on zazen were distributed to us. They concluded with a classification of the four distinct grades of aspiration, which ranged from mental and physical health to enlightenment. "I am interested in kensho, but would consider myself fortunate if he assigns me the counting of my breaths," I convinced myself. "Perhaps a novice like me will merely learn to entangle her legs correctly and sit up straight." With awe I looked around the room at the other participants sitting perfectly erect, legs in half-lotus posture, breathing in deep concentration in front of a white curtain.

Time passed quickly. Yasutani-roshi arrived and we were all invited to come on Sunday for zazen and tea. When I saw the little light man, seventy-seven yet bearing himself like fifty-seven, with the sparkling magnetism of youth in his eyes, all doubts vanished. "This is my master, for whom I was going to search all over India and Japan," I told myself, and was filled with a strange feeling of joy.

That same evening at the Soto Mission Yasutani-roshi spoke on the koan Mu and how to penetrate it. His pantomime was so vivid that I understood without knowing a word of Japanese. It seemed to me to be like the anguished joy of bearing a baby, and I was ready for the labor.

The night before sesshin I couldn't sleep. I knew I was going on the trip of my life, and my heart beat with the wild anticipation I feel before climbing a mountain. The next morning I arose at four, sat two sittings without much trouble, and boldly announced to Yasutani-roshi that I was in the fourth category of aspiration, hoping to reach kensho. To my surprise, he asked me further questions but straightway assigned me the koan Mu. Almost at once I regretted my decision!

For two days I worked on Mu half-heartedly, scared to death to face the roshi at dokusan, because to me he represented the strict disciplinarian father of my youth. On top of this, I could never remember the simple Japanese words for "My koan is Mu."

The third day everything changed. Our interpreter, the serenely smiling, "floating" Tai-san, became the angel of vengeance. "This is no tea party," his voice thundered, "but a sesshin! Today I will teach you the meaning of sesshin!" Whereupon he began cracking everyone with his kyosaku, a flat board used on the shoulders of sleepy monks to rouse them to full concentration. I was anything but sleepy, believe me, I was absolutely panic-stricken. That whole day I saw myself walking on the edge of an abyss with water gushing wildly below. Every breath was Mu. "If you let go even once you will fall," I cautioned myself, "so keep going as though you were starting on a long hike up a steep mountain."

That night I had a strange dream. A table with four cups, cloverleaf fashion, was set for a Japanese tea ceremony. Just as I was lifting my cup, a winged Tai-san descended upon me like an angel with a fiery sword, and with a loud Mu! whacked me. I awoke with a start and immediately fell into zazen, this time in a lying position stretched out on my bed, hands over my belly. "You'll never get anywhere in this panic," I tried to quiet myself. "You must relax. Picture a quiet mountain scene at night beneath the star-studded infinite." Slowly, deeply I inhaled and exhaled, and a wondrous peace enveloped me. My belly seemed to expand into a balloon, and a fog which had shortly before enveloped me slowly began to lift, until a sweet nothingness invaded my whole being. I heard the sound of flowing water and slowly came out of my trance. At dokusan I was told that I was on the verge of the great experience of enlightenment.

The fourth day the tension rose to an even higher pitch. Tai-san told the story of a monk so determined to reach kensho that he meditated with a stick of incense in one hand and a knife in the other. "Either I am enlightened by the time the incense is burned out or I shall kill myself," he vowed. With the pain of the burning stub of incense he became enlightened. Tai-san then made the rounds with his kyosaku, reducing everyone, even my husband, to tears.

"I shall reach kensho at this sesshin," I promised myself and sat three sittings in half-lotus. Then I broke down and sobbed bitterly; even in dokusan I could not stop crying. I went upstairs to rest, and when I got up to wash my face I had the strange sensation of water gushing right through me and blinked my eyes. It sounded like the water I had heard the night I experienced voidness.

The morning of the fifth day I stayed home to take care of the children. I should mention that neither my husband nor I attended sesshin full time. We took turns going to the 4 a.m. sitting and went home for almost all meals. I stayed overnight once, my husband not at all.

A little embarrassed at dokusan that afternoon, I confessed that I had not done zazen at home because of too many interruptions. I was told that two people had already reached kensho and that if I exerted myself to the utmost, I could also get kensho. So that night my husband allowed me to stay overnight.

With Mu I went to bed, with Mu I arose the sixth day. "Don't get nervous," Tai-san cautioned, "just concentrate." I listened to these words of wisdom, but was too tired to meditate. My energies were drained. After breakfast I lay down to rest, doing Mu in a horizontal position, when suddenly a glow appeared in front of my eyes as though sunshine were hitting them directly. I clearly heard sounds I had not heard since I was a little girl sick in bed: my mother's footsteps and the rustling of her boxes.

Having had so many strange experiences already at this sesshin, I paid no further heed but continued my concentration on Mu throughout the entire morning's sitting. As I was awaiting dokusan a familiar aroma tantalized my nostrils; it was the tempting smell of my mother's cooking. My eyes glanced at a red cushion on a brown table, the same colors of my grandmother's living-room furniture. A door slammed, a dog barked, a white cloud sailed through a blue sky—I was reliving my childhood in makyo, hallucinations.

At noon, with the roshi's permission, my husband told me that he had achieved kensho. "Now or never!" I told myself. "A pumpkin wife cannot be married to an enlightened husband!" I vividly recalled the story of the youth with the knife and incense. "Death or deliverance!" became my watchword.

I inhaled deeply and with each exhalation concentrated with all my might on Mu. I felt as though I were all air and would levitate any second. I "crawled" into the belly of a hideous, hairy spider. "Mu! Mu! Mu!" I groaned, and I became a big, black Mu. An angel, it seemed, touched me ever so softly on the shoulder, and I fell backwards. Suddenly I realized that my husband and Tai-san were standing behind me, but I could not move; my feet were absolutely numb. They practically carried me outside, and I sobbed helplessly. "I was already dead," I said to myself. "Why did they have to bring me back to life?" At dokusan the roshi told me that this was but a foretaste of kensho, it was not yet realization.

Then I took a little walk and suddenly the whole experience of the last few days seemed utterly ridiculous to me. "That stupid roshi," I remember thinking, "he and his Oriental hocus-pocus. He just doesn't know what he's talking about." At dinner, half an hour later, as I was fumbling with my chopsticks, I felt like getting up and handing him a fork. "Here, old boy, let's get used to Western ways." I giggled at my own joke. Throughout the evening chanting I could hardly keep a straight face. After the roshi's final words I wanted to pick up my bag and walk out, never to return, so unreal did it all seem.

In his first lecture the roshi had told us that Mu was like a red-hot ball stuck in the throat which one can neither swallow nor spit out. He was right, so right. As I look back, every word, every move was part of the deliberate plan of this venerable teacher. His name, "White Cloud" [Hakuun], indeed fits him. He is the greatest, whitest cloud I have ever experienced, a real antidote to the dark atomic mushroom.

Now I was in bed, doing zazen again. All night long I alternately breathed Mu and fell into trances. I thought of the monk who had reached kensho in just such a state of fatigue. Eventually I must have dozed off in complete exhaustion. Suddenly the same light angel touched me on the shoulder. Only this time I awoke with a bright "Ha!" and realized I was enlightened. The angel was my kind tired husband tapping me on the shoulder to waken me to go to sesshin.

A strange power propelled me. I looked at the clock—twenty minutes to four, just in time to make the morning sitting. I arose and calmly dressed. My mind raced as I solved problem after problem. I arrived at the sesshin before four o'clock and accepted an offer of coffee with such a positive "Yes" that I could not believe my own ears. When Tai-san came around with his "sword" I told him not to bother hitting me. At dokusan I rushed into the little cottage my teacher was occupying and hugged and kissed him and shook Tai-san's hand, and let loose with such a torrent of comical verbosity that all three of us laughed with delight. The roshi tested and passed me, and I was officially ushered through the gateless gate.

A lifetime has been compressed into one week. A thousand new sensations are bombarding my senses, a thousand new paths are opening before me. I live my life minute by minute, but only now does a warm love pervade my whole being, because I know that I am not just my little self but a great big miraculous Self. My constant thought is to have everybody share this deep satisfaction.

I can think of no better way to end this account than with the vows I chanted at sesshin every morning:

All beings, however limitless, I vow to save.
Fantasy and delusion, however endless, I vow to cut off.
Dharma teachings, however immeasurable, I vow to master.
Buddha's Way, however lofty, I vow to attain.[3]

Charles Finney Is Converted to Christ

The next account, comes from a different time and religious tradition. The author is Charles Finney (1792–1875), a great American revival preacher and later a college president. In this narrative he tells of his initial conversion out of which came his vocation to preach.

Evangelical Protestant conversion does not have the same sort of philosophical perspective as much other mysticism. Some might ask whether it should be called mystical. A comparison of this passage with the preceding one raises the question of whether there is a meaningful distinction between mystical experience and other intense religious experiences. Are there any major variables besides the religious world view through which each is expressed; if not, does the different world view make it a different experience?

It is significant to note that the period before Charles Finney's conversion has one important feature in common with the period before the schoolteachers experience. For several days prior to his vision, Finney had been much preoccupied with the question of his salvation, had tried praying and—in an act reminiscent of the commitment of *sesshin* —had vowed that he would give his heart to God that day or die in the attempt.

I went to my dinner, and found I had no appetite to eat. I then went to the office, and found that Squire W————had gone to dinner. I took down my bass-viol, and, as I was accustomed to do, began to play and sing some pieces of sacred music. But as soon as I began to sing those sacred words, I began to weep. It seemed as if my heart was all liquid; and my feelings were in such a state that I could not hear my own voice in singing without causing my sensibility to overflow. I wondered at this, and tried to suppress my tears, but could not. After trying in vain to suppress my tears, I put up my instrument and stopped singing.

After dinner we were engaged in removing our books and furniture to another office. We were very busy in this, and had but little conversation all the afternoon. My mind, however, remained in that profoundly tranquil state. There was a great sweetness and tenderness in my thoughts and feelings. Everything appeared to be going right, and nothing seemed to ruffle or disturb me in the least.

Just before evening the thought took possession of my mind, that as soon as I was left alone in the new office, I would try to pray again—that I was not going to abandon the subject of religion and give it up, at any rate; and therefore, although I no longer had any concern about my soul, still I would continue to pray.

By evening we got the books and furniture adjusted; and I made up, in an open fire-place, a good fire, hoping to spend the evening alone. Just at dark Squire W————, seeing that everything was adjusted, bade me good-night and went to his home. I had accompanied him to the door; and as I closed the door and turned around, my heart seemed to be liquid within me. All my feelings seemed to rise and flow out; and the utterance of my heart was, "I want to pour my whole soul out to God." The rising of my soul was so great that I rushed into the room back of the front office, to pray.

There was no fire, and no light, in the room; nevertheless it appeared to me as if it were perfectly light. As I went in and shut the door after me, it seemed as if I met the Lord Jesus Christ face to face. It did not occur to me then, nor did it for some time afterward, that it was wholly a mental state. On the contrary it seemed to me that I saw him as I would see any other man. He said nothing, but looked at me in such a manner as to break me right down at his feet. I have always since regarded this as a most remarkable state of mind; for it seemed to me a reality, that he stood before me, and I fell down at his feet and poured out my soul to him. I wept aloud like a child, and made such confessions as I could with my chocked utterance. It seemed to me that I bathed his feet with my tears; and yet I had no distinct impression that I touched him, that I recollect.

I must have continued in this state for a good while; but my mind was too much absorbed with the interview to recollect anything that I said. But I know, as soon as my mind became calm enough to break off from the interview, I returned to the front office, and found that the fire that I had made of large wood was nearly burned out. But as I turned and was about to take a seat by the fire, I received a mighty baptism of the Holy Ghost. Without any expectation of it, without ever having the thought in my mind that there was any such thing for me, without any recollection that I had ever heard the thing mentioned by any person in the world, the Holy Spirit descended upon me in a manner that seemed to go through me, body and soul. I could feel the impression, like a wave of electricity, going through and through me. Indeed it seemed to come in waves and waves of liquid love; for I could not express it in any other way. It seemed like the very breath of God. I can recollect distinctly that it seemed to fan me, like immense wings.

No words can express the wonderful love that was shed abroad in my heart. I wept aloud with joy and love; and I do not know but I should say, I literally bellowed out the unutterable gushings of my heart. These waves came over me, and over me, and over me, one after the other, until I recollect I cried out, "I shall die if these waves continue to pass over me." I said, "Lord, I cannot bear any more;" yet I had no fear of death.

How long I continued in this state, with this baptism continuing to roll over me and go through me, I do not know. But I know it was late in the evening when a member of my choir—for I was the leader of the choir—came into the office to see me. He was a member of the church. He found me in this state of loud weeping, and said to me, "Mr. Finney, what ails you?" I could make him no answer for some time. He then said, "Are you in pain?" I gathered myself up as best I could, and replied, "No, but so happy that I cannot live."[4]

A comparison of the American schooltecher's experience and Finney's suggests the importance of considering mystical experience in the context of its religious environment. Both individuals obviously considered what happened an encounter with the spiritual ultimate, and both found religious language congenial to its expression. Both experiences had common phenomena: a full suspension of ordinary time perception and a feeling of deep joy—a joy so great it released itself in tears and laughter. Both experiences were subsequent to a period of intense spiritual questing, study, and practice, including a vow to find a spiritual breakthrough now or never.

Yet the differences related to their religious context and world view compromise their intrinsic similarities. In the Zen case, the goal was to find the absolute unitive state paradoxically represented by *Mu* or Nothingness, the "great big miraculous Self." But dualistic means—

the relation of student to roshi, of present pain to hoped-for future bliss —kept intruding as barriers to be fought through and overcome. Finney, on the other hand, gave an impression of wanting to objectify and to make dualistic an experience inward, ineffable, and unconditioned. He at first took the vision of Christ as external and only later came to realize it was "mental." The rapture like "electricity" and "waves of liquid love" is personified as the Holy Spirit.

Yet it could be argued that the differences between the Zennist schoolteacher and Finney are only relatively technical matters of language and interpretation; that both are experiences of the same generic type. The great mystic Saint Teresa of Avila speaks of a high state of prayer in which the soul and all its faculties are wholly united with God, except that the individual remains consciously aware of God and so can appreciate the great work of love God is doing in this individual's life. This high state of prayer is transcended only by the "prayer of quiet" in which a person is so deeply fused with God any sense of Him as external other than to be enjoyed slips away. Then the person knows only still enjoyment of the supreme good, but "cannot comprehend this good thing," so taken up are his or her faculties with sheer joy.[5]

Yet Teresa would see these two states as close and complementary to each other, indeed blending into each other, not as competitive or radically different kinds of religion or religious experience. It is important to perceive these continuities in her states and in experiences as different in context as those of the Zennist and the evangelist. Yet it is also important to observe how much context and the interpretation it suggests can alter the expression, and perhaps the felt nature, of the experience.

Agehananda Bharati's Experience of Oneness, and Mine of the Mystic Sun

Agehananda Bharati is an Austrian who became a Hindu monk and later an anthropologist—his Indian-sounding name was taken in religion. In his book *The Light at the Center,* Bharati argues that mysticism is just a simple, bare experience of oneness—what he calls a "zero experience." All other feelings, symbols, and interpretations are superimposed on that base. We shall return later to this argument.

Bharati describes four or five such experiences he has had under very different circumstances. As a contrast to the preceding two experiences with their conceptual embellishments, I would like to describe the first of these, which occurred when Bharati was only twelve. It should be noted, though, that he had had some background preparation, for he had been reading Hindu literature such as the Upanishads for about a year.

Bharati reports that one evening, as he was falling asleep, the entire world seemed to become one. There was no drama, no special feelings, just "deadeningly sure oneness," centered in himself. For a fraction of a minute, he felt and knew nothing but that oneness. Then the experience gradually faded. But he knew it was the same oneness he had been reading about in the Upanishads.[6]

Quite different from Bharati's experience was my own. I was lying on my back on a carpet floor one quiet afternoon when I was in my early thirties. I was a graduate student in history of religions at the time. I was deliberately attempting to enter into an experimental religious trance, I think of a spiritualistic nature, but was unprepared for what happened.

My eyes closed, I suddenly perceived inwardly a long cloudbank in an azure sky. A brilliant sun rose above the clouds until it was clear of them; as it rose, it seemed to grow brigher and brighter and I sank deeper and deeper into an intense rapture, a sheer intensity of feeling and concentration excluding all else, even joy. Then, after a timeless moment, the sun gradually began to fade and I gradually became more aware of my surroundings; I began to talk to my wife about what happened. I recall that as the sun faded, more detail appeared. I saw small objects, like planets or planes, circling the sun briefly. Then finally it was lost from view but seared indelibly on my memory. The experience was so powerful that for over an hour afterward I could not do anything, not even read; I just sat in a chair quietly recovering strength and mental orientation.

I have never been quite sure what meaning to give this experience. It was not consciously an experience of oneness, for the sun was simply something I saw, as one might see the sun in the sky, not a cosmic essence I was participating in. It was not even explicitly religious, though I could not help but feel, as soon as I thought about it, that it must have some religious or transcendent meaning. The sun is, of course, a virtually universal symbol of supreme godhead or cosmic essence: Christ is spoken of as the sun, Vairocana is the "Great Sun Buddha" of the East, Surya is the object of daily Hindu devotion, and the Solar Logos is a theme of Hellenistic philosophy. But none of these meanings were emblazoned in my experience. All I knew—and know

—was that because of its unique brilliance and intensity, it must encode something very important for me.

Definitions
of Mysticism

What is it that these and the thousands of other accounts of transcendant experience have or do not have in common? A host of scholars have wrestled with this question in attempting to define mysticism and mystical experience. All have felt that something special is, or can be, indicated by the word *mysticism,* something not covered by words like *religion* or *religious experience* or even terms like *trance* or *rapture.* Much in sociological religion is not subjective experience in a sense as acute as in these narratives; on the other hand, people also speak of nonreligious mysticisms—*nature mysticism, political mysticism,* and so forth.

But many feel words pointing to nonintellectual psychological states like *trance* and *rapture* are too restrictive. While these states may be a part of mysticism, the full meaning of mysticism ought to include conceptual and traditional sides. Mystic states are experiences conjoined with concepts that interpret and set them into a tradition like Buddhism, Christianity, or Hinduism. But such interpretations leave out cases like my own, which, equally intense, seem devoid of direct conceptual and traditional content and suggest open-ended transcendence.

Let us now look at some classic definitions of mysticism to see how some giants in the study of mysticism have dealt with the subject.

The medieval philosopher Thomas Aquinas expressed a theme that has been echoed by a number of others when he spoke of mysticism as "the knowledge of God through experience." Comparably, W. R. Inge, in his study of Christian mysticism at the end of the nineteenth century, spoke of mysticism as "the attempt to realise, in thought or feeling, the immanence of the temporal in the eternal, and of the eternal in the temporal."[7] Mystical experience, in other words, is seeing the timeless within the context of life bounded by time, or seeing all things in their ultimate environment, the infinite and eternal. With a definition like this, Inge was able to include in his study on "nature mystics" poets like William Wordsworth and Robert Browning, who saw flashes of the transcendent in the midst of the ordinary.

A few years later, the American Quaker Rufus Jones wrote that mysticism is "the type of religion which puts the emphasis on immediate awareness of relation with God, on direct and intimate consciousness of the Divine Presence. It is religion in its most acute and living stage."[8] This definition, clearly loaded with metaphysical and value assumptions, is in the lineage of Thomas's "knowledge of God through experience." Undoubtedly, it reflects the self-understanding of most theistic mystics.

Slightly more cautious is the approach of Evelyn Underhill in her very influential book *Mysticism*. A contemporary of Inge and Jones, she spoke of mysticism as a quest for truth and reality that goes beyond merely sensory or intellectual spheres, taking on the aspect of a personal passion that must know directly ultimate reality without mediation of mind or sense. She quoted Coventry Patmore to the effect that mysticism is "the science of *ultimates* . . . the science of self-evident Reality, which cannot be 'reasoned about,' because it is the object of pure reason or perception."[9] Mysticism to her is our way of knowing whatever we can know of that which sense and reason cannot conclusively probe. It is directly knowing the being and meaning of ourselves and all that is, including the consciousness by which we reason itself. It cannot be the object of reason because it is the source or essence of the consciousness that reasons. Mysticism is a mirror by which the eye sees itself and sees the light behind the eye.

Inevitably, when an individual obtains that sort of perception, he or she expresses the answer in the language of unity, for it transcends the subject/object distinction. Many commentators of mysticism have therefore emphasized in their definitions that mysticism is an experience of oneness, even though a criterion like this may veer toward an ideological definition. Yet the suprasensory and suprarational eye of the mystic tends to perceive unions where, to ordinary vision, multiplicity and separateness reign. To this eye the many things of this universe are all God or a divine order; the self is really the Buddha-nature or united with Christ.

Thus, the distinguished philosopher of mysticism Walter T. Stace spoke of mysticism as a different kind of consciousness from the ordinary. It is nonsensory and nonintellectual, has no thoughts in the usual sense, and apprehends "an ultimate nonsensuous unity in all things—the One. Stace proceeded to make a useful distinction between two kinds of mysticism. The extrovertive mystic looks out through the physical senses to find that the world is the One; the introvertive mystic finds the One at the bottom of the self, in the depth of human personality.[10]

Similarly, Geoffrey Parrinder claims mysticism is or seeks union.

He also quotes Ben-Ami Scharfstein's comment that "mysticism is a name for our infinite appetites. Less broadly, it is the assurance these appetites can be satisfied."[11] But Parrinder is careful to remember that different religions seek this union or strive to satisfy these infinite appetites in different ways and with different categories. Parrinder specifies three styles of mysticism.

First, theistic mysticism, Parrinder says, seeks union with God but not identity. This would be the mysticism of, among others, the Christian and Jew, who believe the devotee can become united with God in love, but can never *become* God, even as a mirror can glow with solar light but does not become the sun.

Monistic mysticism, Parrinder continues, seeks identity with a universal principle, which may be called divine. This is the approach of much Eastern mysticism. More precisely, we might add, this mysticism wants to discover, experience, and manifest the identity all beings already have with the One that is the root nature of everything. It is intuiting the essence of the mirror until one discovers it is made of light just as is the sun.

Lastly, nonreligious mysticism, Parrinder says, "seeks union with something, or everything, rather like monism.[12] This mysticism would presumably be when an individual's sense of oneness with nature or a beloved or a political cause acquires that quality of knowing, in a way reason cannot; shares the life of what is known;and makes this knowing comparable to religious mysticism.

Psychological and Sociological Approaches

Other scholars have sought out psychological rather than philosophical criteria for mysticism. The important psychologist William James spoke of mysticism as based on an experience having four marks: ineffability (it cannot really be described), a noetic quality (it is an experience of gaining knowledge), transiency (it does not last long), and passivity (it simply happens to the experiencer).[13] Although one could question the absoluteness of each of these characteristics, they do represent important aspects of much mystical experience and have been basic to much subsequent discussion.

Marghanita Laski made a careful study of the exprience of "transcendent ecstasy," which is related to what we commonly call mystical experience. Ecstasy, she says, names "a range of experiences character-ized by being joyful, transitory, unexpected, rare, valued, and extraordi-nary to the point of often seeming as if derived from a preternatural source."[14]

Her study of ecstatic experiences is based on interviews with 63 people in her circle of acquaintances in contemporary England, com-pared with a similar number of literary and religious accounts of mysti-cal experiences past and present. The trigger for the ecstatic experiences of the interviewers was in some cases religious, in others love, child-birth, nature, aesthetic rapture, and the like. But in all cases terms or categories of feeling like the followed emerged:

> Feelings of new life, satisfaction, joy, salvation, purification, glory; new and/or mystical knowledge; loss of words, images, sense; knowledge by identification; unity, eternity, heaven; loss of worldliness, desire, sorrow, sin; up-feelings [of ascent, soaring etc.]; contact; enlargement and/or im-provement; loss of self; inside-feelings; loss of difference, time, place; light and/or heat feelings; peace, calm, liquidity feelings; ineffability; release; pain-feelings; dark-feelings; loss of limitation.[15]

Laski's work states that ecstasy, as an experience of rare joy sug-gesting contact with ultimate meaning and transcendent origin, is not as restricted as might have been supposed to particular (i.e., religious) triggers or to particular self-interpretations of a philosophical cast, such as universal deity or oneness. At the same time, Laski suggests the experience calls forth the most ultimate and transcendent words avail-able to the individual in the context of his/her background and world view. These words are either religious or religious-substitute ones. Laski believes when one compares the contemporary accounts with the classic literature of mysticism, these parallels in language are obvious. Thus, a sixteen-year-old who said she did not believe in God "or in anything supreme" told Laski about the ecstatic experiences that poetry and music induced in her in words like these: "forgetting oneself . . . oneself ceasing to matter and no longer being connected with everyday things . . . time seems to stop . . . you're not anywhere, and despite not feeling anywhere in particular, feeling in unity with everything . . . it feels to a certain extent like a great climax which has built up—this thing has been seething inside you and suddenly it comes out."[16] The parallels in this account with basic motifs of classic religious mysticism East and West are obvious: the forgetting of self, reminiscent of the "falling away" (fana in the Sufi term) of contemplative or samadhic absorption;

the unitive awareness; the sense of climax and release involving the discovery of a new dimension of inner reality.

For writers of the psychoanalytic school, understanding of mysticism has been intimately bound up with their view of its psychological genesis. Sigmund Freud saw mystical states as "oceanic" consciousness, in which the distinction of subject and object (individual and what is outside) is washed away into a limitless unity. This unity he associated with the primal consciousness of the womb or the newborn; mysticism was a regressive "return" to that state that avoided facing "reality."

The psychoanalyst James H. Leuba defined the experience of mysticism in a way compatible with the definitions of more sympathetic writers. He said it is "any experience taken by the experiencer to be a contact (not through the senses, but 'immediate,' 'intuitive') of union of the self with a larger-than-self, be it called the World-Spirit, God, the Absolute, or otherwise."[17] His explanation emphasized expression of frustrated sexual drives. Leuba conceded, however, that all mysticism is not directly sexual, but he did view it as motivated by the Freudian "pleasure principle"—it was a more pleasureable state of consciousness than available alternatives. But even if it were not what it seems, under certain conditions and in moderation, mystical states could have a beneficial psychological effect.

Other commentators have rightly reminded us that mysticism does not exist apart from the broader context of religion, society, and history. If mysticism naturally produces psychological interpretations, it equally produces sociological and historical interpretations. The range is broad. Some, like Marx, contend that mystical movements are essentially reactions to political exploitation in which people of certain classes have no means of self-fulfillment and vehicles for protest except in religion. Others, like the Hindu philosopher Sri Aurobindo, assert that mystics are in the vanguard of evolution toward a superior humanity and a more perfect social order.

In the eyes of the great sociologist of religion Ernst Troeltsch, mysticism ("simply the insistence upon a direct and present religious experience")[18] fundamentally has no need for religious forms or organization. Yet because persons with a mystical bent still live in society, their desire for direct experience regardless of religious forms and institutions is bound to have an effect on society. The winds of the mystical free spirit may sometimes loosen the seams of the social fabric, or sometimes vitalize it by filling it with billowing energy, but in any case mysticism works at cross-purposes to the tendency of religion to institutionalize.

Mysticism, for Troeltsch, is the third form of religious expression in society, after the church and the sect, both of which in their own ways tend toward the conservatism of all institutions. Mysticism does sometimes form groups, but they are not held to be absolute; instead they are only temporary fraternities in which the emphasis is on the experience rather than the group. Equally, mystics may find no difficulty in worshiping according to the norms of their community, since compared to their inner experiences the outer forms are neither important enough to reject nor embrace. Thus, Troeltsch said mysticism has two forms: a "narrow, technical, concentrated sense" that undercuts structure and forms new groups and a "wider form" that is diffuse and supports the prevailing religious structures since its practice does not oppose them.[19]

Much in this Troeltschean picture is less than adequate. He bases his portrayal too narrowly on Protestant mysticism in Europe before 1800. He avoids the question of what to make of the sociology of mysticism in traditions, such as Hinduism and Buddhism where transcendent mystical experience is ostensibly the central goal, and highly institutionalized forms for attaining it are available.

Nonetheless, Troeltsch's monumental pioneering work, together with that of his contemporaries Max Weber and Emile Durkheim, is basic to any sociology of mysticism. All emphasized that mysticism is part of society, that the mystic does not exist in an empyrean abstracted from society, that instead his experiences have directly or indirectly a social impact, and also that these (an idea stressed by Weber and Durkheim) may in part derive from the feelings of nonrational oneness engendered from living in society. After all, the first and usually most powerful other-than-self with which we are united is society.

Mysticism, Tradition, and Oneness

In an earlier generation, James Bissett Pratt perceived three great elements of religion working together: the traditional, rational, and volitional or mystical. The last, in his definition, embraces the emotional and feeling faculties. This mystical element is either a sense of the presence of a being or a reality attained through means other than the ordinary perception processes or the reason. Mysticisim refers to the *sense* or *feeling* of this presence, not just to intellectual *belief* in it. Pratt perceptively noted that mysticism has much in common with the rational element in religion, in contrast to traditional and actual religion. Both judge traditional and actual religion in terms of an ideal created, each in its own way, within the mind.[20] Both reason and mysticism, then, can oppose tradition. More recently, Frits Staal has argued strongly that mysticism and reason are not incompatible, but come together when mysticism is not merely studied, but actually practiced.[21]

In the introduction to his classic work *Major Trends in Jewish Mysticism,* Gershom Scholem has also developed contextual qualifications concerning mysticism. Mysticism, he says, historically comprises much more than the experience, even though this experience lies at its root. No such thing as mysticism in the abstract exists, only mystics of particular traditions: Jewish, Christian, Buddhist, and so forth. While a common element, which he speaks of as a "pantheistic trend," may be found in them all, each actual mystic can only be understood in the context of his or her religious system. For example, some mysticism is unitive, but theologically Jewish mysticism is not. Finally, Scholem notes, mysticism emerges as a definite stage in religious history. Appearing in its classic forms with the transition from naive archaic belief in anthropomorphic gods to more sophisticated religion, mysticism "seeks to transform the God whom it encounters in its own social environment from an object of dogmatic knowledge into a novel and living experience and intuition."[22]

This relating of mysticism to a particular historical period depends, of course, on how narrow or wide a net one's definition of mysticism is. Is archaic shamanism mystical, or would one restrict the term to the trances and rigorously ascetic practices that are more precisely identifiable with the period of transition from archaism Scholem has in mind? But the perception that mysticism has a history and historical context is very important, particularly because mysticism's claim to contact with transhistorical reality has often so fascinated observers (as well as mystics themselves) that some ignore the importance of its historical context.

Agehananda Bharati's book, *The Light at the Center,* illustrates the importance of context for the mystical experience. The reader will recall that Bharati insists the mystical experience is always the same: a bare experience of *oneness,* which he calls the "zero experience." This experience, he says, is "like distilled water, tasteless." Since there is little to say about this zero experience, what mystics really talk about in discussing it are the "ramifying events, euphoric or visionary" associated in the mystic's consciousness with the experience. The way mystics describe these events derive from context and individual personality; their accounts may be compared to the personal "style" of different artistic performers. But, Bharati claims, variations in style are most apparent when artists perform below their peak; the peak performances of great musicians and dancers, like peak sexual orgasms, are simple, clear, powerful, and selfless; they negate individual and context. It is imperfect performances and orgasms below the peak that inflate the element of personality and context; it is imperfect mysticism that is ridden with personality, ideology, and contextual symbols.[23]

Zero experience itself is transient, lasting, perhaps like Bharati's, less than a minute. However, it makes an indelible imprint on the consciousness that must then be interpreted. In a colorful image, Bharati compares the zero experience to the blastoff of a rocket. Leading up to zero and the moment of lift has been the countdown in decreasing numbers: eight . . . seven . . . six . . . and on down. After blastoff and the spaceship's flight, comes re-entry into the atmosphere of earth.[24] We can compare this re-entry with Laski's assertion that the ecstatic experience is brief; she says it is of two types, *tumescence,* in which the subject feels full of the ecstatic surge, and *withdrawal,* characterized by a sort of blissful quiet emptiness and absence of self-consciousness. The brief ecstasy, however, is induced by a trigger, which may bear resemblance to Bharati's countdown or at least its onset, and is followed by a lingering euphoria that may be like the stage of Bharati's "ramifying events, euphoric or visionary" and the re-entry. Presumably, in this stage, symbols and attitudes much more derived from the personality and context of the mystic would raise their heads to assimilate and express the distilled water of the zero experience itself.

Bharati's book is highly personal, often opinionated, and much less empirical or judicious than Laski's. But the writing is vivid and many of its ideas provocative and worth further development. We can make use of the metaphor of the zero experience, or point experience of ecstasy, surrounded by its numina of trigger, countdown, euphoria, and re-entry.

But considering the empirical data of Laski and others, I am not convinced that cosmic oneness is *necessarily* the basic motif of the zero experience, though it often is a main motif, and even more often is a philosophic interpretation inseparable from the experience in the experiencer's mind.

It seems to me the fundamental nature of the experience is well put in Laski's words "transcendent ecstasy." In the zero experience a person knows he or she is being and perceiving in a profoundly different way from ordinary; he or she is moving to a different state of consciousness that is likely to be ontologically interpreted as moving subjectively to a different reality or angle of perception. This ecstatic state is so intense that, for its brief moment, it is all-absorbing. This absorption gives it a one-pointed, unitive aspect that easily transfers to conscious symbols of oneness: philosophically, the sense of cosmic oneness; in visionary terms, a single focal symbol such as the brilliant sun. Without denying validity to the Jamesian noetic quality of mystical experience, we may thus note that the mystical states characteristic reality-perceptions and corresponding psychological states can be closely linked.

We must be very careful, however, about falling into easy psychogenic explanations of mystical experience. Prematurely turning to them usually involves the use of inadequately examined philosophical presuppositions; even more to the point, this type of explanation inhibits further investigation of mysticism because it establishes barriers to empathy with the mystic and his reality. The relation of mind, sensory awareness, and reality is, so far as I can see, an incredibly complex one to which no one has any easy answer. It is by no means self-evident that all perceptions growing out of a zero experience or mystical state are necessarily invalidated because one understands something about the psychology of that state, anymore than all that has the appearance of reason is actually true. We need to exercise caution in judgment and maintain long the open-minded empathy needed to understand mysticism from the experiencer's point of view.

We must then be aware of the basic characteristics of mysticism as it is experienced. In the examples of experience already presented, we were probably first impressed with their ecstatic intensity. Someone simply had a feeling of really *experiencing* something. Understandably, this led us to believe that something must have been there to be experienced. When we see a cat with our physical senses, we naturally assume a cat is there; when we experience something extraordinary with the mind, we likewise tend to assume something more than the mind, at least the ordinary mind, is there.

One can, of course, be mistaken about these perceptions. The cat might have been a small dog seen out of the corner of the eye or an illusion created by a holograph or a hallucination caused by alcohol. But the presumption of mystics that their experiences are, in Stace's terms, nonsensory and nonintellectual ways of apprehension—knowing by the brain *directly* without the mediation of sensory data or rational processes—is not to be dismissed out of hand as utterly fanciful. It is in fact what *seems* to be happening, as surely as seeing a cat seems to be seeing a cat.

Another characteristic of the mystical experience is its transformative impact. The first two experiences, those of the American schoolteacher and of Charles Finney, deeply affected the subsequent courses of their lives. Bharati argues that the zero experience has no particular effect on a person's subsequent morals or manners—anymore than drinking a glass of distilled water—except as he or she permits it to by associating it with such "lower" things as doctrine and feeling. Undoubtedly, an individual can find an entire gamut of responses to the experience, from none to life-transformation. But it seems that Bharati's attempt to demystify mysticism is overly iconoclastic at this point; I would suggest the experience is so intense that an individual must adjust his or her paradigms of self and reality to take it into account—though conversion to some sort of religion is not necessarily the only way. Yet even if, as Bharati seems to suggest, we can respond to mystical experience in simply an esthetic manner—as something to be enjoyed when it comes but which does not require a change of morals or life-intention—that in itself is a response implying a life-style, a life-style that might not have been actualized without the experiences.

Finally, as we have emphasized, the experience takes place within a context both personal and social that contributes heavily to its interpretation. The experience may speak for itself as authentic and noetic, but the words that it speaks will make it in many cases an experience of Buddhist reality or of conversion to Christ and knowing the Holy Spirit or of the fruits of Upanishadic study—though in some instances, like my own, it may not be so readily identified with a tradition.

Moreover, sometimes in our modern pluralistic world the wires get crossed, so that Westerners have Hindu experiences and Chinese see visions of Christ. But in any case there is likely to be an addendum of what James and Laski called overbelief—a religious or philosophic belief immediately attached to the experience. This overbelief also easily becomes translated into technique—postures, meditation on particular themes, and so on—which as the re-entry code of the initial experience become a countdown system for repeating it, a trigger that comes to function smoothly through continued use, at least until it wears out. Moreover, triggers and techniques, like those of yoga or Zen, may be culturally transmitted and have been used even to produce the initial experience, giving it an almost automatic interpretive overbelief.

Mystical experience then seems to emerge as a sharp point of short duration, a point in itself without intrinsic meaning or even conscious content, but of such a nature as to attract a transcendent meaning and technique to reach it. In this respect one is reminded of the elaborate preparations and culinary symbology that goes into confecting and consuming a gourmet meal for the relatively brief moments spent swallowing the food. But who is to say these anticipatory hours, which make our experiences so different from that of a hypothetically spontaneous "child of nature," are not a part of the experience and as much—or more —its essence to us as social beings than the moment of consummation?

Yet these precedings also leave us with ambiguities. For just as cuisine and styles of lovemaking vary from culture to culture, so does the apparatus of mysticism, and in religious matters at least, doubt is destructive of consummate intensity. But the conclusion seems unavoidable that for all the innumerable meanings given mysticism, one is left with an enigmatic state of consciousness too full or too empty for intrinsic content, but so richly suggestive of transcendence in its very uncompromising absoluteness that it calls for whatever concepts of the ultimate one can bring to it. It is the taste of the God who is known by unknowing.

Some Approaches to Mysticism: Reading Selection

The following passage is from the classic discussion of mysticism by William James (1842–1910), the distinguished American psychologist. Originally given as the Gifford Lectures in Edinburgh in 1901–1902, this material was first published as part of *The Varieties of Religious Experience.* In the passage below James presents the previously cited four characteristics of the mystical state.

Over and over again in these lectures I have raised points and left them open and unfinished until we should have come to the subject of Mysticism. Some of you, I fear, may have smiled as you noted my reiterated postponements. But now the hour has come when mysticism must be faced in good earnest, and those broken threads wound up together. One may say truly, I think that personal religious experience has its root and centre in mystical states of consciousness; so for us, who in these lectures are treating personal experience as the exclusive subject of our study, such states of consciousness ought to form the vital chapter from which

Source: William James, *The Varieties of Religious Experience* (New York: Random House Modern Library), pp. 370–72. Originally published 1902 by Longmans, Green and Company, London.

the other chapters get their light. Whether my treatment of mystical states will shed more light or darkness, I do not know, for my own constitution shuts me out from their enjoyment almost entirely, and I can speak of them only at second hand. But though forced to look upon the subject so externally, I will be as objective and receptive as I can; and I think I shall at least succeed in convincing you of the reality of the states in question, and of the paramount importance of their function.

First of all, then, I ask, What does the expression "mystical states of consciousness" mean? How do we part off mystical states from other states?

The words "mysticism" and "mystical" are often used as terms of mere reproach, to throw at any opinion which we regard as vague and vast and sentimental, and without a base in either facts or logic. For some writers a "mystic" is any person who believes in thought-transference, or spirit-return. Employed in this way the word has little value: there are too many less ambiguous synonyms. So, to keep it useful by restricting it, I will do what I did in the case of the word "religion," and simply propose to you four marks which, when an experience has them, may justify us in calling it mystical for the purpose of the present lectures. In this way we shall save verbal disputation, and the recriminations that generally go therewith.

1. *Ineffability.* —The handiest of the marks by which I classify a state of mind as mystical is negative. The subject of it immediately says that it defies expression, that no adequate report of its contents can be given in words. It follows from this that its quality must be directly experienced; it cannot be imparted or transferred to others. In this peculiarity mystical states are more like states of feeling than like states of intellect. No one can make clear to another who has never had a certain feeling, in what the quality or worth of its consists. One must have musical ears to know the value of a symphony; one must have been in love one's self to understand a lover's state of mind. Lacking the heart or ear, we cannot interpret the musician or the lover justly, and are even likely to consider him weak-minded or absurd. The mystic finds that most of us accord to his experiences an equally incompetent treatment.

2. *Noetic quality.* —Although so similar to states of feeling, mystical states seem to those who experience them to be also states of knowledge. They are states of insight into depths of truth unplumbed by the discursive intellect. They are illuminations, revelations, full of significance and importance, all inarticulate though they remain; and as a rule they carry with them a curious sense of authority for aftertime.

These two characters will entitle any state to be called mystical, in the sense in which I use the word. Two other qualities are less sharply marked, but are usually found. These are:—

3. *Transiency.* —Mystical states cannot be sustained for long. Except in rare instances, half an hour, or at most an hour or two, seems to be the limit beyond which they fade into the light of common day. Often, when faded, their quality can but imperfectly be reproduced in memory;

but when they recur it is recognized; and from one recurrence to another it is susceptible of continuous development in what is felt as inner richness and importance.

4. *Passivity.*—Although the oncoming of mystical states may be facilitated by preliminary voluntary operations, as by fixing the attention, or going through certain bodily performances, or in other ways which manuals of mysticism prescribe; yet when the characteristic sort of consciousness once has set in, the mystic feels as if his own will were in abeyance, and indeed sometimes as if he were grasped and held by a superior power. This latter peculiarity connects mystical states with certain definite phenomena of secondary or alternative personality, such as prophetic speech, automatic writing, or the mediumistic trance. When these latter conditions are well pronounced, however, there may be no recollection whatever of the phenomenon, and it may have no significance for the subject's usual inner life, to which, as it were it makes a mere interruption. Mystical states, strictly so-called, are never merely interruptive. Some memory of their content always remains, and a profound sense of their importance. They modify the inner life of the subject between the times of their recurrence. Sharp divisions in this region are, however, difficult to make, and we find all sorts of gradations and mixtures.

These four characteristics are sufficient to mark out a group of state of consciousness peculiar enough to deserve a special name and to call for careful study. Let it then be called the mystical group.

Notes

[1]Andrew Greeley, "Is America a Nation of Mystics?" *New York Times Magazine,* January 26, 1975.

[2]*Religion in America: The Gallup Opinion Index 1977–1978* (Princeton, N.J.: American Institute of Public Opinion, 1978), pp. 53–55.

[3]From Philip Kapleau, *The Three Pillars of Zen.* New York and Tokyo: John Weatherhill, Inc., 1967. Copyright in Japan 1965 by Philip Kapleau. Pp. 239–45. Reprinted by permission.

[4]From Charles G. Finney, *Memoirs* (New York: A. S. Barnes & Company, 1876), pp. 18–21.

[5]J. M. Cohen, trans. *The Life of St. Teresa* (Harmondsworth, England: Penguin Books, 1957), pp. 117–22.

[6]Agehananda Bharati, *The Light at the Center* (Santa Barbara, Calif.: Ross-Erikson), p. 39.

[7]W. R. Inge, *Christian Mysticism,* 7th ed. (London: Methuen & Co., 1933), p. 5.

[8]Rufus Jones, *Studies in Mystical Religion* (London: Macmillan & Co., 1909), p. xv.

[9]Evelyn Underhill, *Mysticism* (London: Methuen & Co., 1911), p. 29.

[10]Walter T. Stace, *The Teachings of the Mystics* (New York: New American Library, 1960), pp. 13–15.

[11]Ben-Ami Scharftstein, *Mystical Experience* (New York: Penguin Books, 1974), p. 1.

[12]Geoffrey Parrinder, *Mysticism in the World's Religions* (New York: Oxford University Press, 1976), p. 15.

[13]William James, *The Varieties of Religious Experience* (New York: The Modern Library), pp. 371–72. Originally published by Longmans, Green and Company, London, 1902.

[14]Marghanita Laski, *Ecstasy: A Study of Some Secular and Religious Experiences* (London: The Cresset Press, 1961), p. 5.

[15]Laski, *Ecstasy,* p. 41.

[16]Laski, *Ecstasy,* p. 387.

[17]James H. Leuba, *The Psychology of Religious Mysticism* (New York: Harcourt Brace Jovanovich, Inc., 1925), p. 1.

[18]Ernst Troeltsch, *The Social Teaching of the Christian Churches, Volume 2,* trans. Olive Wyon (New York: Macmillan Publishing Co., Inc., 1931), p. 730.

[19]Troeltsch, *Social Teaching,* p. 734.

[20]James Bissett Pratt, *The Religious Consciousness* (New York: Macmillan Publishing Co., Inc., 1921), p. 337.

[21]Frits Staal, *Exploring Mysticism: A Methodological Essay* (Berkeley: University of California Press, 1975).

[22]Gershom Scholem, *Major Trends in Jewish Mysticism* (New York: Schocken Books, Inc., 1946), pp. 5–6, 10.

[23]Bharati, *The Light at the Center,* pp. 80–81.

[24]Bharati, *The Light at the Center,* p. 48.

Mysticism: Religious Encounter with Ultimate Reality

2

Definitions

How can mystical experience be usefully defined? Answering that problem will be the task of the present chapter. We shall first discuss the meaning and limitations of definition. Next we shall present a working definition of mystical experience and discuss how this definition distinguishes between mystical and other religious experiences. We shall then take up the matter of religious context in relation to mysticism, and finally we'll deal with two important qualities of the mystical experience: its tendency for self-validation and its nature as a discrete state of consciousness.

First, let us reflect on just what a definition of mysticism is and is not and for what purpose it is constructed. Presumably, though every human religious experience is in some respects unique, it also possesses important relationships to other religious experiences. Undoubtedly, an infinite number of typological lines could be drawn through this body of material, setting off categories according to diverse variables: content, predominant symbols, emotional tone. Each might be useful for a different task; no set of variables is intrinsically more basic or important than others as interpretative tools. After all, it is not these variables that have reality, but the immense number of unique experiences in human beings themselves. Categories are important only insofar as they provide instruments that isolate and interrelate certain experiences from the others in ways that aid one in understanding.

Our task is that of comprehending religious experiences like those presented in the first chapter, which seem to be so intense they exclude other considerations and which seem to involve immediate contact or even union with absolute reality. The job, then, is first to establish the parameters of a category that, so far as is humanly possible, separates those experiences from others.

We shall call this category mystical experience and refer to the existence of such experiences and their interpretation as mysticism. The reason for this terminology is that, despite its notorious ambiguities, the term *mysticism* has traditionally been used in discussion of similar experiences. Indeed that discussion has been largely responsible for recognition of such experiences as a discrete category. The question remains whether it is an authentic category in that it isolates experiences that actually belong together, or whether mysticism is a false category that obscures more than it clarifies because it glosses over important distinctions or makes faulty distinctions based on subjective preferences.

This is a very important issue. Strong cases can be made—and have been made—that categorizing mysticism confuses more than it clarifies. For instance, it obscures the fact that experience in each religious tradition is unique to that tradition and can only be understood in that context rather than in a world-wide suprareligious category like mysticism. A strong case can also be made that the concept of mysticism implies a covert metaphysical position inappropriate to scholarly religious studies. Furthermore, it can be argued that all religious experience is primarily the same. To call some of it mystical on the basis of the experiencer's self-understanding of it as a union with God or contact with ultimate reality while denying the title to psychologically similar experiences that the experiencer interprets differently, perhaps even nonreligiously, is to confuse philosophical interpretation with psychological state.

I myself accept the thrust of these objections insofar as they apply to the psychological experience. However, these arguments do not vitiate the category "mysticism," because religious experience itself does not exist apart from the interpretation given the experience, however culturally conditioned and metaphysical that interpretation. The fact that we are speaking of *religious* experience means we are speaking of experience *interpreted* in religious language, rather than raw inchoate feeling.

Mysticism, then, is only a subcategory of the already interpretive category of religious experience. In fact, mysticism is more a category of interpretation than experience, though the interpretation may be immediate with the experience. Its interpretation may seem self-evident as the experience occurs and may even deepen the experience for the experiencer. In other words, the explanation becomes inseparable from the experience. Mysticism is, finally, an important category because it illustrates the importance of interpretation to the experiential essence of religion.

We can probably accept the theorem that no significant difference exists between the religious experiences of different cultures or between mystical and nonmystical ecstatic experiences, apart from those differences injected by interpretation. This is a statement that cannot be proved, and indeed must be set against another already stated theorem: every religious experience is in some way unique. On the other hand, a verifiable difference existing between mystical and nonmystical experiences apart from interpretation would be even harder to prove scientifically, though it might be postulated on philosophical or theological grounds.

In any case, the important idea is that in all *religious* experience we *do* have an interpretation as part of that experience, which not only shapes its internal development and its psycho-social impact, but also shapes the "visible" face by which it is known to the world. Moreover, this interpretation provides a way to compare and contrast various experiences. When we say, for example, that particular Christian, Muslim, and Hindu experiences have mysticism in common however much they may differ in other respects, we really point to the similarity or difference in the experiencer's interpretation. Mysticism, then, is an interpretive category. Here is our definition:

> Mystical experience is experience in a religious context that is immediately or subsequently interpreted by the experiencer as encounter with ultimate divine reality in a direct nonrational way that engenders a deep sense of unity and of living during the experience on a level of being other than the ordinary.

The Meaning
of the Definition

Let us consider each of these qualifications in our definition. First, the "encounter with ultimate divine reality" means the experience has a quality of unconditionedness; in other words, one feels there is nothing more that could be contacted. The experiencer feels he or she has touched the reality behind the outward manifestations of religion. He or she uses, then, whatever is the relevant language of ultimacy, which in traditional societies will generally be religious and metaphysical. This language suggests the powers that made, sustain, and are the "being" of all things. Speaking of this encounter as divine indicates a religious interpretation, though the interpretation may make it God, God above God, the Void, and so forth.

This characteristic does not necessarily exclude from mysticism encounters with angelic beings or with one of the gods within a polytheistic system. After all, such encounters are often described in terms that make it clear the engagement was as absolute an experience as any couched in monistic or monotheistic phraseology. In these instances, it seems the particular place of the encountered entity in the pantheon is less important than whether the experience was a breakthrough to the ultimate, and consequently transformed the individual. Later in this book we shall, for example, confront the case of a Brazilian woman who was healed of mental illness in an at least quasi-mystical experience of possession by a minor deity of one of the Afro-Brazilian cults. We will also read of a similar encounter with the ancient goddess Astarte in the context of modern ceremonial magic. In each case it will appear that, for the experiencer, the theoretically polytheistic deity was, for the moment, *the* god with which the individual was in transformative contact.

The next part of our definition (that we perceive this encounter in a direct, nonrational way) indicates that though the experience communicates a sense of being a real awareness, it seems to happen during a partial or full suspension of the normal means of perception. The senses and ordinary awareness of time and space have mostly faded. While a total eclipse of awareness may not occur, the experiencer is so engaged in the transcendent experience as to pay little heed to the many things one usually sees and hears; an hour, for instance, may pass in what seemed a few minutes.

All these symptoms of nonrational awareness suggest the individual sees the object of the experience with some nonsensory organ of perception. It implies simply "having" the experience without the engagement of the rational "figuring it out" mind. Such a rational mind can keep track of time and the meaning of things comprehended with the common senses, but is out of its depth in transcendent experiences and can only "let it happen"—James' "passivity" as a characteristic of mysticism, or Teresa's enjoyment without comprehension of what is enjoyed.

What is that nonsensory organ of perception? The answer is perhaps indicated by the next criterion of our definition of mystical experience: the sense of unity or of "being one with the ultimate." If one knows divine reality in the experience, yet not by sensory or rational means, perhaps it is because they are no longer necessary. After all, if one *united* with the reality being experienced one would know it from inside, in the same way that reality knows its own self and I know myself. Thus, many descriptions of mystical experience (though not all) are replete with language of union with God or a god, with the All, with nature or the universe, with the Absolute.

One must be cautious in taking such language as directly indicative of what happened in the experience itself, for sometimes it is doubtless a metaphysical or conventional explanation. Yet obviously the experiencer must select such language because it points to something important about the experience. The language of oneness between the experience and the object must derive, as indicated, from the logic of a nonsensory and nonrational way of knowing.

When the individual uses language of oneness with the one divine reality, it likewise derives from the absoluteness of the experience. That experience is of a nature that excludes consideration of anything but itself while it is going on. It thus proclaims both psychologically and metaphysically that its reality is the only reality on a level of meaning as powerful as is the experience itself.

The experience suggests one is now operating on a different level from the ordinary. Often the experiencer expresses that realization in talk of uncommon laws and principles and unusual entities (like the seraphim seen by Isaiah). This other world may seem like a reversal of the ordinary: it is light where the ordinary is dark, inner where the ordinary is outer, blessed where the ordinary is cursed. Though laws on this level are hidden and occult and their purposes not widely known, they explain much about the outer world and its destiny. This quality of mystical experience may provide the beginnings of the mystic's message to the world.

Experience Religious
But Not Mystical

In order to clarify the mystical experience, let us consider what would be an experience interpreted as religious, but *not* mystical. Some examples might be these:

1. A joyful and deeply felt acceptance of salvation as already granted by God. This instance might be a Christian who accepts a highly "forensic" or predestinarian theory of atonement or a Pure Land Buddhist who accepts through simple faith the saving grace already offered in Amida. This experience might be profoundly transformative for the individual yet might involve no actual encounter with the ultimate or direct nonrational perception.

2. Intellectual enthusiasm for the ideas of religion or spiritual philosophy (such as the excitement one can feel while reading a book that makes everything fall wonderfully into place) yet which is still an encounter with the ideas of religion rather than the reality behind them.

3. A strong experience of commitment to certain moral or ethical principles that derive from one's religious world view. This experience would obviously be a deep one related to religion, but would not involve direct encounter with its ultimate reality.

4. Warm feelings in a religious context caused by something validly a religious means of communication but not the absolute: the aesthetic, social, and sensory means of religious expression. Examples would be response to a religious painting, to participation in a religious rite (in which the effect was highly positive but less than divine contact), or to acceptance in a religious group. But if the experiencer *thinks* it was an encounter with the religious reality, we must accept the experience as mystical, because mysticism is a category based on the experiencer's own interpretation of what happened.

5. Activity interpreted as involving real gods and spiritual powers that are perhaps intensely felt and believed in, yet in which the style is one of the calculated manipulation of these gods and powers, so that the experience becomes distanced control, rather than unconditioned encounter, direct perception, and oneness. Much shamanism is "spirit wrestling" of this sort, and so are many rites such as those of Vedic India and ancient Rome. In these rites the experiencer really feels these divine powers but thinks they are subject to the rite, making their ultimacy negated rather than encountered. However, one should not be hasty in judging this category: much of what seems manipulative in shamanism

and Vedism can unexpectedly flower into experiences that seem as mystical as any, given the cultural milieu. On the other hand, advanced mysticism can also contain subtle manipulative aspects.

When is Experience
Interpreted Mystically?

The next question we might ask is what determines whether one is likely to interpret a religious experience in a mystical way. Two factors would seem to give an experience the necessary "raw material" for the mystic's sort of rhetoric.

First, the experience must have sufficient intensity—the requisite singleness and disengagement—to allow immediate interpretation as encounter with full spiritual reality. Moreover, it should possess the capacity to suspend conflicting "realities" within sense or mind, and so have a sense of unity, though it does not necessarily need to have the intensity of an exotic "trance." If the interpretive conditions are right, this experience may be no more intense than the absorption one has in deep thought or the "high" one feels in dancing.

Second, the experience must be in a context that makes the mystical interpretation the most available, so that one "knows" his or her altered consciousness is not only religious in meaning, but also a direct, uniting encounter with the religious ultimate reality.

Apart from these two criteria, no other determinants seem necessary. It should be noted that these two leave a wide variety of religious experiences and settings potentially able to qualify as mystical. The mystical experience certainly need not be in the context of conventional prayer or meditation nor the almost equally conventional walk in the woods. Later in this book, we shall find sacred dance and even participation in "sacred" war included among techniques of mysticism. These entries may surprise some readers, but it cannot be denied that some, though not all, sacred dancers and warriors have experienced and interpreted the fervent and sometimes trancelike passion of their actions as indicating union with the ultimate divine power, even as does the meditator in his monastic cell. A nonmystical experience may, on the other hand, be of equal power to a mystical one, in its own way, but it will have only one, not both, of these characteristics.

At the same time, we should note in passing here, as we will again, that in this discussion we do not *primarily* have in mind spontaneous mystical experiences. These certainly occur, but they are rare compared to other mystical events that happen. To put it as plainly as possible, these spontaneous experiences take place because the experiencers wanted them to happen and set them up by arranging circumstances that would tend to induce psychic breaks and suggest immediately religious-mystical interpretations. In other words, these experiencers practice disciplines like yoga or Zen, go to churches or temples, meet to meditate with like-minded friends, or even just take walks in the woods —all to bring on these mystical breaks.

The Religious Context

We spoke of mystical experience as experience in a religious context in our definition. It remains to discuss what is meant by "religious context" or the social and personal climate that makes most available to the interpreter a religious and mystical interpretation. By interpreting the experience religiously, the mystic gives it both ultimacy and legitimacy in a social tradition. This assigned meaning enhances the experience while making it less private. Now we must determine exactly what is meant by "religion" within the present discussion.

The investigation of mysticism clearly shows religion a matter of *language* in the broadest sense. (Perhaps *symbolic expression* would be a better term: while language is the fundamental model and vehicle for communicating what we think, nonverbal media—music, art, rites, styles of groups—are also such communication.)

There is little reason to doubt that in physiological and behavioral terms, secular and religious ecstasy are about the same: the same glands are activitated, and the same raw feelings are engaged. What differs is the trigger and the symbolic interpretations used to sustain the state of consciousness and feeling. In mysticism, that interpretation is religious.

Religion is defined as systems that are understood to be, in Frederick Streng's phrase, "means toward ultimate transformation."[1] They also exhibit Joachim Wach's three forms of religious expression: theoretical, practical, and sociological.[2] A religious state, idea, practice (worship), or group must offer a means toward ultimate transformation of self or world or both, and do so through a combination of symbols involving ideas, practices (worship), and interpersonal or group life. It must, to use more common religious terms, offer conversion, salvation, or other means of integrating oneself absolutely into the true nature of the universe (whether God, gods, or subtle forces) and tapping this ultimate's power.

This definition of religion is not, in my opinion, unnecessarily complex, despite its use of several criteria, for the simple reason all these factors always go together. Whenever a theory, practice, or group is present as a *means* toward *ultimate transformation* it seems *always* to have all of Wach's three forms of expression.

The word *religion,* then, is useful both philosophically and sociologically because it enables us to isolate the highly visible and immensely important systems of human culture that combine theory, practice, and sociology, and in all these employ symbols of process, absoluteness, and transcendence that indicate the system is intentionally a "means toward ultimate transformation."

Mysticism is experience linked to this matrix. It may be regarded as itself *the* cardinal means toward ultimate transformation; it may be interpreted simply as a contact with the deity or plane that offers it through other means. But it any case, a mystical experience is a state of consciousness whose dominant symbols and structures of thought, behavior, and expression relate to ultimate transformation of self and world, and whose same symbols and structures derive from or construct a system with theoretical, practical, and sociological components also pointing toward ultimate transformation. These three Wachian forms need not, of course, be present explicitly in the experience, but they would be implied by the terms, the symbols and structures, through which the mystic experiencer interpreted the experience to himself/herself and others.

Mystical Experience as Self-Validating

An important quality of mystical experience, and one to which we will be referring frequently, is that it is self-validating. The psychologist Abraham Maslow included the concept of self-validation in his discussion of the peak experience, B-states, and deprivation versus nondeprivation states of consciousness. Maslow contended we experience two alternative kinds of consciousness, what he called D-states (deprivation states) and B-states (being states). In the D-state, some need outside the present essentially motivates the person: he or she is hungry or is working toward a future benefit or needs love or security. In the B-state, people are fulfilled in the present. Like a cat well-fed and asleep, the individual is totally content in the here and now. In humans, the B-state is not merely passive. In fact, it can lead to a whole new surge of activity. Out of it, Maslow said, creativity and ecstasy can flow. When a B-state wells up to its highest pitch, it becomes a "peak experience."

Maslow deliberately pointed to many similarities between the peak experience and the classical mystical experience. He said that in it a person feels integrated with the world, functions effortlessly, is free of blocks and fears, is spontaneously creative, and at the height of his or her powers. He or she expresses freely in poetic and rhapsodic terms, has a playful nonstriving joy, and is most intensely himself or herself. These characteristics seem extensions of the oneness and reality-touching qualities of the mystical experiences we have surveyed.

One of Maslow's features of the peak experience is that it is "self-validating." That is, the experience bears its own meaning and requires no explanation or justification itself.[3]

Maslow's peak experience is not identical with religious mystical experience, though it comes close to Laski's moment of ecstasy and is reminiscent of Bharati's term *peak.* The Maslovian peak includes many "high" experiences, such as moments of artistic creativity, musical performance, or love, which are only marginal to classical religious mysticism; they are joyous and fulfilling, but are not punctiliar moments of stunning ecstasy or clear realization. Neither could one call religious mystical states B-states, for as psychoanalytic commentators have pointed out, it cannot be denied we often associate mystical experiences with such deprivation situations as fasting and sexual frustration. Nonetheless, all these states are akin, and in fact too much eagerness to make distinctions in such subtle matters—except for such objective points as whether or not traditional religious language is used—may lead to the reifying of categories that are artificial.

In any case, the concept of self-validation is one we can use to help define mystical experience and mysticism. Maslow tells us that "the peak-experience is felt as a self-validating, self-justifying moment which carries its own intrinsic value with it." He adds that often even an attempt to justify this peak experience seems to take something away; in fact, many find the experience not only justifies itself, but the whole of life.[4]

The basic point here is simple. In a self-validating state, one makes no justifying appeal to anything *outside* the experience to say *why* the experience is good, or even why it is happening. One does not say to oneself, "This will be good for me later on," or "This will help me get ahead in my career," or "This will improve my mental health," or "This was caused by something I ate or something I did as a child." The experience is so overwhelming, nonrational, and unitive, it leaves no room for such side considerations. For the moment, one takes it just as what it says, in its own language or symbolism—a manifestation of the oneness of all, a vision of a transcendent sun, an influx of divine love. One is too busy *having* the experience to reflect on it.

Statements defining the experience may all be true and may occur to the experiencer later. The literature is full of mystics who agonized over whether their experiences were valid or delusional. But the real mystical experience does not *feel* oriented toward an outside need or cause. It just *is.* And while happening, it is *all* that is. This mystical experience justifies the events that lead to it and sanctifies the events that follow, for even if induced by prayer, fasting, and technique, the mystical peak experience always *feels* spontaneous when it comes. The experience may not even have an explicit meaning, like Teresa's prayer of quiet, and may still seem self-validating.

In the case of my own vision of the transcendent sun, no meaning was apparent, and yet I have never felt much need to seek for physical, psychological, or philosophical interpretations. It was simply something that just *is,* a cardinal light in my memory like falling in love and seeing the births of my children. As with these latter events, their sovereign meaning seems better approached through an exploration of what it means to be human than through psychological analysis. Nothing is wrong with the psychological approach; it is just that the appreciation of some personal things in life does not require it. That I take to be the simple meaning of self-validation. If one did *not* feel a joyous intensity in falling in love or at the birth of one's child, it would be cause for concern and psychological analysis. So one should regard the self-validation of mystical and ecstatic peak experiences. Of course, the societal valuation of love, childbirth, and ecstasy is part of personal response to them.

Yet it seems certain that the quality of self-validation is what is expressed in metaphysical language when the mystic speaks of contact with eternity, and when he or she talks of oneness or union with that which is greater than self. For these words are names for the universal that is absolute, self-validating, dependent for meaning on nothing else. The language of union tells us of participation in the unconditioned and self-validating, of neither knowing nor needing anything else.

States
of Consciousness

A mystical event can be thought of as a state of consciousness. What is a state of consciousness? Following Charles Tart's definition, I mean a discrete configuration of the various subsystems or elements of awareness.[5] These elements include emotion, memory, time sense, perception, and motor activity. They arrange themselves differently in response to such diverse factors as culture, personal life history, and interpersonal relations. Also such physiological conditions as fatigue or illness can deeply affect these parts of awareness. The possible combinations of these elements are almost infinite, as are the possible combinations of the limited number of keys on a piano. The continual shifting of these awareness elements makes up the kaleidoscope of feeling or tone that constitutes all our days and our dreams. During the course of an hour, one passes through a number of such shifts: from concentration on work to relaxed daydreaming, from a wave of joy to one of weariness, from a flash of anger to a moment of anxiety. These states of consciousness can be gathered up into categories, ranging from lethargy, fugue, and reverie through emotional states, concentration, and joy, to the unusual states of consciousness reported by drug "trippers," the insane, and mystics.[6]

Each state, Tart insists, has its own world of perception, meaning, and value; none can be considered "normal" or "altered," "higher," or "lower," except by criteria external to the state itself. Each should, he says, be studied by what he calls a "state specific science," a technique able to enter each state of awareness and work according to that state's logic.

Nevertheless, Tart believes most states of consciousness are conditioned by factors outside, not inside, the self. These external factors justify, validate, or even cause these states of consciousness. For example, an external event—someone or something—creates conditions like fear and anger in an individual; these emotions do not spring automatically from within. Even states like dreaming have the same quality in that they usually recount the particulars of one's existence; they express the separation of the present from the past and the self from others.

External events do not stimulate all states of awareness, however. For instance, they do not affect those of psychic equilibrium or unity. In Maslow's B-state nothing is feared or desired outside the experiencing self, whether in past, present, or future. Because this state validates itself and the individual knows nothing outside could give greater value, the mind is not divided. It does not see various ideas or objects as rationalizations for the experience, nor are they competing desires. Moreover, the individual does not view these states as plumbing the wells of memory; in them one feels very much "here now" and spontaneous. Even when deprivation, such as fasting or frustration, aids the state, one does not *feel* deprived because the consciousness does not focus on this abstention, but appears overwhelmingly complete in itself.

This state of psychic equilibrium is close to the ecstatic or mystical one. Even ordinary moments of self-validating joy are similar to mysticism by their merging of pleasure with half-articulated feelings of oneness and special reality. The sports car addict unites with the fast vehicle he enjoys driving; a gorgeous view makes one say "This is *really* spectacular," with just a hint of elevated ontology lurking in the adverb.

Conditions for Mystical States

Out of the state of psychic equilibrium genuine mystical and ecstatic states arise. Under the right conditions this "natural" state of equilibrium, joy, or calm concentration can develop until it is like those experienced by the Zennist schoolteacher or Charles Finney. What are the right conditions? These will be explored throughout the book. Briefly, they are of two types: inner psychological force and outer symbolic and social support.

Regarding the first, we may recall that one of William James's four characteristics of the mystical state was transiency. That is not surprising, for every state of consciousness in a normal person lasts for only a limited duration and then another state replaces it; the failure of such a replacement to happen is a sign of serious mental illness. One does not remain depressed, lethargic, or gleefully happy forever. Instead, psychological dynamics generally cause us to replace one state with an alleviating one: wakefulness with sleep, intense emotion with calm, alertness and concentration with fatigue and daydreaming. It is as though we were seeking an overall equilibrium, but through continual alternation.

Sometimes mystical states are parts of this process. There is much they can alleviate: fragmentation and frustration, depression, anxiety, and deprivation. For instance, preliminary mystical states are probably most common among adolescents and young adults. Such occurrences may be their way of finding alleviation after testing the extremes of feeling that often characterize those years. Such states may also be a relief from the vast awakening of sexual and emotional life that makes that period so tumultuous. These awakenings can produce such intense fragmentation, depression, and loss of self-control that the young person needs an equally intense alleviation—well provided by intense ecstatic and mystical experience.

Ecstatic and mystical experience seems, however, to require a specific "trigger" as well as this generalized internal need for relief. Unfortunately, depression or anxiety do not terminate automatically by switching to their opposite—ecstasy. But a person who is anxious or depressed may be particularly susceptible to a trigger appropriate to him or her; this person "needs" an experience and so will respond as does a starving man to food. Yet a person who is balanced probably will not respond to the same trigger because he or she has no corresponding demand.

Besides these internal triggers caused by a need for alleviation, there are external ones. An external trigger is a symbol that powerfully evokes ideas and feelings of transcendence and oneness. Churches, temples, sacred art, and holy people are such symbols. The interior of a sacred building reinforces mystical states for people attuned to that particular spiritual tradition. Perhaps it was no accident Isaiah was in the temple when he saw the Lord "high and lifted up." The whole panoply of religious painting, images, shrines, and ornaments also offers such reinforcement. So, often forcefully, does religious music—from a shaman's drumbeat to an oratorio of Handel—and types of worship—pilgrimage, prayer, or public worship.

Though the external acts of religion have more purposes than inducing mystical consciousness, the majority of religious symbols point in that direction. But the effect is quite different on different people because of the relation their cultural setting to these symbols. Whether this person is best stimulated by the familiar or the exotic is another possible cause for the difference.

Words and ideas, equally, can function as trigger symbols. Reading scriptures and mystical books, reflecting on them, and above all memorizing them for prayer and meditation, can encourage mystical states.

All these symbols remind us, finally, that we are social beings. We live not alone but in society, even in our most inward thoughts and experiences, including transcendent ones. After all, the very concepts and private symbols by which we communicate our mystical experiences come ultimately from society—through language, childhood play, talk, books, religion.

Moreover, society conditions even nonreligious ecstatic experiences. The greater part of those tabulated by Laski were induced by phenomena just as social in origin as religion: music, poetry, sports. Modern "nature mysticism" is undoubtedly as much influenced by socially transmitted romantic attitudes about nature as by nature itself. Ecstatic experiences triggered by love and childbirth certainly have a biological base, but even here, social attitudes toward these experiences can color their meaning.

If society's influence is strong on "secular" and "biological" ecstasy, how much more is it on religious mysticism. If the use of explicit religious language separates mysticism from other ecstasy, the experiencer is deliberately trying to find a culturally legitimated meaning for his/her experience. Usually, the use of religious language means both an attempt to give the experience the most transcendent interpretation available and an attempt to place it in some tradition (familiar or exotic) meaning that legitimates its meaning. The mystic, then, *wants* his/her experience to be less private, less limited to self and this world than does the secular ecstatic.

Conversely, a third external condition triggering mystical experience would be the attitude of the surrounding society toward mysticism. If it encourages and expects some kind of mystical experience, or even if mysticism is a recognized form of protest, mysticism will be reinforced.

Finally, we should mention the ultimate trigger for mysticism. Maybe there *is* a transcendent reality here, there, and everywhere that can be experienced in the mystical state. Perhaps mystical experience happens and is self-validating simply because the reality that can be experienced in this way is truly valid. That is how mystics themselves would understand the matter. But acceptance of mystical validity is not denigrated by looking at the psychological and symbolic factors inducing mystical experience, anymore than studying mechanics casts doubt on whether a car really moves.

Notes

[1]Frederick J. Streng, *Understanding Religious Life,* 2nd. ed. (Encino, Calif.: Dickenson Publishing Co. Inc., 1976), pp. 7–9.

[2]Joachim Wach, *Sociology of Religion* (Chicago: University of Chicago Press, 1944), pp. 17–34.

[3]Abraham H. Maslow, *Toward a Psychology of Being* (New York: Van Norstrand Reinhold Company, 1968), pp. 103–104. See also his *Religion, Values, and Peak Experiences* (Columbus: Ohio State University Press, 1964).

[4]Maslow, *Religion, Values, and Peak Experiences,* p. 62.

[5]Charles T. Tart, *States of Consciousness* (New York: E. P. Dutton & Co., Inc., 1975).

[6]The psychologist Stanley Krippner has listed twenty definable types of states of consciousness: the dreaming state, the sleeping state, the hypnogogic state, the hypno-pompic state, the lethargic state, states of rapture, states of hysteria, states of fragmentation, regressive states, meditative states, trance states, reverie, the daydreaming state, internal scanning, stupor, coma, stored memory, expanded consciousness states, and the normal everyday waking states. Stanley Krippner, "Altered States of Consciousness," in *The Highest State of Consciousness,* ed. John White (Garden City, N.Y.: Doubleday & Co., Inc. 1972), pp. 1–5.

A
History
of
Mysticism

3

Historical Patterns

The essence of mysticism, Bharati's bare zero experience, may be as beyond history as its transcendent reference. But the circumstances in which it is known and the ways it is expressed are certainly conditioned by history. If mysticism expresses the encounter with ultimate reality in a religious context, these religious contexts have shifted and varied decisively within history. Our purpose in this chapter will be to see what patterns or stages can be detected amid this historical flux.

To be sure, the contours of spiritual periods and patterns are often deceptive. Once highly regarded schemes of religious evolution are now laughingstocks. Nowhere is this more true than in mysticism, where forms sometimes seem to have lives independent of the vicissitudes of history and culture. Like yoga in India, they continue long past their origin; like Zen in modern America, they recur in unexpected times and places.

Nonetheless, we can perceive major periods in the history of mystical experience. In each of these periods a new mystical language (a new conceptualization and articulation of the mystical experience) appeared on center stage in the main religious cultures of the world.

It should always be remembered, however, that the forms of earlier eras have generally persisted, often very prominently, alongside the new. The history of mysticism is more a matter of accumulation than of the new replacing the old. Shamans still go into trances today as they did in the Old Stone Age, and mystics of ancient wisdom share the shrines of the world with those of more modern devotion.

Shamanism and Initiation

The starting point of our history is primal or primitive religion. Diverse yet not without certain widespread themes, this type of religion was the spiritual way of our ancestors for countless centuries. These primitive beliefs are full of expressions of transcendent ecstasy suggesting mystical oneness with various objects: animals, plants, tribes, ancestors, even the universe itself with all its subtle powers. But the most important expression of ecstasy, and at least the prototype of mysticism, is in the life of the shaman.

The term *shaman* is generally used for a type of religious specialist found in many parts of that archaic world. The shaman is a human custodian of spiritual power, an individual who has gained mastery over spirits and who knows the paths of the dead by means of a great initiatory experience. He or she uses this power primarily for healing and divination. In popular terms the shaman is called medicine man or witch doctor.

Typically, the shaman is an individual who as a young man or woman exhibited strange, dissociated behavior. He or she displayed disturbing fits and trances, spent days wandering in the woods, and occasionally broke into berserk rampages in the villages. This young person would report the voices of gods and spirits. These voices would command all sorts of contradictions, forcing the individual to cry out for relief. This hysteria was a sign the individual must either become a shaman (one who controls such spirits) or end his or her life in insanity and early death.

The next stage is the initiation of this person as a shaman or controller of spirits, either by a master shaman or by an internal spirit guide. The initiation essentially intends to produce a liaison—even one-ness—with the tutelary deity through whose aid the shaman can control the riot of spirits within and without. This initiation is a difficult and painful process, which often is represented by vivid symbolism of death and rebirth—gods take apart the initiate shamans, the novices count their own bones, the spirits then write a new language inside the nov-ices' skulls and replace their organs with quartz.

But when the initiate shamans come through, they are able to go into trances and, with the help of their spirit guides, display some new talents. They can now discover the cause of illness (usually as the loss of soul or the work of evil spirits), they can embark on magical flights to the world of the gods or the dead, or they can receive spirits from other worlds who can communicate reasons for disaster or plague.

For example, with the initiation and the work of the Eskimo sha-man, the candidate either is selected by a senior shaman or manifests his call by strikingly unusual behavior. He or she may see visions, desire to prowl about in solitude, or fall into trances. Inwardly, the future shaman gains awareness that a company of spirits seek to procure entry and control. This awareness is a critical time in the initiation: the pro-spective shaman must either win control of these spirits, making them allies, or he or she will become their slave and end in madness.

Taught by an old shaman, the candidate goes to a lonely place—in the wilds or by a lake—and rubs two stones together while waiting for an initiatory event. According to some tribes, a great white bear comes to eat away the flesh of the novice until only a skeleton remains. He or she remains "dead" for three days; then new flesh finds its way to the novice and he or she is reborn as a shaman.

Others tell of the young person sitting and waiting for a spirit to descend. This is called "learning to see." When the initiate's guardian spirit arrives, he illumines him like a mighty searchlight. The candidate now feels as though he has eyes set on all sides of his head, piercing eyes by which he can see through the earth as though it were one flat plain, eyes that can even see to the hidden lands of the gods and the dead to find strayed or stolen souls.[1]

In either case, it is as an Eskimo shaman who told the Danish explorer Rasmussen: "All true wisdom is only to be found far from men, out in the great solitude, and it can only be acquired by suffering. Privations and sufferings are the only things that can open a man's mind to that which is hidden from others."[2]

The mystic power that the shaman receives in this wilderness session is called *sila,* a word of three different yet interlocking mean-ings. *Sila* is the universe, the weather (good or bad), and intelligence, understanding, or wisdom. The shaman, then, is one who *has the universe, has the weather,* and *has wisdom.* [3] The shaman is a person of power. What does the shaman then do? When he or she is called upon to perform, either to heal or to handle some problem such as famine, the shaman begins by entering into a trance, using the droning sound of his or her drum and chanting. In this trance, the shaman invokes spirit aides and asks them questions; often it is said the shaman travels far away to the land of these deities. If someone is sick, the shaman exorcises the evil causing the illness. Through this dramatic presence—the shaman's words and art—the shaman creates an alternative world. In this world he gives the cause of the suffering or evil a tangible meaning—divine anger or a broken taboo—and on the same level a cure can be wrought.

The shaman's initiation trance is of most interest to us. Clearly when genuine it is a self-validating experience because the shaman is preoccupied with it to the exclusion of all else, and because he or she finds that it transforms reality. While a shaman can do much to induce and even simulate it, when initiation or trance really happens, it happens on its own terms. So far as one can tell from literature about shamanism, it has the basic structure of mystical experience: a trigger (whatever induces the trance), a high point of divine contact, an afterglow of return from the trance to ordinary reality. However, the stages may be longer and more dramatically contrived or expressed in shamanism than in modern "spontaneous" mysticism, since the shaman enacts his trance for a sick person or the community with the intention of bringing them into, if not the experience, the world of belief expressed and sustained by the trance. Yet at the same time the shaman's trance clearly implies the model, if not the reconstruction, of authentic mystical experience.

It is, I think, best to leave shamanism on this level of paradox: it is both a performance and authentic religious experience. Even if the shaman simulates his trance, he does not necessarily disbelieve in the spirits, but rather he wishes to enhance belief in them through certain technical adjustments that make their reality more apparent to himself and others. His performance is not radically different from the rhetoric, lighting, music and art used in other religions to enhance belief.

In fact, it is this performance that helps relate the shaman's experience to our definition of mysticism, for whenever it does induce a self-validating state of consciousness, it is certainly in a religious context. In other words, culture and tradition help express and validate the shaman's seance. The shaman's call and trances are considered sacred rather than pathological because the culture has a sacred understanding of them. For that reason, the shaman believes that, however disturbing these seizures, they are divinely inspired and make the shaman sacred rather than psychotic. Likewise, the shaman's belief in the divinity of these trances deepens the authenticity of the performances. It is certainly possible for a religious trance to begin somewhat contrived, then become real as the performer becomes what he or she acts out.

Moreover, the religious tradition makes it clear the shaman's trances are means toward ultimate transformation; the shaman becomes one with the transcendent powers of the universe. Indeed, the Eskimo shaman, attaining *sila,* gains the universe, weather, and transcendent wisdom—occult energies beyond the finite gods of that culture.

The importance of taking shamanism seriously in understanding religion, and especially mysticism, can hardly be overestimated. In shamanism something distinctively human expresses itself and does so with explosive power. It is the deliberate transformation of self for spiritual reasons as well as the deliberate enjoyment of special states of consciousness to gain knowledge and ability from the universe and the transcendent. From the shaman comes the basic furnishings of religion: gods, rites, processes of subjective transformation. Also from the shaman comes the basic discovery underlying mysticism: the ecstatic experience aligned to religious meaning.

Ancient Mysticism

The central shamanistic idea, then, was of the individual with power, an idea cryptically embedded in all mysticism. The shaman was able through wizardry and trance to modify reality—or at least his perception of it and that of his followers. The motif of power remains central with the advent of the next stage: the mysticism of the ancient civilizations of India, China, western Asia, and the Mediterranean. But to this next stage of mysticism were added the benefits that flowed from one of the most decisive makers of civilization—writing.

Many of the first books written have come to be regarded as religiously authoritative scriptures. Just as important, writing enabled language to develop enhanced capacities for abstract thought through sustained logical discourse. Now the outlook of the man of power and vision began to take the shape of philosophy and theology. The shaman's oneness with the universe became a vision of the cosmos as a mystic unity, and his spirit allies the population of a defined heaven.

Equally important, techniques could be made precise and transcribed for future references. Even though writing was an aid to mysticism in some ancient cultures, others—such as that of Vedic India—used writing very sparingly, and novices continued to receive sacred lore essentially through oral transmission.

Besides writing, the ancient civilizations also benefited from another important change, one which depended on writing for the long-distance communication and trade it required. This change was the emergence of large societal units, the ancient empires and widespread culture areas.

In the empires or integrated economic and culture realms of China, India, and the Near East, exchange of ideas was relatively easy and division of labor was sufficiently extensive to allow for the appearance of an educated, scholarly, and religious specialist class. This religious class consolidated the old shaman's lore, or its equivalents, into forms compatible with literate, historical civilizations. Likewise, this lore had to agree with an agricultural civilization's need for spiritual stability, and the need for its elaborate institutions to be legitimated by transcendence. But the very necessity in these ancient civilizations for stability (for rational rather than charismatic leadership) meant that the mediumistic aspect of shamanism was downplayed. Instead emphasis was put on the trance because it validated an eternal, changeless reality, perceived by the mystic and made highly contingent the changes on the stage of history. That is more to be desired than the shamanistic oracles, like those of the sibyl or the imperial shamaness of ancient Japan, who gave mediumistic advice on matters of state.

Ancient mysticism, then, in this transition from primal societies to the great empires and history centered (with numerous exceptions) on the mystic's trance as a supreme good and giver of a wisdom in which the cosmos is unified and the mystic has a position of pivotal power.

An example of this emphasis on the unity found in a trance is the Upanishads, the last and most philosophical part of the Vedic scriptures of ancient India. The Katha Upanishad, for example, suggests the old vision of universal unity:

And now, O Nachiketa, will I tell thee of the unseen, the eternal Brahman, and of what befalls the Self after death.

Of those ignorant of the Self, some enter into beings possessed of wombs, others enter into plants—according to their deeds and the growth of their intelligence.

That which is awake in us even while we sleep, shaping in dream the objects of our desire—that indeed is pure, that is Brahman, and that verily is called the Immortal. All the worlds have their being in that, and no one can transcend it. That is the Self.

As fire, though one, takes the shape of every object which it consumes, so the Self, though one, takes the shape of every object in which it dwells.

As air, though one, takes the shape of every object which it enters, so the Self, though one, takes the shape of every object in which it dwells.

As the sun, revealer of all objects to the seer, is not harmed by the sinful eye, nor by the impurities of the objects it gazes on, so the one Self, dwelling in all, is not touched by the evils of the world. For he transcends all.

He is one, the lord and innermost Self of all; of one form, he makes of himself many forms. To him who sees the Self revealed in his own heart belongs eternal bliss— to none else, to none else!

Intelligence of the intelligent, eternal among the transient, he, though one, makes possible the desires of many. To him who sees the Self revealed in his own heart belongs eternal peace—to none else, to none else![4]

This vision clearly derives initially from a self-validating experience of oneness of the sort raised by the archaic shaman in his dark wood. The word *Brahman,* a Sanskrit term for the Absolute, God as the ground and being of all, is very similar to the name of the brahmans, the priestly caste most concerned with such matters. Both words appear to come from a root meaning a magical force or spell. It is as though the unity that the mystics discovered within was the great magical force keeping the universe together, and the spells of the brahmans in their rites were drawn from this force.

From the Svetasvatara Upanishad comes an account of an ancient yogic method for knowing this Brahman in all:

Control the vital force. Set fire to the Self within by the practice of meditation. Be drunk with the wine of divine love. Thus shall you reach perfection.

Be devoted to the eternal Brahman. Unite the light within you with the light of Brahman. Thus will the source of ignorance be destroyed, and you will rise above karma.

Sit upright, holding the chest, throat, and head erect. Turn the senses and the mind inward to the lotus of the heart. Meditate on Brahman with the help of the syllable OM. Cross the fearful currents of the ocean of worldliness by means of the raft of Brahman—the sacred syllable OM.

With earnest effort hold the senses in check. Controlling the breath, regulate the vital activities. As a charioteer holds back his restive horses, so does a persevering aspirant hold back his mind.

Retire to a solitary place, such as a mountain cave or a sacred spot.

The place must be protected from the wind and rain, and it must have a smooth, clean floor, free from pebbles and dust. It must not be damp, and it must be free from disturbing noises. It must be pleasing to the eye and quieting to the mind. Seated there, practice meditation and other spiritual exercises.

As you practice meditation, you may see in vision forms resembling snow, crystals, smoke, fire, lightning, fireflies, the sun, the moon. These are signs that you are on your way to the revelation of Brahman.

As you become absorbed in meditation, you will realize that the Self is separate from the body and for this reason will not be affected by disease, old age, or death.

The first signs of progress on the path of yoga are health, a sense of physical lightness, clearness of complexion, a beautiful voice, an agreeable odor of the person, and freedom from craving.

As a soiled piece of metal, when it has been cleaned, shines brightly, so the dweller in the body, when he has realized the truth of the Self, loses his sorrow and becomes radiant with bliss.

The yogi experiences directly the truth of Brahman by realizing the light of the Self within. He is freed from all impurities—he the pure, the birthless, the bright.

He is the one God, present in the north, the east, the south, and the west. He is the creator. He enters into all wombs. He alone is now born as all beings, and he alone is to be born as all beings in the future. He is within all persons as the Inner Self, facing in all directions.

Let us adore the Lord, the luminous one, who is in fire, who is in water, who is in plants and trees, who pervades the whole universe.[5]

Similar wisdom and comparable techniques—though never quite so fully described as in India—can be found in the Pythagoreanism and Platonism of ancient Greece (philosophies also rooted in shamanism and resulting in metaphysical vision) and in the quasi-shamanistic traditions that lead to Taoism and the metaphysics of Confucianism in China.

The climax of this stage of religious history is the appearance of the great religious founders and their movements: the Buddha, Lao-tzu, Confucious, Jesus, Muhammad. These are historical persons, because the emergence of records allowed for a "discovery of history" and a corresponding need to defeat the terror of history by allowing the transcendent a historical pivot. One way or another, these persons focus the spiritual culture of their respective societies. Also, through their strong personalities, they transformed their cultures into world views a new age of history and change could appreciate.

These personalities had much in common with the archaic shamans. Each of their teachings affirmed oneness, altered consciousness and self-validating experiences. All these qualities were still ultimate hallmarks of spiritual legitimacy: the Buddha's enlightenment gave him unlimited vision; Jesus experienced himself and the Father as one.

Nonetheless society perceived these persons in a new way, not *just* as shamans or mystics, but as sacred pivots of history, as apertures through which a new sacred work was being done. Thus, their movements in the beginning emphasized not so much mystical experience as the new messages of the founders and the organization of institutions that were for the first time intercultural. However, the transhistorical, transcultural, and transreligious call of mystical experience could not long be quelled.

Wisdom Mysticism

Within a few centuries after the initiation of these new founder-religions, these new faiths have assimilated much of the surrounding religious culture and have weakened in their historical novelty. They merged not only with thaumaturgic folk religions and seasonal agricultural rites, but also with unitary visions and transformational techniques of ancient mysticism. Thus, these religions became a new package for spiritual motifs with roots in primal shamanism and ancient unitive and nonhistorical mysticism.

Present-day Christians continue to use and to supply with Christian meaning such pre-Christian seasonal symbols as Christmas trees and Easter eggs; Islam retained the symbolic star and crescent of the preceding astral worship. In the same way, the quest for mystical experience reappears in new faiths. Mystics find in the new gospel or dharma a fresh language for a perspective that sees eternal oneness beyond the historical. To these mystics the pivotal personality and the distinctive teachings of the new religion are symbols of those eternal realities beneath them. Very often, wisdom— *sophia* in the West, *prajna or prajnaparamita* in the East—is a key concept for this mystical transformation of meaning.

In Buddhism, the first few centuries after the Buddha's passing from this world saw the full flowering of Mahayana: the subtle philosophy and manifold practices centered on *prajnaparamita* ("wisdom that has gone beyond" or "perfection of wisdom"). The perfection of wisdom is sharp intuitive insight that grasps all in a flash because it is free from any clinging to partialities and is sheer consciousness without "support." Zen enlightenment is the attainment of this wisdom. All the historical Buddhas, as the Lotus Sutra in particular makes clear, are countless emanations of this one indescribable universal nature, descending everywhere like the rain.

In a comparable way, Greek and Egyptian Christian mystics came to see the advent of God in Christ essentially as a manifestation of an eternal realm that the mystic could reach deep in meditation when he was bathed in the uncreated light.[6] This mysticism was very much influenced by the complex web of Eastern, Gnostic, and Jewish strands that crisscrossed the Hellenistic spiritual world and by Neoplatonism. In Gnostic and Jewish mysticism of the time, Sophia or Wisdom (personified as feminine and an expression of God creative in the world, an idea going back to Proverbs 8:22–31) was a major symbol. Similarly, Neoplatonism spoke of emanations from the inexpressible godhead.

The most influential statement for later European mysticism of Christian Neoplatonism was the writings of the fifth-century Syrian monk who went under the pseudonym Dionysius the Areopagite. Dionysius spoke of the Super-Essential Godhead (a godhead beyond all concept even of Essence) in perfect Unity, from which the Trinity of Differentiated Godhood—Father, Son, and Holy Spirit—derives, like a chalice overbrimming with goodness. Below, proceed the created order: a ladder of angels, humans, and the creatures of earth—each step on the ladder farther away from the godhead and thus less divine than the step above it. The task of the mystic was to reverse this descent of glory by inwardly working his way back up the ladder to the light of Super-Essential Deity.[7]

A similar development in Judaism was the Kabbala, also ultimately rooted in the Neoplatonic and Jewish Gnostic mysticism of the Hellenistic age. Kabbalism came to full flower in the Middle Ages. It presented a vision of a creation which unfolded itself through a gradated series of divine attributes, *sephiroth,* from the One, Ein Soph, beyond form or concept. Scripture and its history are allegorical of these realities, or a kind of code that buried them in the esoteric meanings of words and even of Hebrew letters.

The Sufi mystics of Islam, heirs of a complex tradition that probably included both Neoplatonism and Asiatic shamanism, found the oneness of God that Muhammad revealed historically to be also revealed mystically in their moments of ecstasy. Sufism apparently began within a hundred years of the death of Muhammed as a reaction against the allegedly increasing worldliness and laxity of the new faith. But its asceticism quickly expanded into a mystical tradition with characteristics common to wisdom mysticism: emphasis on the incomprehensible One everywhere and on a series of spiritual steps by which one could rise to lose oneself in the One; a veneration of saints as men of power who radiate this divine within; and a desire to transcend what is historically conditioned. For the Sufis the outer forms of Muslim practice were but veils hiding while revealing the presence of God everywhere. They meditated especially on the verse of the Koran, "Whichever way you turn there is the face of Allah." One of their poets, Ibn al-Farid, sang of the wine of divine love, which lovers of God quaffed before the grape was made.

Devotional Mysticism

Wisdom mysticism, however profound, does not meet the religious needs of everyone. Beside the negative way which approaches God by spiritually removing everything that is not God—taught by wisdom mystics such as Dionysius and many Sufis—stands the affirmative way which uses visible and conceptual supports, images, stories, ideas of God, as ladders toward the infinite. In mysticism, one such ladder is devotional love, wherein oneness is attained in the ecstatic union of human and divine lovers, and the rapture of this merging through love is its own validation.

The implicit premise of devotionalism is that for most people the drives for expression through love—ranging from the sexual to the philanthropic—are the most intense of those by which we can forget ourselves and live for and feel with another. Therefore, devotionalists say, let these drives be used to power the supreme quest, the quest for liberation in the divine from all that constrains.

In devotionalism individuals seek liberation within an interpersonal relationship. Its achievement in those moments of love is so intense that only the beloved—or perhaps only the emotion of love—exists in a timeless now. But here the beloved is not of flesh but divine. Devotion seeks the combination of two of the most common media of ecstatic experience, eros and religion. The object of love is the concept or image of a transcendent person who has all the charm and perfection of a lover's dream yet who also has immortality and the power of the universe. That object is the Jesus, Virgin Mary, Krishna, Parvati (or Amida of devotional piety) or the One who is the Eternal Friend of Sufism.

Devotional mysticism is generally focused on only one face of God, because its style of love, as well as its search for ultimate oneness, comports best with singleness of heart. Its love is not far from that hard-to-define quality of religion called faith, which for devotionalism has overtones of its meaning for courtly love. In chivalry the lover has absolute trust in the beloved's promise, simply because life would be worth nothing without such commitments to go with one's fullness of heart.

In fact, it is no happenstance that ancient devotional mysticism came to maturity in several major spiritual cultures in the high Middle Ages, when wisdom mysticism had run its creative course and the literature of chivalry or courtly love flourished. Chivalry was not the cause of devotionalism; its roots are far older and deeper. Yet a relationship exists. Both courtly love and devotionalism represent a powerful discovery of the individual as a center of feelings at once potent and pathetic, capable of firing heroic accomplishment yet also subject to deep frustration on the human level. Devotionalism and courtly love both led people away from various kinds of identity—with clan, caste, duty, even the mystic One—to an exploration of the emotions and configurations of relationships, both human and divine. Chivalry and devotionalism then were steps toward the modern isolation of the individual as a unique center of feelings with unprecedented responsibiliy for his/her own subjectivity and happiness. At the same time, devotionalism offered its own powerful balms for the healing of that aloneness.

The devotionalism of Hindu India, called bhakti, provides an excellent example. Bhakti is the path to liberation through the arousal of love powerful enough to effect freedom from ego and oneness with the divine beloved. It makes use of names and forms. Common bhakti practices are repeating the name of the cherished deity over and over and worshiping before this holy image with affectionate gestures such as fanning the deity's image. But these outward shows are not necessary, and the supreme meaning of such bhaktic deities as Vishnu and Krishna is that they are inwardly one's "chosen ideal," personifying the identity of the highest within one with infinite God. According to some teachers, the ultimate goal of bhakti was identity with the beloved; according to others, love paradoxically requires both separateness and union, so the love itself rather than absorption was the goal. The complexities of love are poorly put into words, but every lover will understand.

Rich understanding of love as it leads to liberation can be found in the Bhakti Aphorisms of Narada. He was a half-legendary sage of ancient India whose book, in its present form extremely influential in the development of bhakti, is probably from the early Middle Ages. Narada tells us that bhakti is the greatest way to self-realization because God loves humility and dislikes those who are proud of their attainment, a failing common among enthusiasts of the paths of yoga, action, and knowledge. Bhakti, like all devotional tracks, is a way open to great and small alike; it does not matter how wealthy, powerful, learned, or skillful in religious techniques a person is—all that counts is how much he or she loves the Lord. And this love, Narada goes on to say, offers no reward but itself ("Spiritual realization is its own fruit"). An individual achieves devotion by renunciation of mundane pleasures, by ceaseless concentration on the Lord, by singing and hearing of him in simple adoration, and by the mediation of a teacher who is a great devotee.[8]

The great theologian of bhakti, Ramanuja (eleventh century), emphasized that a profound need, bestowed by divine grace, drives the devotees, for they cannot sustain their souls without continually worshiping God. They must continually give gifts to God, even if it is so humble and accessible an object as a leaf or a song in praise of him. Another side of Ramanuja's teachings is a bit more surprising. He also says that God is himself dependent upon these devotees and longs for their love, as though each represented mutual parts of the other, God sustaining the mystics and the mystics sustaining God.[9] In bhakti, the deep roots of devotionalism in the analogies and ecstasies of human love become intertwined with mysticism's tendency to discover God in one's own subjectivity.

In the Buddhism of China and Japan, the same medieval period gave the tradition known as Pure Land Buddhism. This type of Buddhism affirms that the Buddha Amitabha (Amida in Japanese), who in Pure Land represents the Buddhahood latent in all persons and things, has vowed that all who call upon his name will be reborn in his Western Paradise or Pure Land, where attainment of Nirvana is easy. Faith and the devotion that expresses this call is needed—a loving trust in the prior infinite mercy of the Buddha being superior to elaborate intellectualism or technique. In this need for faith it is comparable to the saving love of bhakti. But so simple is the faith required that one may wonder whether it really involves a mystical experience at all. The clean pointlike faith of masters of this tradition like Shang-tao in China and Shinran in Japan has a very different quality from the effusive love of Hindu bhakti. Yet these teachers have seen in true faith's clear unemotional quality a contact with the ultimate reality of the universe, and many have attained from Pure Land a peace not unlike that of Zen enlightenment. Perhaps for some it is like Laski's brief ecstasy, or Bharati's zero experience, but without the emotional afterglow.

Sufism in Islam had a devotional as well as a wisdom side, though the object of devotion was of course not represented in human form.

The great poet and mystic Jalal al-Din Rumi (1207–1273) spoke of the joy and delight of God as riches and of bitter things being made sweet by love, like copper turning into gold. "The faith of love," he said, "is separated from all religion. For lovers the faith and the religion is God." For the devotional mood of Sufism as well as its wisdom side (and the two are less separable here than in any other mystical tradition), the face of Allah is everywhere, beneath all the outer forms of the world, but it is love for the supreme Friend that best lifts the veil.

Of special interest is the poet Kabir (1440–1518) of India, who was deeply influenced by both Hindu bhakti and Islamic Sufism. Kabir found a way to a devotional mysticism toward the universal God behind all names and all religions; God, he says, was neither in mosque nor in temple, but was everywhere, "the breath of all breath."

The Judaic movement called Hasidism, which started in eastern Europe in the eighteenth century as a devotional expression of both orthodox following of the Law and kabbalistic lore, was a comparable successor to wisdom mysticism. Using music, dance, and ecstatic behavior, Hasids taught the greater value of simple loving devotion to cold learning and infused following the commandments with feeling.

Christian devotionalism as we now know it started in the Middle Ages. It was ultimately based on such New Testament experiences as Paul's crucifixion burial and resurrection through Jesus Christ. Thus, Paul no longer lived as a separate entity, but as one in Christ. Francis of Assisi and the Franciscan movement were influential in encouraging medieval devotionalism, as was the great Cistercian monk Bernard of Clairvaux (the latter was author of hymns like the famous one beginning, "Jesus, the very thought of Thee, with sweetness fills the breast").

Legend has it that Francis made the first Christmas nativity crèche and worshiped before the infant Jesus, a gesture that strikes near the heart of a pure devotional mood: homely, unintellectual, unselfconscious, often childlike in its expression of the love burning within. But we are also told that later Francis had another, grimmer experience: deep in prayer on a mountain, he was visited by a seraph who imprinted in his hands and feet the nails and wounds of Christ, the stigmata. This mysterious episode suggests another characteristic of Christian devotional mysticism, the worshiper's experience of identity with Christ.

After Francis and Bernard, Catholic devotionalism underwent a complex course through the visions of Teresa of Avila and the spiritual marriage of Catherine of Genoa to more recent piety of the Sacred Heart and the fullness of Marian devotion. Protestantism has been scarcely less affected by devotionalism. Martin Luther's original teaching of justification by faith may have been closer to the punctiliar experience of Pure Land Buddhism than to that fervor that delights in prolonged feelings of love. To him it was faith in spite of ourselves, not our feelings, that saves. But soon movements called pietism, and later English and American evangelicalism, widely emphasized and enjoyed the devotional feeling engendered by the Protestant stress on the centrality of Christ and the felt power of the Holy Spirit. The conversion of Charles Finney exemplifies evangelical piety, so also does the great collection of devotion-oriented Protestant hymnody, with lines like Charles Wesley's "Jesus, lover of my soul, let me to thy bosom fly."

Modern Mysticism

The modern period has been characterized by a complex of factors deeply affecting religion, some of them reinforcing mysticism and others destroying it. In some cases mysticism appears as a reaction to the modern experience, in others as a way of fully experiencing what it offers. In some cases mystical experience reinforced traditional religion through felt experience; in others, it abetted the erosion of tradition.

Several characteristics of the modern experience especially relate to the fortunes of mysticism within it.

First is the enhancement of individualism, already cited as incipient in the new devotionalism of the Middle Ages. This focus on the individual has only increased as time has gone on, emphasizing individual conversion, experience, and responsibility for one's own subjectivity and spiritual life. Ernst Troeltsch wrote, "Whereas the older mysticism has absorbed the Neo-Platonic doctrine of deification, and natural philosophy, the new mysticism [post-romantic] now drew into itself the modern conception of humanity and aesthetic individualism."[10] Mysticism, in other words, becomes as much a way of finding and experiencing one's individuality, of reifying and authenticating it in a world void of community, as a way of losing oneself in the One—though for many the two poles, even if logically inconsistent, become experientially identical.

A second factor is the experience of change. Changes there have always been, of course, as armies have marched back and forth across the face of earth and civilizations have risen and fallen. But because modern change has been joined with accelerating technological and social innovation, it has given many a dizzying sense of rapid and irreversible alteration of nearly all the conditions of life. We moderns have a correspondingly acute sense of history. We are much aware of the linear nature of time; things are moving from the past into a different future and whatever happens, good or bad, they will not go back exactly to what they were before.

Mysticism has sometimes been experienced as a contrast to this pace of change; it has been sought in reaction to it, for zero experience promises contact with changeless and absolute reality. Amid all the vicissitudes of history and the related experience of pluralism, modern advocates of mysticism like Aldous Huxley,[11] Alan Watts,[12] and Arthur Osborne[13] have found the best option in mysticism. These writers have argued for mysticism as a perspective that sees an immutable reality underlying all history and all religions. Next to this reality all historical particulars and individual religions are relative and imperfect, only pointing those who have eyes to see in the right direction.

Yet for others virtually an opposite effect has occurred: mysticism has been a way of deeply participating in and even modifying the process of change. For Mohandas Gandhi mysticism was the dynamic of a political program leading to the creation of a modern state, independent India. Shapers of the modern historically conscious mind like Hegel and Teilhard de Chardin found that something like a mystical vision enabled them to see the contours of process in history; a modern "mysticism of progress," much influenced by the Hegelian idea of history as Spirit coming to know itself, has made awareness of the meaning of historical change something of a teleological self-validating ecstasy, making one experientially a part of oneness and infinite reality in the midst of change.

Closely related is the thought of people like Sri Aurobindo in the East[14] and Sir Francis Younghusband in the West[15] who have argued that the great mystics are actually in the vanguard of human evolution, that they indicate the direction humanity must go if it is to survive and fulfill its ultimate destiny. Far from being anachronisms, the yogin or mystic is hard for most of us to understand because he or she is so far ahead of us in the course of evolution.

Another modern motif is technology. The creation and use of the scientific apparatus that dominates our lives and the complex bureaucratic organization it makes necessary in business and government virtually require a rational, pragmatic attitude of mind, at least toward technology and social organization. Technology does not run on ecstacy or poetry, but on skill in mathematics and mechanics. Increasingly, the same ideal of the cool engineer determines the mood, especially on their functional levels, of other institutions that serve a technological society:

government, education, business. The rational, pragmatic mentality works best in such a world and appears here to stay as long as technology does. Romantic reactions against it, such as fascism, have ended disastrously. Is it possible to be a mystic and at the same time to hold the rational, pragmatic, cool mentality necessary to function in any important way in the technological world? Or can mystics only be marginal "drop outs"?

Before answering, let us pursue the discussion a step or two further. Another modern motif, deriving directly from technology and the mind-set that goes with it, is alienation. It is the tendency of a modern person to feel he or she is an individual separate from all others first, and a member of a nation, community, or even family second. (Consider the high rate of divorce.) We are detached from one another by mobility, life-style, and increasing division of labor and consumption. We are then very much aware of our individualities, our singular yearnings and abilities. We talk of the need for individual fulfillment.

At the same time, we have lost the awareness of a mystical oneness with family and community that past cultures had. Among premoderns, the family and community were almost as much part of their identities as their names. This community matrix provided role-models, inner support, participation in festivity and sorrow, and access to transcendence in thousands of ways we have forgotten.

Compared to our ancestors, we are alienated from the world. We may be able to manipulate it better than they did, but the sense of being one with the sacred lines of force that the Eskimo shaman knew is not ours.

Rational pragmatism and this double alienation may seem to offer poor prospects indeed for mysticism in the modern world. But there is another twist to the argument, and one probably responsible for the obstinate fact that the modern world is in fact awash with mystical movements and claims to mystical experience. The isolation of the individual from community and world has forced upon each individual a new responsibility for his or her own destiny and subjectivity, as we have seen. No longer can one count upon a satisfactory subjective life being created by an intimate relation to the social and natural environment. One must do it for oneself.

This attitude can be traced back to medieval chivalry and devotion and even more to romanticism. However, it has been abetted by the ways in which the pragmatic, rational attitudes and the technological control that is their cause and effect serve to desacralize ties to world and other people. When compared to the mystic's experience of oneness, we are isolated from union with the world and people even though our knowledge and technology has increased a thousandfold over that of the archaic shaman.

The modern responsibility for one's interior self has led to rebirths of mysticism and paramystical processes from psychotherapy to positive thinking. Because religious institutions have also been affected with the cool engineering model of organization, they too have often seemed unable to deliver with past assurance an adequate self-validating subjectivity. But in the face of alienation never have people needed such subjectivity more. We have then on our own responsibility turned to techniques that seem to offer something, many of them brought out of mystical traditions of the past.

Another modern motif is universalism. We are much less culturally isolated than before. Through the mass media we have instant awareness of what is going on around the world and some impressionistic knowledge of other cultures and religions. It may not be knowledge in depth, but at least we are much more aware than our ancestors who probably never ventured far from the village. History, too, is available to us with a new immediacy. After all, it has only been a century or so since more than a small elite in nearly all societies have been able to read and write. Both synchronically and diachronically, we live in Marshall McLuhan's "global village."

The new universalism has enabled people to ransack the religions of the world for techniques and insights to cope with the alienation wrought by the same technological advances. Some understandably find the mystical traditions in those religions the most appealing dimensions because mysticism is usable in meeting the modern responsibility for subjectivity. These people, like Aldous Huxley and others, have perceived a universal mysticism beneath the surface of nearly all religion, and they have seen it as the gold which justifies mining these substrata.

This "universal mysticism" ideology, though not without precedent, is a significant indicator of the modern mood. So is the simple eclecticism of those who take one feature of an old tradition that appears usable, say a method of meditation or chanting, and leave the rest. Another indicator is the reaction of those who find the pluralism of the global village baffling and ignore it in favor of either sheer rational pragmatic secularism or a return to traditional religion. But even in this return to tradition, a rebirth of experience orientation is evident, such as in Pentecostalism and "born again" evangelicalism in America. From an empirical perspective, it seems very likely the inner core of ecstatic experience in these phenomena is nearly identical to that of transient

transcendent ecstasy of all sorts, but here the associations and the interpretive code favor alignment with traditionalism rather than universalism. Either way, people are countering the cool rational mood required
by the workaday technological world and the cosmic and social alienation that goes with it and are doing so by setting the bricks of ecstasy
with the diverse mortars of universalism and integralist traditionalism.

The structure of the modern world is thus at once closed and open
to mysticism. However skillful we are in managing the world, we do not
yet fully know our own human nature and the full spectrum of its
potentials.

A History
of Mysticism:
Reading Selection

This passage gives a vivid impression of shamanism, describing
how the shaman goes into the transic state and journeys to the other
world.

Shamanizing begins with the shaman putting himself in a trance by various
means, chiefly by monotonous, repetitive sounds produced by a drum or
rattle, and by dancing movements. Consciousness is eliminated and the
productive subconscious levels of the mind find expression. Not only does
this enable the shaman's power of artistic creation to work upon his audience by presenting the image of the community's vision of the world to the
consciousness of the spectators, the listeners, the sick and the mentally
disturbed. It seems also that in a state of trance the shaman is able to
transfer on to the others, better or more lastingly, the power of healing
which he has gained for himself.

The shaman always operates in a state of trance.

He voluntarily puts himself in this state, in which his unconscious
power of image-making speaks and through which he enables the others
to participate in this act of creation.

The new powers which he has acquired through shamanizing may
be transmitted to others, or else similar powers are aroused in them.

From Andreas Lommel, *Shamanism: The Beginnings of Art,* Transl. Michael
Bullock. New York: McGraw-Hill, 1967, pp. 63–69. Explanatory notes omitted.
Reprinted by permission of Andreas Lommel.

The mentally sick person heals himself by functioning first not as a priest and doctor but as an artist. He gives artistic form to his inner images, composes poetry, dances, mimes, and so on.

The trance, the process of giving shape to inner images, is experienced by the shaman as communication with spirits; the displacement of the level of consciousness is seen as a "journey" into the "beyond." The "spirits" and the "journey" are never conceived of as phenomena of the shaman's own mind. The spirits are presumed to speak through the shaman to the community, to bestow good hunting and health. On the journey undertaken by his soul, while his body lies "like dead," the shaman is able to visit "distant lands," the "beyond," the "gods," or the "underworld," and to bring back important information.

It seems, therefore, that what we have here is a special psychological technique. Communication with the "spirits" seems to be an activation of levels of the mind not available to these people—or to anyone—in full consciousness. It is evidently a very ancient technique which is not yet accessible to modern psychology, but which represents a means of curing certain depressive states, based on thousands of years of experience. The essence of this process of self-healing consists in imposing order and form upon these confused and chaotic images, which threaten to overwhelm the individual.

The content of experience during this process, according to all reports, is very similar over wide areas.

Radloff describes the state of excitement into which a Siberian shaman puts himself by dancing, and of which he was an eyewitness, as follows: "Some shamans dance so wildly that in the end they sink down as though dead; others get into such a violent ecstasy that they have to be held fast and bound, which can be done only by several men exerting all their strength. Then the bound shaman often trembles and twitches for a long time and tries to twist himself free, until the drum falls from his hands and he lies for hours as though dead."[a]

Mikhailovskii also gives a good description of an ecstatic state, this time from among the Buryat. "The longer the action continues, the stronger will be the inspiration."

An example in which possession by an animal spirit is manifested —for example by the spirit of a wolf—is given by Jochelson, who witnessed a shamanistic performance among the Koryak: "Suddenly the shaman commenced to beat the drum softly and to sing in a plantive voice; then the beating of the drum grew stronger and stronger, and his song— in which could be heard sounds imitating the howling of the wolf, the groaning of the cargoose, and the voices of the other animals, his guardian spirits—appeared to come, sometimes from the corner nearest to my seat,

---

[a]Wilhelm Radloff, *Aus Sibirien.* Leipzig, 1884, p. 52.

then from the opposite end, then again from the middle of the house, and then it seemed to proceed from the ceiling . . . The wild fits of ecstasy which would possess him during his performance frightened me."[b]

A detailed description of a Yakut shamanistic performance, in which the shaman goes into an ecstasy and is possessed by a spirit, is presented by Czaplicka after Siero-szewski: "Only the gentle sound of the voice of the drum, like the humming of a gnat, announces that the shaman has begun to play . . . The audience scarcely breathes, and only the unintelligible mutterings and hiccoughs of the shaman can be heard; gradually even this sinks into a profound silence. Then the music grows louder and louder and, like peals of thunder, wild shouts rend the air; the crow calls, the grebe laughs, the seamews complain, snipes whistle, eagles and hawks scream. The music swells and rises to the highest pitch. The numberless small bells (on the shaman's garment) ring and clang . . . It is a whole cascade of sounds, enough to overwhelm all the listeners . . . Then sombrely the voice of the shaman chants the following obscure fragments:

Mighty bull of the earth . . . Horse of the steppes!
I, the mighty bull, bellow!
I, the horse of the steppes, neigh!
I, the man set above all other beings!

"In the ensuing prayers the shaman addresses his *ämägyat* and other protective spirits; he talks with the *kaliany,* asks them questions, and gives answers in their names. Sometimes the shaman must pray and beat the drum a long time before the spirits come; often their appearance is so sudden and so impetuous that the shaman is overcome and falls down.

"When the *ämägyat* comes down to a shaman, he arises and begins to leap and dance . . . and beats the drum uninterruptedly . . . Those who hold him by the leather thongs (he is bound) sometimes have great difficulty in controlling his movements. The head of the shaman is bowed, his eyes are half-closed; his hair is tumbled and in wild disorder lies on his sweating face, his mouth is twisted strangely, saliva streams down his chin, often he foams at the mouth."[c]

Further descriptions of the shaman's abnormal state while shamanizing are to be found in Jochelson and Schirokogorow.[d]

The shaman's psychological experiences during the ecstasy are generally pictured as a journey into the land of souls, the beyond, the underworld or the sky or over wide geographical areas—real, known regions. Similar psychic experiences must underlie these accounts of

[b]Waldemar Jochelson, *Religion and Myths of the Koryaks.* Publ. of Jesup North Pacific Expedition. Vol. VI, Memoir of the American Museum of Natural History, 10, Leiden/New York, 1905–08, p. 49.

[c]Marie Antoinette Czaplicka, *Aboriginal Siberia,* Oxford, 1914, p. 235.

[d]S. M. Schirokogorow, "Versuch einer Erforshung der Grundlagen des Schamanentums bei den Tungusen," *Baessler Archiv,* Vol. XVIII, p. 74.

travel, which are astonishingly alike from Siberia and North America to Australia.

Also common to all these regions is the fact that the inner experiences are so intense that they are unquestioningly taken for outside "real" events and described as such.

The power of suggestion of these experiences and their artistic formulation is so great tha.ᵗ the bystanders often participate in them.ᵉ

Notes

[1]Mircea Eliade, *Shamanism: Archaic Techniques of Ecstasy,* trans. Willard R. Trask (New York: Bollengen Foundation Pantheon Books, 1964), pp. 58–62.

[2]Andreas Lommel, *Shamanism: The Beginnings of Art.* Transl. Michael Bullock. New York: McGraw-Hill, 1967, p. 29.

[3]Andreas Lommel, *Shaminism: The Beginnings of Art.* Transl. Michael Bullock, New York: McGraw-Hill, 1967, p. 29.

[4]Swami Prabhavananda and Frederick Manchester, trans., *The Upanishads: Breath of the Eternal.* New York: Mentor Books. Copyright © 1948, 1957 by The Vedanta Society of Southern California, and reprinted by its permission, pp. 22–23.

[5]Swami Prabhavananda and Frederick Manchester, trans., *The Upanishads: Breath of the Eternal.* New York: Mentor Books, Copyright © 1948, 1957 by The Vedanta Society of Southern California, and reprinted by its permission, pp. 120–21.

[6]Helen Waddell in *The Desert Fathers* (Ann Arbor: University of Michigan Press, 1957), pp. 127–28, states that Christian mysticism of the "uncreated light" reached its fullest expression in the teaching of Hesychast mystics on Mount Athos such as Gregory Palamas (1296–1359) who taught that the mystic can perceive the "Light of Tabor," that is, the divine light with which Christ was bathed at the Transfiguration. But the tradition goes back to the Desert Fathers of the third and fourth centuries; we are told that a certain abbot Sisois was seen with his face shining with radiance like the sun, and he told his companions he was conversing with saints, angels, and Christ.

[7]C. E. Rolt, trans., *Dionysius the Areopagite on the Divine Names and the Mystical Theology* (1920; reprint ed., London: Society for the Promotion of Christian Knowledge, 1966).

[8]Swami Prabhavananda, *Narada's Way of Divine Love* (Hollywood: Vedanta Press, 1971).

[9]John Braisted Carmen, *The Theology of Ramanuja* (New Haven: Yale University Press, 1974), pp. 191–93.

[10]Troeltsch, *Social Teachings,: Volume II,* trans. Olive Wyon (New York: Macmillan Publishing Co., Inc., 1931), p. 794.

[11]Aldous Huxley, *The Perenniel Philosophy* (London: Chatto and Windus, 1946).

ᵉPut together after Ursula Knoll-Greiling, "Beitrag zur Psychologie des Schamanismus bei einigen Völkern des nördlichen Asiens und Amerikas," Inaugural Dissertation, Friedrich-Wilhelms-Universität zu Berlin, Berlin, 1944.

[12]See especially Alan Watts, *The Supreme Identity* (New York: The Noonday Press, 1957).

[13]Arthur Osborne, *The Axis and the Rim* (London: Vincent Stuart, 1963).

[14]Sri Aurobindo Ghose, *The Life Divine,* 8th ed. (Pondicherry, India: Sri Aurobindo Ashram, 1973).

[15]Sir Francis Younghusband, *Modern Mystics* (New York: E. P. Dutton & Co., Inc., 1935).

The
Structure
of
Mystical
Experience

4

Types and Structures

Many books of mysticism draw colorful typologies of mystical experience, distinguishing theistic and monistic mysticism, illuminative and unitive stages, individual and collective mysticism. After much reflection and experimentation, I concluded that classifications of this sort should not be made fundamental to the present study.

All these terms and others like them are essentially categories of interpretation of mystical experience. Since mysticism is itself an interpretive category, these terms are certainly legitimate as subcategories of this larger one. We have suggested some of them in connection with the history of mysticism, and we will again, but these categories tend to isolate mysticism from religion and emphasize the ideological or institutional *expression* of mysticism. We are concerned with this expression, but we are also concerned with the complex interaction of mysticism and surrounding religion, including ways various religions "trigger" mystical experience as well as interpret it.

It seems best, then, to analyze the structure of the mystical experience itself rather than its ideological expression. In this chapter we'll undertake that analysis. Then we shall examine mysticism and its relation to religion, not so much in terms of mystical ideologies, as in terms of the Wachian three forms of religious expression: theory, practice, sociology.

The basic movement of mystical experience, suggested by the work of Laski, Bharati, and many others, is comprised of three stages.

First, there is what Laski calls the *trigger.* This term may be somewhat unfortunate in that it seems to imply an overly mechanical, reductionistic explanation for mystical experience. The writings of the mystics themselves, who should know, are full of expressions of the wonder, subtlety, and unexpectedness of their encounters with the transcendent. These seers find them beyond any earthly cause, attributing them to the workings of divine grace, or to the unveiling of the marvellous divine within.

Nonetheless, few spiritual writers would deny it is also true that one's reading, devotion, exposure to sacred symbols, and general way of life can at least prepare one to receive the grace of mystical experience when it is bestowed. From the psychological point of view, it seems equally reasonable to assume that the sort of symbolic stimuli one has —sacred or profane, of this culture or that—should have some relation at the least to the interpretation one gives mystical or ecstatic experience. Catholic writers on prayer speak of both remote and proximate preparation for meditation, well aware that the general as well as immediate tenor of one's thoughts will affect the quality of spiritual exercises, and that this is a matter within one's control. In some cases, certainly, the direct antecedent of mystical experience seems to be so sharp and direct as to deserve the word *trigger:* a sudden vista of natural beauty, a Zen master's slap. We shall use both the terms *background influence* and *trigger.*

Background influence might be one's reading, religious acts, or an impending crisis in one's life. The immediate influence or trigger controls the actual time and setting of the experience. It could be an inspiring natural environment, or a religious setting such as church or monastery. It could include interpersonal relation with a spiritual director or master. It might involve the deliberate induction of a prayerful or meditative state, in which foci of attention other than the sacred are excluded or the experiencer "centers down" mentally, permitting God, or the depths of the self, to surface into consciousness.

The background influence contributes to the interpreted meaning of the experience, since it will naturally suggest a cause, and will probably control to some extent the experiencer's way of thinking about the event afterward. This will particularly be the case the more explicitly religious is the influence. However, the experiencer does not necessarily bring all influences into the interpretation. Some seem to be overshadowed by either surfacing unconscious material or post-experience suggestions for interpretation. Nothing definitive can be said on this point.

Second, there comes the first moment in the mystical experience proper and its most intense point: a sudden, seemingly spontaneous flash of absolute power or ecstasy. It does not last long in its intense phase, but it imparts enough intensity to leave the experiencer shaken yet enraptured for minutes or even hours afterward. It might make an impression that will last a lifetime, especially when associated inseparably with a meaningful interpretation. But in itself it is brief, like the initial high experience of the Clear Light of the Void at the beginning of the Tibetan Book of the Dead, or—the peak seemed to come twice in this experience—Finney's vision of Christ and his baptism of the Holy Spirit. In both cases Finney commented he could not say how long the intensive experiences lasted. They were probably briefer than they seemed. Though a gradual release of intensity followed his brief experiences, rich joy continued to develop.

Finney thought he had a vision of Christ during the intensive moment, but later realized it was a "mental state." In my case, the climax of the intensive stage still seemed to be associated with a particular visual content, the brilliant sun rising above clouds. The matter of visual, audial, or conceptual content in the ecstatic moment is, however, problematical. Others report only a marvellous emptiness of thought, a void of bliss. Possibly, since memory abhors a vacuum, it immediately reads back to the ecstatic moment ideas or images that really surfaced a few moments later as the afterglow stage began. Also, there may be different kinds of ecstatic moments, not all equally formless. Laski, as we have seen, distinguishes between a "tumescent" ecstasy in which the experiencer seems to overburst with joy and reality, and a quieter "withdrawal" ecstasy in which all senses and ideas fall away leaving only bliss.

The third stage is then the afterglow, when the intensity recedes and associated ideas and images appear. This afterglow particularly happens if the experience is to be a true mystical experience by our definition, having a religious context governing its interpretation. While we may ignore some ecstatic moments, it would be a logical impossibility for us to overlook a religious experience since to give it religious meaning is in itself to interpret it and to say it is important.

The afterglow is still a stage of heightened consciousness, perhaps much higher than anything else the experiencer has known. In many cases it will seem to be the mystical experience. The ecstatic moment may pass so rapidly as to *be* virtually undetected, but it will leave an afterglow full of joyous ideas, associations, images, and feelings.

The greatest mystical writers, of course, knew better. The classic *Cloud of Unknowing* says of the work of grace in the Christian mystic's soul:

> It is always a sudden impulse and comes without warning, springing up to God like some spark from the fire. An incredible number of such impulses arise in one brief hour in the soul who has a will to this work! In one such flash the soul may completely forget the created world outside.[1]

This authority tells us not to try to figure out these experiences intellectually, and above all not to allow them to slide into what we have called the afterglow: it is better to hold to this "blind outreaching love to God himself" piercing the cloud of unknowing with these sharp momentary arrows, than to "gaze on the angels and saints in heaven, and hear the happy music of the blessed."

Yet even this profoundly austere work does not disdain to connect with subtle experience with such symbols of supreme significance as the name God, and that is at the minimum what the afterglow does. It is not primarily a rational state. It is not the point at which an individual figures out the meaning of what is happening to him or her; it is rather an associative state, when the experiencer begins the work of relating the experience to other experiences or ideas, particularly those that give meaning to the experience and his or her life. The individual accomplishes the associative task quietly and passively. Because it is not done rationally, the experiencer has no recollection of having thought it out and so no reason to suspect the associated images and ideas may not have been in the momentary spark of the actual experience. Yet the human desire to have something to hold on to and to give meaning to important events—and let them give meaning to other events—is not absent.

The associations are from three sources: first, the remote influences —the experiencer's recent spiritual background, his or her reading and practice; second, the proximate and immediate influences—the present sights and symbols, the immediate state of mind, even the physiology of the experience itself; third, the afterglow. This last nonrational emotionality and susceptibility can easily lower the threshhold of consciousness to evoke content from the individual's more distant past: images from childhood, problems to be solved, archetypal forms from wherever derived. Thus, the experience can be reconversion to a faith almost forgotten, or it can call up a sacred picture on the wall of one's childhood home. If the experience seemed ultimate enough to evoke transformation symbols, the individual will be enabled by the melting of rigid structures wrought by the afterglow warmth to reach for whatever symbols of ultimacy are available in the attic of the mind. For most people, it is probably still religion in some form or another that supplies such symbols, and the experience will become mystical.

It should not be forgotten, however, that most mystical experiences are not the lonely and climactic conversions of apostates. In most cases the experiencer will prepare quite deliberately for a religious interpretation. The atmosphere of religious worship—music, preaching, prayer, and architecture—in its suggestion of ecstasy make such an experience unavoidable or at least it will be the conclusion of habitual piety.

Interpretation has several stages. First is the afterglow associative interpretation, in which fundamental images and block-concepts align with the experience.

Next, shortly following the afterglow may come a period of seeking meaningful reinforcement outside of the experience. At this point the experiencer will probably not turn toward critical or higher philosophical or psychological perspectives, but seek the counsel of others whose world view and personal experiences correspond to the afterglow associations. Depending on his or her bent, the experiencer will probably turn toward reading congenial books or seeking social reinforcement in a religious circle (if he/she was not already in one on the occasion of the experience).

In the last stage of interpretation—weeks, months, or even years later—the individual moves toward a more rational or universal interpretation, and finds that the experience's meaning might shift somewhat without diminishing in power. Its true meaning becomes something other than what it seemed at the time and transforms to something rationally integrated with a world view relevant to all humans and all human experience, including mystical ones. This integration into a world view may not, however, mean a change in what we call theological opinion; instead it may be simply a slowly changing attitude toward the definitiveness of the experience for one's life-style, work, attitude toward people, and self-image.

The Experience
of R. M. Bucke

An example of this integration of the mystical with the rational is the first-hand account (though written in third person) of the mystical experience of Richard M. Bucke, author of the well-known book *Cosmic Consciousness*. This event took place in Victorian England.

It was in the early spring at the beginning of his thirty-sixth year. He and two friends had spent the evening reading Wordsworth, Shelley, Keats, Browning, and especially Whitman. They parted at midnight, and he had a long drive in a hansom (it was in an English city). His mind deeply under the influence of the ideas, images and emotions called up by the reading and talk of the evening, was calm and peaceful. He was in a state of quiet, almost passive enjoyment. All at once, without warning of any kind, he found himself wrapped around as it were by a flame colored cloud. For an instant he thought of fire, some sudden conflagration in the great city, the next he knew that the light was within himself. Directly afterwards came upon him a sense of exultation of immense joyousness accompanied or immediately followed by an intellectual illumination quite impossible to describe. Into his brain streamed one momentary lightning-flash of the Brahmic Splendor which has ever since lightened his life; upon his heart fell one drop of Brahmic Bliss, leaving thenceforward for always an after taste of heaven. Among other things he did not come to believe, he saw and knew that the Cosmos is not dead matter but a living Presence, that the soul of man is immortal, that the universe is so built and ordered that without any peradventure all things work together for the good of each and all, that the foundation principle of the world is what we call love and that the happiness of every one is in the long run absolutely certain. He claims that he learned more within the few seconds during which the illumination lasted than in previous months or even years of study, and that he learned much that no study could ever have taught.

The illumination itself continued not more than a few moments, but its effects proved ineffaceable; it was impossible for him ever to forget what he at that time saw and knew, neither did he, or could he, ever doubt the truth of what was then presented to his mind. There was no return that night or at any other time of the experience. He subsequently wrote a book in which he sought to embody the teaching of the illumination. Some who read it thought very highly of it, but (as was to be expected for many reasons) it had little circulation.

The supreme occurrence of that night was his real and sole initiation to the new and higher order of ideas. But it was only an initiation. He saw the light but had no more idea whence it came and what it meant than had the first creature that saw the light of the sun. Years afterwards he met C. P., of whom he had often heard as having extraordinary spiritual insight. He found that C. P. had entered the higher life of which he had had a glimpse and had had a large experience of its phenomena. His conversation with C. P. threw a flood of light upon the true meaning of what he had himself experienced.[2]

In this striking account, the remote preparation in reading and discussing elevated poetry—and, even earlier, in perusing mystical and philosophical writings—is obvious. So is the proximate trigger of the condition of being finally alone and still, though happy, after an exhilarating evening.

We observe then the sudden brief flash of ecstasy. Bucke does not explicitly describe the afterglow stage, but what follows in the way of interpretation strongly indicates it. The cognitive ideas that the experience communicates—including such terms as *Brahmic Bliss*—seem too complex to have been formed verbally in the momentary ecstasy. Still one can well believe that this lightning flash suggested their essence and opened the channels for their reception.

We note also the several stages of the interpretive process. First was an immediate interpretation, while the afterglow nimbus still surrounded the experiencer in this excerpt. At this stage the ideas of Brahmic Splendor and immortality surged in raw but verbalized form through his mind. Then an intermediate stage occurred in which he wrote a book putting forth the teachings. The last stage happened years later when he met C. P. and found the experience actually had even a higher and larger meaning than had originally appeared.

Mystical Liminality and Communitas

The three stages we have defined in the mystical experience—background influence or trigger, ecstatic moment, and afterglow—can be compared to the three stages of traditional initiatory ritual procedure of the distinguished anthropologists Gerardus van Gennep and Victor Turner.[3]

In the traditional initiatory process for young men in a primitive tribe, the first step is to separate the novices from the rest of the population. Older men in divine or demonic masks summon them, or call them from the village by the beat of drums and the whirl of bull-roarers. Then the initiates go to a lodge deep in the bush, where either a monster devours them and they die or they wait until they see a vision of their guardian deity. Finally, after this period of isolation the young men return from the dead or their encounter with their guardian deity. Through some kind of ceremony the tribe readmits them—but now with a new status, as men rather than boys.

This separation of the novices can also be broken into three stages: separation, liminality, and reincorporation or reaggregation. Of these, the middle stage, extensively discussed by Victor Turner, is the most interesting for us. It is the middle stage of an initiatory transition, after separation from the community when the young man leaves his old status and yet before his reincorporation with a new status. At this stage he does not have structural status in society, but perhaps because his structure in society is broken, he is more accessible to vertical relationships—to impingements by gods and ancestors, to oracular dreams and visions, to mystical transports, even to nonstructural intimacy with other initiates leading to special life-long ties.

Liminality then is the stage where an individual is betwixt and between. It is when a youth undergoes initiation in the lodge in the woods or alone on a vision-quest. It is when a king or queen kneel before the altar in their coronation, or a knight kneels in lonely nocturnal vigil in the chapel. It is when a pilgrim is en route to a holy destination. It is a state embodied permanently and symbolically by certain persons—monks, friars, ascetics, hoboes, minorities—against the rest of society, although they may have their own internal counter-structures: leaders, rules, customs.

Liminality is represented in a social ideal as well as individual process. This ideal Victor Turner calls *communitas*. *Communitas* indicates human relations when all the structures that separate people are abolished, and one is in "I-thou" relations with everyone. Intersubjectivity and the inward desire to actualize love can take their full course without hindrance from social convention, rank, or institution. *Communitas* is not fully attainable, but the glowing image of such a society has been an immensely powerful force in human affairs. It fulfills the promise latent in liminality-creating events such as pilgrimage, initiations, and holy orders. It has inspired the planning of countless utopias and religious communities, and is the motive behind the symbolic breaking of ordinary structure of festival and pilgrimage. In such festivities people briefly act as though *communitas* existed, greeting and even embracing strangers, and losing inhibitions to drink or dance in the streets.

The antistructure of liminality and *communitas* is, as Turner emphasizes, not a negative term, but implies certain primordial human yearnings for more than what structure gives. Indeed, the force that causes individuals to break with structure and taste liminality and *communitas* is close to mysticism. After all, an experience must be a direct perception and self-validating if it is to exist unsupported by any structure.

To compare categories for the interpretation of rites and other social processes, such as those of Turner, with those of subjective processes, such as mystical experience, is a difficult matter. But it could be an extremely important venture. For social and individual processes cannot be sealed off from each other. Each is a reflex or projection of the other, thus helps to understand the other, as well as the intimate connection of inner and outer in human affairs. If yoga is, as Mircea Eliade said, an interiorization of the old Vedic sacrificial rites, a study of those rites can help us to understand yogic mysticism. If Christian sacraments are, in the words of the Anglican catechism, an "outward and visible sign of an inward and spiritual grace," study of them might help us to understand mystical rebirth and communion with God through Jesus Christ.

Categories from the study of rite can, then, be extremely valuable metaphors for the structure of mystical experience, so long as we keep the distinctions in mind. For they offer, as do those of van Gennepp and Turner, not only vivid and memorable terms, but also possible insights into why rites are structured as they are and why mystical experience often seems like an inward reflection of religious events in the experiencer's society.

If we compare the structure of liminality occasions to those of mystical experiences, the zenith of liminality when it breaks into *communitas* corresponds to the ecstatic moment. By the same token, both have an afterglow or reaggregation process, in which the individual interprets the experience, associating it with words and symbols that link it to a personal and social grid of meaning. This association is necessary for either experience to be remembered because we can only remember those things that have verbal or symbolic baskets. These baskets will come out of a meaning-matrix derived out of the very structures from which the experience seemed to break. Experiences with no symbolic associations may well happen and be immensely important for the experiencer's psychic process, but like the experiences of preverbal infancy, they will not be explicitly discrete remembered events.

Literary Interpretation

A literary example of this process of interpretation of mystical experience is the following verses from a poem by the great Spanish mystic John of the Cross (1542–1591). Here John of the Cross describes the mystic quest as a maiden leaving her home secretly late at night to meet her lover in the woods. We are reminded of the gopis or milkmaids leaving their homes and husbands to frolic with the devastatingly beautiful god Krishna in the forest. Leaving house and family, breaking the rules, is an ecstatic break with propriety, ideas, and structures. It also offers an interpretation of mystical experience as a comparable inward break with the ordinary structures of thought.

The language of the poem is sensual, but John, an austere Carmelite friar, does not intend to express divine love sensually. The explication of this poem is the purpose of his entire book, *The Dark Night of the Soul*. Elsewhere John of the Cross writes, ". . . even the greatest loveliness and delight that the soul enjoys is not God. God is beyond everything that can be grasped." To this realization, worthy of Buddha or Dionysius, the sensual rapture of devotion toward the Eternal Beloved is but a portal. Yet it is important. The surges of erotic love suggested by these lines tell in their own way of a counterstructure, as soft and emotive and inward as the outer institutional structures are hard and legalistic. Erotically, this counterstructure is the trail leading toward emotional and sexual climax, in which the experiencer forgets all for ecstatic intensity; spiritually, this counterstructure marks the stages of a descent deeper and deeper into divine darkness and unknowing, where the individual meets the God beyond everything that can be grasped.

> Upon that night of bliss,
> When none beheld, I parted secretly,
> Nor looked on that or this,
> And nothing guided me
> But light that brimmed my heart so ardently . . .

> O night that in her spell
> Beloved and Lover caught!
> Into the Lover the beloved was wrought!
> He lay upon the breast
> I kept for Him immaculate and fair.
> He closed His eyes in rest,

And I caressed Him there,
And fans of cedar branches moved the air.

And when the dawning flung
Her wind among His locks and spread them wide,
His gentle fingers clung
About my neck—O tide
Of ecstasy in which my senses died!

And then I bowed my head
On my Beloved, forget my self, and all
Else ceased, my self I shed,
and shed was every pall;
Forgotten where the lilies hold in thrall.[4]

We note the initial theme of separation—the departure—and, after the proximate trigger of a night of warm love, the ecstatic moment that the arising dawn and its breezes fan into flame. In the image of interpersonal love, we sense the *communitas* ideal; in the ecstatic loss of self-awareness, we sense transcendence beyond the separateness of the human plane.

Polarities
for Interpretation

Next comes the process (beginning with the afterglow and proceeding for years) of integrating a major experience into the rest of the experiencer's life. Such integration is what John was doing in *The Dark Night of the Soul.* Everyone who makes ecstatic experience into religious experience must undertake this process. We can find a striking example of this process in the accounts of the medieval Swiss mystic Nicklaus von Flue (1417–1487), discussed by C. G. Jung.

On a memorable occasion Nicklaus had a vision he later regarded as God of Holy Trinity. In his earliest reports, however, he describes the vision as simply a tremendously intense apparition of light in the form of a human face. The visage seemed full of wrath, striking such fear and terror into the sage's heart that he turned away instantly and fell to the ground. As Jung pointed out, the sight clearly impressed Nicklaus as being of the most supreme and otherworldly subject conceiveable, which in his time and place could only be the Holy Trinity, God himself in three persons. In later accounts by Nicklaus of the vision, the experiencer tones down the sheer and stark terror of the piercing light and elaborates the description to include three wheels around the deific face.

This process brings it into line with contemporary representations of God as Trinity, in which spoked concentric circles were a popular motif. Nicklaus himself possessed a devotional book illustrating the Trinity in this manner, and a nearby parish church displays a similar old painting of such a Trinity.[5]

Two stages appear in this mystic's articulation of his vision . . . of which we know nothing but what he tells us. Not only is there movement from the vision to the later descriptive expression of it in words, but also there is a development in the description itself. This development starts with an initial inchoate but powerful account, in which—unlike most of the accounts with which we have dealt—the ecstasy seems highly unpleasant, but no less self-validating. It ends with an understanding of the theological meaning of what was seen.

Perhaps the wrathful face was an afterglow association with the wave of unbounded terror that swept over Nicklaus—a terror that he associated with the primoridially sacred. However that may be, we clearly see a subsequent stage in which he assimilates his vision to the religion of the time—in which terror at the wrath of God was a far from unfamiliar feeling.

During the immediate afterglow stage the motifs, from memory and perhaps reality, seem to spill over backward into the ecstatic moment, to give the whole experience its primary, associative rather than rational, religious tone. This afterglow is the matrix of the mystical experience taking shape as visionary or void, as love or monistic oneness, and the like. Some possible primary associations with the ecstatic moment are of many different orders and can conveniently be presented in terms of polarities.

1. *Love–Infinity.* We have already examined the mysticism of devotional love, which emphasizes interpersonal relations, and the mysticism of the Upanishadic type, in which awareness of the infinity of divine being seems to be the dominant theme. While, as in Sufism and John of the Cross, these types of mysticism are by no means mutually exclusive, and Christian mysticism of the type of *The Cloud of Unknowing* makes love the arrow to penetrate the infinite divine dark, much mysticism seems in its associations to be tilted one way or the other.

2. *Technique–Spontaneous Grace.* This is a polarity in which the character of the trigger has a decided impact on the afterglow associations. While the ecstatic moment of all real mysticism *seems* spontaneous—a gift of grace—only some experiences occur quite surprisingly; others follow a deliberate prayer or meditation. One way or another, where the experience falls along the spectrum of this polarity will shape its interpretation.

3. *Hard–Easy.* Related to the foregoing is the simple but important matter of whether the experience seems to come only after strenuous effort toward a spiritual breakthrough, or if it flows out without arduous preparation.

Entire mystical systems and life-styles revolve around this polarity. The shaman goes through a difficult and painful initiation. Countless later techniques for mystical experience have shown it to be a slow hard process, requiring extraordinary feats of asceticism and perseverence. Understandably, the teachers of these techniques have often not been slow to rebuke the mysticism of those to whom such effort seemed alien. In China, the *feng liu* school of Neo-Taoists exalted living by impulse to express the spontaneity and evolution that was the essence of the Tao, the undifferentiated universal principle. For them, such acts as going to a friend's house in the snow and returning without knocking or drinking wine among the pigs were expressions of immediate awareness of the ultimate. Yet they are quite antithetical to any idea that mystical experience has to be the product of stern discipline.

4. *Visual–Dark.* We have already observed that some mystical experiences seem to be of light, others of divine darkness. Some, like Finney's, have an important visionary feature; others, like that of the American schoolteacher, alter only more subtly the tone of what is seen with the eyes. The religious significance of this polarity is of course great. It may determine whether the experience leads to a following of the negative way of taking away all that is not God and the philosophical emphasis on divine infinity and incomprehensibility that goes with it; or whether the experience leads toward devotion to visually conceptualized gods and saviours.

5. *Socially Isolating–Socially Integrating.* This is a sociological polarity. It refers to the immensely significant interpretive factor of whether the experience leads the experiencer to see himself/herself as now more isolated from society (called to a different life) or as more integrated because he or she has had an experience that confirms and integrates him/her into the dominant faith.

Of course, these poles can represent not final choices but a process in which the extremes have different relationships to the individual at

different stages. Sri Ramana, a great modern Hindu mystic, after his
initial spiritual experiences as an adolescent, left home in the traditional
Hindu way—though not without deception to his family—and dwelt
alone in the woods and then in a temple for several years. By the time
he was twenty, followers, drawn by his evident sanctity, had already
begun to gather around him or visit informally. In time the following
developed into an ashram, the well-known institution of Hinduism
made up of disciples, family, and visitors drawn to a charismatic personality. This household served to reintegrate Ramana into a society, yet
not principally the natural one (his family and home) he had left. In a
broader sense it did integrate him through the role of holy man into the
tradition of Hindu society as a whole, which has ever made a place for
such persons.

6. *Intellectual–Paradoxical.* For some mystics the ecstatic experience leads to a rationalized intellectual position; for others the unique-
ness and transcendence of the experience can only be expressed in the
language of paradox. Some, like Nicklaus of Flue and R. M. Bucke,
cannot leave the memory of their mystical vision alone until they have
constructed or discovered a rationalized and universalized world view
integrating the ordinary with the transcendent. Only with such inter-
gration can their experience have a meaningful place and appear as a
meaningful perception of the transcendent above the ordinary. Others,
while not denying the meaningfulness of the experience, give its meaning obliquely and paradoxically. While a Zen master, for instance, was
weighing out flax in the field, he was asked what was the Buddha. He
responded, "Three pounds of flax." The paradoxists believe with the
Sufi Haji Bektash:

> For him who has perception, a mere sign is enough.
> For him who does not really heed, a thousand explanations
>   are not enough.

As another Sufi put it, faith and experience is sheer truth without
form, and its mysterious appearances and disappearances in this world
—and in oneself—is best explained by this verse of Hasan of Basra:

> I saw a child carrying a light
> I asked him where he had brought it from.
> He put it out, and said:
> "Now you tell me where it is gone."[6]

Three Forms
of Religious Expression

Whatever the interpretive style, whether along the axes of one or more of these polarities, we can be certain that the experiencer adds something interpretive to any mystical experience when communicated to another or when he rationalizes it to himself. The interpretation will be a part of the work of reaggregation, of the way the mystic makes himself or herself into a newly initiated person—one who must now live as an individual who has had this powerful and unforgetable experience.

We do not imply that the interpretation is simply extraneous to the experience. Much about the physiology, psychology, and neurology of ecstatic experience is far from well understood, and it would be premature to deny that variables within its intrinsic nature could suggest interpretation, just as do the specific trigger and cultural setting. Physiology sometimes associated with ecstasy may be relevant to the waves phenomenon some mystics report. Such widespread intrinsic experiences as dazzling light and loss of time and space orientation may have neurological grounding and be subject to variation, for all individuals do not report them in the same way. Yet they have become extremely important for the intellectual and symbolic expressions of mysticism.

However, the interpretations most significant for history (both personal and social) are those verbalized and symbolized interpretations of the afterglow stage, which seek to facilitate the process of reaggregation. They reflect a highly complex process of mixing the dynamic of the experience (which in itself briefly but totally isolates the individual) with the realities of world and ordinary life. It is a complex but creative process, out of which have come many remarkable self-transformations and many cultural goods of great value.

This mixing process is basically one of seeking expression. It strives to communicate the experience in some sort of language common to the world and to the individual experiencer. The communication is not just in words, for people do not live by words alone. What we have to say about our experiences of all sorts we say not only in verbal language, but also in the languages of symbols, art, actions, and social relations. A mystic will undoubtedly employ more than one of these languages, even as the experience may have any one of them influential in its genesis.

Most of the remainder of this book will be a study of the background and expression of religious mysticism in terms of the three forms of religious expression described by the sociologist of religion Joachim Wach. These forms are the theoretical, practical, and sociological.[7]

The theoretical refers to the verbal and conceptual expression of religion and includes myth, normative stories and history, doctrine, theology, religious philosophy, and mental attitudes. Basically, the theoretical expression constructs conceptually a world view in which its experiences are meaningful because they connect with what is and what gives meaning to all else. In the form of myth and mythic history, theoretical expression conveys the world view through exemplary narrative; in doctrine and philosophy, which usually come later, it essays a greater degree of abstraction and self-conscious system-building.

The practical form of religious expression, *praxis,* refers to what is done. It embraces worship and services, pilgrimages and festivals, and private prayer and meditation—whatever involves doing something. Ordinarily these gestures will take stylized forms that mark them as religious in the culture, and because of this will be—like the other forms of expression—links to the traditional past as well as to the transcendent.

The sociological form of expression means the way individuals articulate religion through the kinds of groups it supports or forms, leadership it actualizes, and interpersonal relationships it makes concrete. The experience, for example, might communicate very different messages about the nature of a religious experience, if he or she became more devout in the parish church, or if the experiencer withdrew from society to become a holy hermit or form a new sect.

As understood from a history of religions or a social scientific perspective, all religion has these forms of expression in one guise or another. Each of them gives, in its own language, its message about the fundamental experience and perception of reality underlying the faith. However, these messages may not always be consistent, nor may their interface with either the environing society or the life-experience of individuals always work the same way. Tensions in these areas give dynamic to religious history.

By the same token, we can safely say that mystical experience, being religious, will always have a context of theoretical, practical, and sociological forms of religious expression. They will all be part of the experience's remote and perhaps proximate triggering, and the experiencer will always express the interpretation of the experience in one, or two, or all three of the forms. Deliberately or not, it will undoubtedly have some interaction with all three. A mystic's implicit or explicit decision *not* to form a new doctrine, rite, or society is as important for understanding the religious history and culture of his time as his decision to do so.

We shall now examine the three forms of expression and their interaction with mysticism in detail.

Notes

[1]Clifton Walters, trans., *The Cloud of Unknowing* (Baltimore: Penguin Books, 1961).

[2]Richard Maurice Bucke, *Cosmic Consciousness,* (New Hyde Park, N.Y.: University Books, Inc., 1961), pp. 7–8.

[3]Arnold van Gennep, *The Rites of Passage* (Chicago: University of Chicago Press, 1960); Victor Turner, *The Ritual Process* (Chicago: Aldine Publishing Company, 1969).

[4]H. A. Reinhold, ed., *The Soul Afire* (Garden City, N.Y.: Doubleday Image Books, 1973), pp. 307–8.

[5]C. G. Jung, "Brother Klaus," in *The Collected Works of C. G. Jung,* Volume 11, *Psychology and Religion: West and East,* 2nd ed. (Princeton: Princeton University Press, 1969), pp. 316–23.

[6]Sufi quotes from Idries Shah, *The Way of the Sufi.* Copyright © 1968 by Idries Shah. Reprinted by permission of the publishers, E. P. Dutton, New York and of A. P. Watt Limited, pp. 222, 227.

[7]Joachim Wach, *Sociology of Religion* (Chicago: University of Chicago Press, 1944), pp. 17–34.

Mysticism and Religious Thought

5

Words About the Unutterable

The distinguished theologian Paul Tillich once wrote that, apart from the statement that God is being-itself, all we say about God is symbolic.[1] This does not mean that words about God are untrue, for Tillich emphasizes that symbols participate in what they symbolize; instead it means that we humans can only utter what they symbolize in elusive symbolic ways.

Our talk about God may be true, but it is not the *whole* truth. The finite can only point toward the infinite greater than all words and concepts. An old Zen saying tells us that words and concepts are only fingers pointing at the moon. They are to God's reality as the reflection of the moon in a well is to the orb sailing high overhead, or the moon's brightness to the sun from whence it draws light.

Nowhere are these cautions more in order than regarding the language of mysticism. If mysticism indeed expresses an experience of ecstasy and oneness uncluttered by linear thought, or an awareness of invisible reality unmediated by the outer senses, the gulf between the experience and how it is expressed is imposing.

Nonetheless, the amount of literature describing mystical experience as well as presenting views of the cosmos and of human nature related to mysticism is correspondingly imposing. One almost wonders if a paradoxical law requires that the bulk of mystical writing expand in proportion to the inexpressibility of the experiences underlying it. The mystic often feels that she or he must speak, even if all rivers of language run into the sand before they cover the terrain of the experience. It seems the writer tries to compensate for the one word that cannot be spoken with a vast volume of words and ideas.

Yet we should not suppose the theoretical expressions of mysticism are worthless. Indeed, the frequent protestations of the experience's inexpressibility sometimes becomes a rather misleading convention, for in fact much that is important about mysticism and its experiences can be said.

Mystical writings are an important aspect of the whole phenomenon, both for what they reveal of the experience and for their general impact on religion and culture. As we have seen, expression—including writing about it—is an important part of the reaggregation process for the experiencer. Through its theoretical articulation the mystic completes and shares the experience. When it is actually put into words an experience becomes effectively cognitive—that is, a way of knowing. For we do not know what we know until we put it into words, first of all to ourselves. But to speak it we need to put what we "know" into some sort of language, which is necessarily symbolic. The symbolic language need not, perhaps, be verbal. It can be in an acted out, even an emotional, code.

But after an individual has acquired a verbal language, symbolization in words will almost always inevitably be a part of the expression of mystical experience. The symbolization will describe a universe and its transcendent realities in which the experience is possible, as well as interpret the experiencer's life making it clear why the experience occurred when it did.

The life history side of the experience makes it not only cognitive, but also transformative. It is the symbolic completion of the experience as one that makes the experiencer a new person. Language suggesting being "born again," becoming "God-realized," or being given a mission that alters one's life is barely strong enough for the climactic effect of major mystical experience. In these instances, though, an individual needs verbalization to complete the transformative process; the experience itself may work deeply to restructure one's psyche, yet part of such a change is the individual's *knowing* that it is happening. Knowing how we are changed, like understanding what we know, must be said in words. We do not really know or become until we can *say* what we have learned or what we have become. The mind worries over these things until it resolves them in words as well as feelings.

Primordial Symbol and Concept

An important distinction within the theoretical expression of mysticism is between what we may call primordial symbol and the conceptual expression. The primordial symbol, in some ways comparable to S. C. Pepper's "root metaphor," is the fundamental image or attitude—a raw picture of a divine vision or vague impression of experiencing height or depth. It is the most immediate and strongest mental association with the experience. This primordial symbol will simply exist in no way rationalized or explained, but it will provide the basic problem for interpretation. The conceptual expression, then, will endeavor to interpret the experience with its primordial symbol, making it consistent with the rest of the experiencer's life, and with a coherent world view he or she can come to accept, or has already accepted.

As an example of this giving theoretical expression to mystical experience and of moving from primordial symbol to concept, we might recall the medieval Swiss mystic Nicklaus von Flue. We noted two stages in the mystic's verbal articulation of his vision. Not only was there a movement from the vision to the descriptive expression, but within this expression a movement appears from an initial inchoate but powerful account to an understanding of what was seen the Holy Trinity—the most sacred concept in the visionary's culture. The process can be thought of as movement from symbol in the full sense to concept. All religious ideas are doubtless symbolic in character, in that they follow Tillich's definition by participating in what they represent without covering it all. But we distinguish between a primordial symbol and a concept that strives to rationalize and explain the meaning of the pure symbol, in the process probably fitting it into existing patterns of thought and cultural values.

The symbol in the primary form is close to the experience and may not be verbal. However, it may be a primordial experience capable of later verbal articulation, such as an experience of light or darkness. But even if not a verbal expression, it may still find itself associated with some sort of visual symbol, such as the cross or an image of the Buddha. These symbols did not exclude subsequent verbal expression. The followers of Jesus who witnessed the crucifixion, or those who heard the Buddha return to preach in the Deer Park after his enlightenment, required words of symbolic weight immediately to register and transmit what had happened. In the case of the Blessed Nicklaus, even his first great vision he burdened with awesome and mysterious language. Even primal language is the first step on the road from primordial symbol to concept. But the first preaching *(kerygma)* of the disciples of Jesus, the Buddha's Deer Park sermon, and Nicklaus's first vision account, are languages that still retain the character of primordial symbol. The words are not ordinary words, nor philosophical ones; they are words that do not so much explain as enable the speaker or hearer to participate in the mystery beyond words. That is, they convey a part of its enigmatic power.

A religious symbol—even if verbal—is different from and in many ways opposite to a religious concept. The symbol, as Mircea Eliade has pointed out, "is not a mere reflection of objective reality," but "reveals something more profound and more basic," and does so in a way that brings out the complexity of inner meanings.[2] A symbol is multivalent; it expresses simultaneously a number of meanings whose relationships may not be immediately apparent, yet which are joined in the fullness of the religious experience. The cross expresses death and life, individual salvation and the institution of the church, among much else.

Symbols, verbal and otherwise, are then capable of bearing the ambivalence or paradox that exists in great religious intuitions when they are aware they have touched something beyond ordinary human capacity. It is only through symbols, in fact, that we can express the diversity yet underlying oneness of the paradoxical complexes that make up religion.

Symbols strive to be inclusive, to carry meanings on several levels and to reconcile or transcend seeming inconsistencies. Concepts, on the other hand, strive to clarify and rationalize. Descending to the plane of ordinary life and thought, they emphasize distinctions, establish themselves on only one side of inconsistencies and polarities, and align themselves with one logical, philosophical, or theological system. In this way they allow mysticism (and the mystic) to be reconciled to the external norms.

A fascinating example is the Japanese Zen master Hakuin (1685–1768). He reports that when he was thirty-two, he came to a dilapidated temple, fell asleep inside, and had a dream. His mother appeared to him and presented him with a robe. When he lifted it, both sleeves seemed very heavy; on examining them he found in each an old mirror five or six inches in diameter. One, as he looked into it, showed everything imaginable: mountains and rivers, all that existed on earth, and even his own internal organs and mind. The other mirror displayed no reflection, yet as he looked its luster seemed to become many times brighter than the other mirror.

The two mirrors clearly represent two aspects of the universal Buddha-nature or the reality seen by a Buddha. This reality comprises all things, yet it is radiant undifferentiated essence, a continuous stream of vibrations like a single roar of thunder, and finally is identified with the mirror of the mind. Thus, after this vision, Hakuin said, "When I looked at all things, it was as though I were seeing my own face. For the first time I understood the meaning of the saying, 'The Tathagata [the Buddha] sees the Buddha-nature within his eye.' "[3] He added that afterwards he read again the Lotus Sutra and other classic Mahayana Buddhist texts and fully understood them for the first time.

That indicates that this dream-vision with its symbol of the two mirrors somehow encapsulated in a brief and simple scene an immense wealth of the convoluted riches of Mahayana philosophy, or at least somehow turned a mental key that made them accessible to this wandering monk. The two mirrors bore the paradoxes of the one and the many, of inner and outer, and of mind and matter, in a facile manner that enabled them to be solved on the level of experience, and a bit later, on the level of logic. Significantly it was the primordial symbols of the experience that opened the gateways of intellectual solution.

The Ideas
of Mysticism

But however wrapped in symbolic envelopes the cognitions of mystics are, including sometimes the symbolic envelope of rational clarity, we may still ask ourselves what does the theoretical expression of mysticism *say?* What does it tell us about the universe and humankind?

First let us remember that two basic types of writing and speaking by mystics can be found: philosophical and theological expression describing the *universe* perceived by the mystic, and discussion of *mysticism* itself. Both may be based on first-hand experience, though it should be remembered that philosophers may deal in the concepts of mysticism without being mystics themselves. The second category includes autobiography and objectified disquisitions on the spiritual life.

We shall examine each of these intellectual expressions. First, however, in the following lines, the Hindu mystic Shankara (c.700–750 A.D.) considerably mixes these expressions. This passage is immensely valuable, for it shows that the view of the universe does determine the life-style of the accomplished mystic, and his life-style is one which makes a certain perception of universal truth discoverable.

This Atman shines with its own light. Its power is infinite. It is beyond sense-knowledge. It is the source of all experience. He who knows the Atman is free from every kind of bondage. He is full of glory. He is the greatest of the great.

The things perceived by the sense cause him neither grief nor pleasure. He is not attached to them. Neither does he shun them. Constantly delighting in the Atman he is always at play within himself. He tastes the sweet, unending bliss of the Atman and is satisfied.

The child plays with his toys, forgetting even hunger and physical pain. In like manner, the knower of Brahman takes his delight in the Atman, forgetting all thought of "I" and "mine."

He gets his food easily by begging alms, without anxiety or care. He drinks from the clear stream. He lives unfettered and independent. He sleeps without fear in the forest or on the cremation-ground. He does not need to wash or dry his clothes, for he wears none. The earth is his bed. He walks the highway of Vedanta. His playmate is Brahman, the everlasting.

The knower of the Atman does not identify himself with his body. He rests within it, as if within a carriage. If people provide him with comforts and luxuries, he enjoys them and plays with them like a child. He bears no outward mark of a holy man. He remains quite unattached to the things of this world.

He may wear costly clothing, or none. He may be dressed in deer or tiger skin or clothed in pure knowledge. He may seem like a madman, or like a child, or sometimes like an unclean spirit. Thus, he wanders the earth.

The man of contemplation walks alone. He lives desireless amidst the objects of desire. The Atman is his eternal satisfaction. He sees the Atman present in all things.

Sometimes he appears to be a fool, sometimes a wise man. Sometimes he seems splendid as a king, sometimes feeble-minded. Sometimes he is calm and silent. Sometimes he draws men to him, as a python attracts its prey. Sometimes people honor him greatly, sometimes they insult him. Sometimes they ignore him. That is how the illumined soul lives, always absorbed in the highest bliss.

He has no riches, yet he is always contented. He is helpless, yet of mighty power. He enjoys nothing, yet he is continually rejoicing. He has no equal, yet he sees all men as his equals.

He acts, yet is not bound by his action. He reaps the fruit of past actions, yet is unaffected by them. He has a body, but does not identify himself with it. He appears to be an individual, yet he is present in all things, everywhere.

The knower of Brahman, who lives in freedom from body-consciousness, is never touched by pleasure of pain, good or evil.

If a man identified himself with the gross and subtle coverings within which he dwells, he will experience pleasure and pain, good or evil. But nothing is either good or evil to the contemplative sage, because he has realized the Atman and his bonds have fallen from him.

During an eclipse, the shadow of the earth falls upon the sun. The ignorant, who do not understand what has happened, say that the sun has been swallowed up by the darkness of the eclipse—but the sun can never be swallowed up.

In the same manner, the ignorant see the body of a knower of Brahman and identify him with it. Actually, he is free from the body and every other kind of bondage. To him, the body is merely a shadow.

He dwells in the body, but regards it as a thing apart from himself —like the cast-off skin of a snake. The body moves hither and thither, impelled by the vital force.[4]

God:
Love or Infinity

The preceding passage shows the ideal interaction of world view and life-style of the mystic, both being intellectual expressions of mysticism articulated as philosophy and personal narrative. We might also note a related interaction, having both ideological and mystical praxis expressions: the mystic's relation to the languages of love and infinity. As we have seen, love–infinity is one of mysticism's axes of interpretation, even as is the cognate matter of whether God is personal or impersonal, and whether or not the individual self is personal or impersonal.

A good example is the mysticism of Islam. Sufism began with a

dualistic emphasis on love between the devotee and God as two different entities. But soon it became apparent that the real thrust of such
devotion was toward the oneness of God alone; so by both logical and
devotional necessity it was also toward his hidden presence as the sole
reality within all things, including the heart of the mystic. In such ways
does mystical experience shape doctrine, or at least the understood
meanings of doctrine, even as the contextual religious culture may shape
the interpretation of the experience. Mysticism, in the intensive flash
itself, has a singularity about it that leads naturally to the accentuating
of doctrines of divine oneness and omnipresence.

The high point of developed Sufism as a mystical philosophical
system was in the work of the great Andalusian scholar Ibn al-Arabi (d.
1240). His work builds on sources going back to Neo-Platonism and
embracing the experience of diverse Sufis and the increasingly unitary
philosophical systems of Muslims like Ibn Rashid (Averroës) and al-
Ghazzali. Nonetheless, al-Arabi's work is strikingly original, and he
bases it on his own rich illuminative visions.

Al-Arabi saw the Beloved everywhere, including the self.
Through an individual's own eyes God looks at the world and finally
back at himself. God loves himself through us. In God's being, then, lies
the transcendent unity of existence. All separate things are God knowing himself. The Andalusian seer also perceived a transcendent unity of
religions; each prophet has a particular perspective on truth, he said, and
is a particular channel through which God knows himself.

Within this divine sea of oneness are also different vertical levels
of being. Between the mortal plane and the ultimate essence of God are
spiritual worlds known by the imagination and mystical insight. But
these realms of angels, archetypes, and blessed souls are also mere
aspects of God, "the breath of the merciful" flowing through a universe
in which "every atom is his throne." "We ourselves," wrote al-Arabi,
"are the attributes by which we describe God; our existence is merely
an objectivization of His existence. God is necessary to us in order that
we may exist, while we are necessary to Him in order that He may be
manifested to Himself."[5]

But the way to this knowledge, for Ibn al-Arabi, is love for God,
an ardent thirst for the Real, more than by quiet contemplation. Human
love is for him a valid analogy for this passionate quest for the omni-
present Beloved; he uses the analogy often in his own poems. But while
the love is the same, he says, the objects are different, for "they loved
a phenomenon, whereas I love the Real." Yet the love of God rising to
knowledge that He is all in all, should have the same fire, the same
"transport and rapture," as the joining of human lovers.

Even in a mystical intellectual system as attuned to the infinity and omnipresence of God as this one, the use of love as a major dynamic for attaining realization—along with the theistic theological bent of Islam—gives the world view a personal touch. God must be personal and so meet his devotees as the Beloved, even as he is also in them and loving himself through them. In other words, concepts have a positive meaning, especially those of personality and emotion, for they are stepping-stones to the infinite God, not separate from him.

Another mystical system that gives great place to the infinity and omnipresence of the Absolute is that of the Hwa-yen (Avatamsaka; Kegon) or Garland Sutra, taught pre-eminently by such Chinese masters as Fa Tsang. The latter once illustrated the Sutra's breath-taking vision of totality to the Empress Wu Tse-T'ien, showing her that the absolute Buddha-nature permeates all things large and small.

The Buddhist monk took the Empress into a room lined with mirrors—on the walls, in the corners, over the floor and ceiling, all facing one another. In the center of the room, the master placed an image of the Buddha, putting a torch beside it.

With a gasp of wonder, the lady instantly grasped the Buddhist teaching of totality. In all the mirrors were reflections of the Buddha, and in each reflections of all the other mirrors, infinity upon infinity without end. So is the Hwa-yen Buddhist cosmos, an inconceiveably vast realm made up of infinite universes of all shapes and durations, each containing a billion solar systems. Even their dimensions are infinite, for the atoms of one universe are universes themselves. Some of these universes are paradisal, and others, like ours, contain suffering owing to evil karma. But all accommodate the Buddha-nature, which infuses every blade of grass and every grain of sand.

The small contains the large and the large contains the small. To demonstrate this, Fa Tsang took a tiny crystal ball from his sleeve and placed it on the palm of his hand. Now the Empress Wu could see that, just as the mirrors reflected the small Buddha-image endlessly around the room, so could a minute crystal capture the entire panorama.

How does an individual attain this vision of ultimate reality, and share in the wonder and freedom that flows through it, and its scriptural descriptions? The answer in Hwa-yen is nonobstruction of mind. Nonobstruction is the quality mind has when it is thoroughly egoless and so nonclinging (for we cling to things or ideas, name-and-form, as props for ego) and nonattached. The primal mode of clinging and attachment, according to Buddhism, is to ego. It is an idea that one's separate self is the center of concern, or indeed has an existence other than being one nexus of light in the endless reflecting game of the infinite universe.

Attachment and ego distort perception of reality, leaving only a tiny beclouded world comprised of petty things and ideas.

Living in the infinite universe requires the "exhaustion of all realizations," the giving up of even the greatest beliefs or truths that are enwrapped with one's ego-identity. Only after an individual gives up beliefs can direct perception arise—seeing without symbols. By this doctrine a Buddha, and only a Buddha, has completely transcended ego and so sees all things precisely as they are. The Buddha needs none of the symbolic web of words, concepts, likes and dislikes, traumatic attraction and repulsions, which lie like a dense screen between our mental eyes and the infinite universe. Only a Buddha, then, can be perfectly compassionate, for compassion is the ethical expression of the egolessness and infinite awareness of liberation. The same ego attachments that inhibit our vision also inhibit our capacity to love without fear.

Buddhahood and all that goes with it, the nonobstructed mind and all its wonder and love, arises out of deep meditation, samadhi. It is in meditation that the Buddha counters ego and exhausts symbols. In meditation a new dawn of symbol-free light can arise that then never leaves the Buddha, whatever he is doing.[6]

For both the Buddhist and the Muslim mystic, love and infinity go together. Each opens the way for the other; each flows out of a true realization of the other. Yet a certain difference and tone and imagery does exist between al-Arabi and the Hwa-yen Sutra. For the al-Arabi, a strong sense of divine personality dwelling in the infinite presence confirms love as a path; for the Hwa-yen Sutra, love was to be freed from attachment with any concept of personality, divine or otherwise, in order truly to range to infinity, the ultimate absolute.

The Self:
Personal or Impersonal

It must never be forgotten that such issues as these are not, for the mystic, mere philosophical debates, but ways of understanding experiences he/she has actually sustained. It is a matter of whether the mystic has *known* overwhelming love for the Divine Other, or known infinite expansion of awareness and compassion in the wide and wondrous Buddhist universe.

Because the question of whether God is personal or impersonal or both is a matter of experience, it cannot be separated from the matter of how the mystic regards his/her own human self. For usually we conceive of God as an infinite analogue of what we take to be our nature. If we think of ourselves as everlasting centers of personal awareness and will, so is God defined; if we are each simply a nexus of reflections drawn from the universe, only imagining that we are separate selves rather than the universe itself, God is that transpersonal universal glory that finite personality only distorts.

Thus, in one of his earlier writings, the great modern Catholic mystic Thomas Merton said:

> For me to be a saint means to be myself. Therefore the problem of sanctity and salvation is in fact the problem of finding out who I am and of discovering my true self . . . *God alone possesses the secret of my identity. He alone can make me who I am* or rather, He alone can make me who I will be when I at last fully begin to be.

And again, speaking of the Christian contemplative experience:

> A door opens in the center of our being and we seem to fall through it into immense depths which, although they are infinite, are all accessible to us; all eternity seems to have become ours in this one placid and breathless contact . . . You seem to be the same person and you are the same person that you have always been: in fact you are more yourself than you have ever been before. You have only just begun to exist.[7]

This discovery of the depth and fullness of the true self may be compared with the Theravada Buddhist Vipassana meditation, whose purpose is to discover experientially that one's self is impermanent, suffering, and not a real entity. In Vipassana the experiencer calmly and carefully observes the actual workings of the self—the passage of events and separate entities we only barely manage to string together by desperate acts of memory and will. The experiencer discovers the very rough fit between sense-data, perception in the mind, and emotional responses. The strange independence of consciousness seems the flat mirror in which all this reflects. Finally, the meditator understands he/she is not a self but a collection of physico-psychological elements that only loosely hang together, though leaving the illusion of being a separate self. Their arrangement is actually transitory, however, born of ignorance, and subject to old age, sickness, and death. For one with any wit at all, this condition is unsatisfactory—suffering—and leads to yearning for the steady light of Nirvana, the transcendence of all impermanent and conditioned reality.[8]

Is the contrast between Christian and Buddhist meditation regarding discoveries about the self as great as it seems at first glance? Perhaps not, for the language of mysticism is elusive. Similar experiences can be veiled in disparate language; actual differences can be smoothed over with an oil of words. Even that observation does not end the problem. We can query further to what extent different words *make* different experiences and different interpretations.

We may compare to Buddhism lines of the Christian mystical classic of the fourteenth century, *The Cloud of Unknowing,* which inquire how one shall destroy the "naked knowing and feeling of your own being." The text comments that, "Perhaps you finally realize that if you destroyed this, every other obstacle would be destroyed. If you really do understand this you have done well." For this awareness of self-being, the *Cloud* tells us, is a sorrow, and the individual alone authentically feels that sorrow who "realizes not only *what he is* but *that he is.*" Yet through feeling this primordial sorrow one "prepares his heart to receive that joy through which he will finally transcend the knowing and feeling of his being."[9]

This passage—seemingly so much closer in concept and tone to Buddhism—nevertheless shares with the earlier Merton passage the belief that so long as the self is experienced *only* as the separate, isolated self, it is shallow and sorrowful. Only by negating that isolation and putting what we think of as the self in a larger context of infinite reality is it overcome, whether the language implies "God alone possesses the secret of my identity" or separate selfhood is impermanent, suffering, and unreal.

Thomas Merton himself, when toward the end of his life he became deeply interested in Christian dialogue with Buddhism, remarked that the Buddhist "no-self" doctrine is not necessarily in conflict with Christianity. He seems to have compared it with insights from sources like *The Cloud of Unknowing,* John of the Cross, Catherine of Genoa, and also the Apostle Paul's "It is no longer I who live, but Christ who lives in me" (Gal. 2:20).[10]

Words and Concepts: Pro and Con

Parallel to the concept of God and self and equally grounded in the realities of meditation for authentic mystics is the attitude that conceptual thinking and ideologies are valid carriers of the cognitions of mystical experience.

If we do not comprehend God or self as a personal self, it is understandable that we would want to disperse concepts like clouds of mist. For concepts are the rigid building-blocks of ego. (We build up the ego structure by clinging to concepts like "I'm a person who knows this, believes that, thinks in a certain way, likes this and not that.") The *Book of Privy Counselling,* by the anonymous English author of the more famous *Cloud of Unknowing,* tells us in prayer to "reject all thoughts, be they good or be they evil."[11] Countless other mystics have said much the same, from Zen masters teaching us to hold to the "unborn mind" to the contemporary Krishnamurti advocating "choiceless awareness."

But not all mysticism is so stark in its rejection of words and ideas. Psalm 119, breathing the spirit of traditional Judaism in its devotion to study of the Law as means to elevating the soul, says: "Lord, what love have I unto thy law! all the day long is my study in it . . . Thy word is a lantern unto my feet, and a light unto my paths . . . Thy testimonies have I claimed as mine heritage for ever; and why? they are the very joy of my heart."

Study of sacred texts and meditation on sacred ideas, even as do the postures of yoga or Zen, can induce a state of blissful concentration on the transcendent. Medieval Jewish kabbalistic mystics explored esoteric meanings latent in the Hebrew words, letters, and even strokes and spaces within single letters of the scriptures. The difference between this mysticism and that of the rejection of words and ideas in the mystical state is not that the latter is less intellectual. Yogins and Zen masters can be as rich verbally as anyone else when explaining their ultimate ideas. Rather, they qualify the experience of verbal mysticism by the different kind of ultimate reference it postulates—a God who expresses *himself* through words and the ideas behind them, and so can be known through the manipulation of verbal concepts.

A middle ground may be found in those mystical practices in which individuals focus attention by short and repeated prayer phrases, such as the Christian repetition of the name of Jesus, the short invocation of Jesus (the "Jesus prayer" of the Eastern church), or the mantra of Hinduism and Buddhism.

A key theme that typically divides the mysticism of words from the mysticism rejecting words is the attitude toward nature. Wordless spirituality tends to see the divine immanent in nature and continuous with it. The divine is, like nature, numinous but dumb, something perceived by the wise but not something that announces itself in plain language. The Upanishads of ancient India sing of Brahman, the divine absolute Spirit in all things, in this way:

O Brahman Supreme!
Formless art thou, and yet
(Though the reason none knows)

Thou bringest forth many forms;
Thou bringest them forth, and then
Withdrawest them to thyself.
Fill us with thoughts of thee!

Thou art the fire,
Thou art the sun,
Thou art the air,
Thou art the moon,
Thou art the starry firmament,
Thou art Brahman Supreme:

Thou art the waters—thou,
The creator of all!

Thou art woman, thou art man,
Thou art the youth, thou art the maiden,
Thou art the old man tottering with his staff;
Thou facest everywhere.

Thou art the dark butterfly,
Thou art the green parrot with red eyes,
Thou art the thunder cloud, the seasons, the seas.
Without beginning art thou,
Beyond time, beyond space.
Thou art he from whom sprang
The three worlds.[12]

Thus, because the Upanishadic sage perceives the divine as immanent in nature, he fully appreciates it and sees it in a good light.

These lines may be compared with a powerful passage from the Old Testament, in which the prophet Jeremiah describes poignantly the suffering of humanity and animals in a drought:

This came to Jeremiah as the word of the Lord concerning the drought:
Judah droops, her cities languish,
    her men sink to the ground;
  Jerusalem's cry goes up.
Their flock-masters send their boys for water;
they come to the pools but find no water there.
  Back they go, with empty vessels;
the produce of the land has failed,
because there is no rain.
The farmers' hopes are wrecked,

they uncover their heads for grief.
The hind calves in the open country
    and forsakes her young
    because there is no grass;
for lack of herbage, wild asses stand on the high bare places
    and snuff the wind for moisture,
    as wolves do, and their eyes begin to fail.
    Though our sins testify against us,
    yet act, O Lord, for thy own name's sake.
Our disloyalties indeed are many; we have sinned against thee.
    O hope of Israel, their saviour in time of trouble,
must thou be like a stranger in the land,
    a traveller pitching his tent for a night?
Must thou be like a man suddenly overcome,
    like a man powerless to save himself?
    Thou art in our midst, O Lord,
and thou hast named us thine; do not forsake us.
The Lord speaks thus of this people: They love to stray from my
ways, they wander where they will. Therefore he has no more
pleasure in them; he remembers their guilt now, and punishes
their sins.[13]

Here nature is a realm of distress in which God is *not* immanently
present, much as one might yearn for that to be the case: "Must thou
be a stranger in the land, a traveller pitching his tent for a night?" God
is, nonetheless, sovereign over nature. He can begin and end droughts.
But God's power is not expressed wordlessly through nature or the soul.
It is, rather, communicated to the prophet in words, words having to do
with other divine words, God's covenant and Law.

The Spiritual Path
as Intellectual Expression
of Mysticism

A metaphysical account of the universe, in which the supernal
realities contemplated by the mystic are properly placed, is not the only
form the intellectual expression of the experience can take. It can also
be a generalized account of the spiritual path, in which the experiencer
progressively presents its realities as the narrative tries to show others

how to encounter the same transcendence. Closely related are the rules of monastic or devotional fellowships. These rules express the spiritual experiences most important to their traditions. They do so through a stated way of life that assumes the supreme importance of mystical states.

A good example of a book on the spiritual path is *The Interior Castle* by the Spanish Saint Teresa of Avila (1515–1582).[14] Teresa affirms that the soul in the depths of the self is "formed of a single diamond or a very transparent crystal." But this radiant being, in which God dwells, is at the heart of an interior castle comprised of seven mansions; this jewel is like a sleeping fairy-tale princess surrounded by a ring of fire.

Passage through the outer three mansions is merely a probing of the soul's exterior defenses. The first is purgative, full of reptilian animals that must be cast out of one's inward life. The individual must remember that to be on this journey, even if only beginning, is a great thing. In the second house, a different kind of problem sets in; the seeker is full of growing doubts. But in the third house, he or she finds a preliminary reward for perseverence.

The fourth mansion begins a change in the nature of the quest, for it initiates the contemplative stages. The individual reaches it by meditation. In the Roman Catholic tradition meditation generally means a quite structured and deliberate process of inducing internal images and affects, a process that can lead into the more profound and formless stage known as contemplation. The fourth mansion goes beyond the hard purgative work and gross vacillations of the earlier steps; it is said to be a time of delicate delights, of subtle pleasures hard to describe.

In the fifth mansion comes an advanced and subtle replication of the second—a time of retrenchment. In it God deprives the soul of its senses so it may be more attuned to his wisdom. It is the stripping, even the initiatory death, that leads to rebirth. We shall later re-examine it as the Dark Night of the Soul.

The sixth house brings many rich mystical experiences—some not genuine—and the soul is wounded by love. The consummation of the inward journey is the seventh, the mystical marriage, when God rewards the questor by a final union with the Beloved beyond all distraction or dissolution.

This process can well be compared with the famous "Eight Limbs of Yoga" of Patanjali's *Yoga Sutras* (c. 100 B.C.–A.D.100).[15]

Its eight steps to spiritual realization and union with the Absolute also start with a course of purgation and control of mental disequilibrium. These courses of purgation and control are the two steps of *yama*

—abstention from evil-doing such as harm, falsehood, theft, incontinence, or greed—and *niyama*—good observances, including purity, contentment, mortification, and devotion to God. In the third step one can,
under the guidance of a master, begin the yogic practices of *asana,* the
well-known physical postures, and *pranayama,* control of the *prana* or
vital energy through breathing exercises.

The fifth step is a point of transition to an interior movement such
as we also noted in Teresa's schema. It is a withdrawal of attention from
the outer senses to direct one's study inward. All the earlier stages have
been preparatory for this stage. The real point of purgation, and likewise
of *asana* and *pranayama,* is to gain such control over one's body, feelings, and flitting thoughts. The experiencer quiets these diversions so
they will not distract from the real quest for inward liberation.

The individual reaches this liberation through the last three steps:
concentration, meditation, and samadhi. The supreme stage of samadhi
is the breakthrough to that perfect mental equilibrium in which all
barriers to horizonless awareness and bliss are demolished. It can undoubtedly be compared to the highest ecstasy of any mystical path, the
supreme or absolute moment.

It is clear that an analysis of the central experience—samadhi—has
led to the sequence that repeats it. If samadhi has an immobile calmness,
steady postures must help induce it. If in it the breathing is deep and
quiet, control of breath must energize the self striving toward it. If
above all it is unconditioned by the modulations of mind, (whether
externally or internally produced), the path toward it must provide for
progressive withdrawal from outward or changeable things. It begins
with withdrawal from erratic or sensual ways of life in *yama* and
niyama, and ends with withdrawal from the outer senses altogether.

In the same way, the supreme goal of Teresa's *Interior Castle,* the
mystic nuptials, conditions the comparable but more romantic tone of
the entire book. Influenced by literature of the chivalric quest, it has
subtle hints of spiritual equivalents to sensual delights.

Both books reflect a life-long progression toward spiritual
maturity and realization. We can probably assume the authors of such
classics realize that in practice the spiritual life is not quite as schematic
as their systems make out. One may experience a flash of meditation
or even token samadhi early on; one may complete one's course without
seeming to advance beyond the preliminary stages, yet find in them a
great peace. Even if one takes a circuitous route on a journey, a map
showing the straight path can be helpful; and even preliminary encouraging flashes of the final glory may not be stabilized until much, much
later. For this reason these guidebooks to the quest are not so much

maps to guide everyone, as intellectual expressions of mysticism. In these expressions the author articulates his experience as narrative sequence rather than as metaphysical system.

Spiritual Rules
As Intellectual Expression
of Mysticism

Similarly, those dedicated to a spiritual path often make structures of group life a factor in the analysis of the experience and its replication. Some intentional communities related to mysticism seek to create for the aspirant the supportive atmosphere of what Erving Goffmann calls *total institution*—a tendency fully realized in the religious order. A total institution, according to Goffmann, is an organization like prisons, insane asylums, hospitals, monasteries, convents, armies, or boarding schools that controls much more than a portion of a member's life (as do ordinary jobs, churches, recreations); instead it comes near complete control. It manages diet, sex and marriage, dress, occupation, personal effects, and daily schedule. Often explicitly, and even more implicitly, total institution determines the pattern of thinking and emotional values of its members. It does so intentionally through the community and indirectly through its conditioning of life-style and environment.[16]

As the list indicates, total institutions are highly diverse in nature and purpose. Only the religious ones interest us, particularly those whose religious focus is the mystical event. In such communities we may expect a statement of a total way of life, because some individuals through experience have found such control productive of a holy life.

The Buddhist Vinaya or monastic discipline discusses the annual period of withdrawal for three months during the rainy season when monks engage in secluded intensive practice and gives precepts regarding the dangers and problems of this experience.[17] The Christian Benedictine rule presents itself as "a school of the Lord's service" containing nothing that is harsh or burdensome but only that which works to amend evil habits and preserve charity. Its life centers on the Opus Dei —the Divine Work or the communal psalms and prayers—and with it stability in community, simplicity of life, poverty, obedience, and chastity for the monks. The Benedictine rule spells out the practice of all these though not in detail.[18] The central motif of rules of Islamic mystical orders is generally to provide opportunity for the aspirant to receive guidance from the shaykh or spiritual master who governs it. Yet it is understood that this is not always an easy matter. To receive and understand spiritual guidance requires far more conditioning than reading a newspaper. Thus, Sufi aspirants generally underwent a three-year probation, in which the masters might treat them rudely. Even after becoming inner-circle disciples of a Sufi master, they still had to pass through several steps or "stations" before achieving the wisdom and love of *fana,* absorption into God.[19]

In these and other examples, we must note the endeavor to order not only life, but also emotional feelings and spiritual experience. The mystics structure emotion and experience into signs and stages to make them part of a meaning-laden psychocosmic reality. At the same time, we must note that mystical experience is not always the only, or even main, purpose of religious orders. Often they are established far more for the service of God and humanity than for mystical pursuits. Yet their ascetic character and religious intentionality suggests a high value given to mystical experience as part of the monastic world view.

Mystical Autobiography

Another genre using an intellectual expression of mysticism is the autobiography. In this genre the recounting of mystical quest and experience is the major theme. Like accounts of the spiritual path and the religious rule, the autobiography lays a grid of meaning over otherwise haphazard ecstasies. It shows they have a progression that can be categorized into purgation, path, and climax, and have a relation to belief and life-style.

A goodly company of mystics from many traditions have left accounts, often very intimate, of their lives and inward banes and blessings. For whatever reason, it seems that mystics are more prone to autobiography than any other class of religionist. The exceedingly personal nature of mysticism lends itself to the expression of its sacred cosmos and philosophy in this form.

The autobiography of the Tibetan Milarepa (1040–1123) paints a vivid vista of a land of shamanlike wizards with magical powers. In this world humans share the towering snowcapped peaks of the mystic's homeland with gods, demons, and calm transcendent Buddhas. However, Milarepa realizes this strange cosmos really derives only from mind.

Like many, if not most, mystical autobiographies, Milarepa's begins with a happy childhood interrupted by a crucial and traumatic turning point, in this case the death of his father. He then tasted bitterness and sorrow as an evil uncle stole the patrimony of himself and his mother. Milarepa practiced the black arts to punish the dispoiler with curses, but after some success became sick of deviltry and turned to true religion instead. This he learned under Marpa, a harsh but celebrated guru who forced incredible trials upon Milarepa, but finally rewarded him with the initiation he sought. Thereafter Milarepa, on his own in the wilderness, grew in spiritual power until he became Tibet's greatest mystic and poet.[20]

Another autobiography from a different culture and a more modern time is that of Maria José, a medium in an Afro-Brazilian spirit cult. She had suffered a terrible headache that would not go away. Doctors were no help. She lost contact with reality and was taken to a mental hospital. For a while her hospitalization helped; then she became nervous and unable to sleep and eat. Eventually, she went out of her mind. Her family took her to a *terreiro*, or center of the spiritist faith, for assistance by a *pai de santo*, saint-father, a spiritist priest and healer. Through his help she began receiving a guardian deity, Rompe Mato, in trance. Thereafter she no longer had headaches or the other symptoms; she believed the deity had driven out the evil spirits.[21]

This oral account by a barely literate contemporary is only marginally mystical, but has themes common to many such narratives past and present: a growing inner crisis, a breakthrough by a transformative experience under suggestive environmental and interpersonal triggers. The extent to which the experience was transformative suggests that Rompe Mato was functionally the ultimate divine reality at that moment, not just a spirit to be manipulated or used.

This case indicates the practical and therapeutic value mystical and religious experience can have. It also shows the role of the experience as a transformative pivot in the autobiography to give meaning to what was obtained before and after. After the experience—and in light of her unsuccessful experiences with doctors and the mental hospital—Maria José could say what "really" had occurred before was domination by evil spirits, which now Rompe Mato was able to keep at bay.

We have glanced at the schematization of the spiritual life given in Teresa's *Interior Castle*. This saint also composed a story of her life, and it might be of value to compare her two texts.

Like the life of Milarepa and that of the German-Jewish American schoolteacher, the *Life* of Teresa begins with her happy, secure childhood with loving parents, a happiness that was shattered in her adolescence. In the case of Teresa the trauma was the death of her mother when Teresa was twelve, though she remained close to her father whom she greatly admired. Subsequently, she lived a life that she later saw as sinful and frivolous, though it seems to have been no more than a normal teenage girl's love of dancing, intimate friendships, and light and gossipy conversation. But later this period seemed to her a life far from God; in relation to her ultimate vocation it was. At sixteen, after spiritual reading, she entered the convent. Her first twenty years was a time of trouble. She endured much from sickness, hardship, and spiritual dryness. But in her mid-thirties she experienced visions and raptures—culminating in the piercing of her heart by a cherub—that fired the writing of her books and her life as an active reformer of the Carmelite order.[22]

We can easily correlate *The Interior Castle* with the *Life.* In the *Castle*, God is a gracious king who gives favors, but the soul—like a knight filled with the spirit of chivalry—must attract the sovereign's benign attention by acts of faith and daring. Such was the meaning Teresa gave her twenty-year period of purgation in the outer mansions of the castle. Her religious experience translated easily into the feudal social order and its chivalric code, which—though already passing in the Spain of her day—still charged its literature and ideals.

Other images and correlations, however, arise as the seeker presses deeper into the inner stronghold and into the life. In the seventh and most inward of the heavenly mansions, God sets aside his kingly sceptre to become maternal breasts, pouring out grace like streams of milk. Turning to these fountains, like the mystical marriage, represents the oneness of the soul with God in the joy of the castle's profoundest secret. These images, effective metaphors of spiritual realization, might also be the climax of the writer's reconciliation with very powerful but buried rememberings: the teenage romanticism she left behind for the convent; the maternal love she early lost to death.

Science and Mysticism

A quite different way of understanding the intellectual expression of mysticism is that body of literature relating mysticism to scientific thought and findings. That this is an important area of investigation may be surprising to some, yet it should not be. Correlations between the perspectives of the more philosophical strands of both mysticism and science have long been apparent, especially when they are compared to other alternatives. Both tend to share a mood that has been eloquently expressed by Albert Einstein:

> There are moments when one feels free from one's own identification with human limitations and inadequacies. At such moments one imagines that one stands on some spot of a small planet, gazing in amazement at the cold yet profoundly moving beauty of the eternal, the unfathomable: life and death flow into one, and there is neither evolution nor destiny; only Being.[23]

Compared to religions stressing God's self-revelation and activity in history, mysticism in its traditional forms of intellectual expression, like science, tends with Einstein to reach for something transcending the historical moment: the nature of reality itself, the beginnings and ends of things, the immutable laws that condition apparent change. As Aldous Huxley put it, the scientist searches out "not the universe of given appearances, but the world of inferred fine structures, not the experienced world of unique events and diverse qualities, but the world of quantified regularities."[24]

Clearly, if the religion of God acting in events tends to value most the world of given appearances, the mystic shares with the scientist a concern with what is behind these appearances. These underlying secrets are more stable, predictable, and real in that the appearances depend upon them. Both the mystic and the scientist tend to see unity in the cosmos, either because it is an expression of one mind or because it operates by the same norms and is built from the same orders of subatomic particles. Whether mystical, metaphysical, or mathematical, the language and presuppositions of serious mysticism and science often have more in common than with other styles or religion or literature. After all, the historical roots of modern science are not so much in mainstream European religion as in Renaissance alchemy and occultism, disciplines intended partly to induce mystical experience and were rooted in mystical Neoplatonism and Pythagoreanism. These disciplines presumed on the basis of experience the cosmos of unity, regularity, and "being" of the mystic. They created protoscience to reinforce these suppositions.

The important difference, of course, between mysticism and modern science is in the method of investigation. Mystics depend on the ecstatic moment and the associations of the afterglow. Scientists may still get an initial idea in this way or through calmer reflection and intuition. In fact scientists obtain their ideas in all sorts of ways—in bright flashes of insight, even in dreams. But the scientist proceeds to express the insight according to the canons of mathematics or scientific description and to verify it by careful observation or experimentation. What cannot be so expressed and verified has been regarded outside the province of science.

Yet even this qualified distinction between science and mysticism may be too simple. Since the Einsteinian relativity revolution, scientists have increasingly recognized the inseparability of the observer and his conceptual paradigms from the observation. This revolution has led in turn to a still nascent realization that we cannot avoid the question of the origin and nature of consciousness in any unified theory of the universe, even in cosmology or physics. Commentators have not lacked to point to convergence between this requirement and the mystic's oneness in a universe alive and conscious because it expresses unifying mind perceived in flashes of "cosmic consciousness."

In the universe of modern theoretical physics matter does not always operate as though it were nothing but lifeless and mindless entities banging around in static space and time. Rather it is a cosmos in which space, time, the forces we perceive as matter, the observer's mind, and whatever in the universe answers to the role of mind—all interplay in a bewilderingly subtle and shifting pattern. Only the farther reaches of mathematics begin to sort out this complexity.

We can do no more here than hint at the emerging universe of the new physics and cosmology. But it seems evident that space, time, and matter are very far from what they seem, and that all the universe—including consciousness—is profoundly and necessarily interrelated. All is one to a degree that would satisfy the most nondualist mystic, if not perhaps in the way he expected. Yet it is not one in a dull determinstic way, but in the harmony of a universe with an astonishing degree of openness and freedom.

Perhaps such a harmony should not be surprising, for we are speaking of the same universe that has, after all, produced the human mind with its complicated mixture of freedom and determinism. We are children of the universe, and one would think that we could be at variance from our origin only to a certain extent, not totally. Is there then consciousness, or some seed or potential for consciousness, built into the universe at large? Is it somehow part—maybe even the cohesive —of the space-time-energy structure itself?

Arthur M. Young, in *The Reflexive Universe,* has advanced a remarkable proposition based on the theoretical physics of Max Planck and the philosophy of Leibniz. Leibniz held that each fundamental monad or particle reflects the whole universe—a view we shall encounter in a new form in a moment. Leibniz may have been through his careful study of Chinese philosophy indirectly influenced by the Hwa-yen Sutra already discussed.[25]

Likewise, Young suggests that light is conscious—or at least acts as if it were.[26] Light is, after all, the basic universal constant of modern physics whose fundamental units, quanta or photons, are close to a modern equivalent of primordial monads. Out of all possible curves, a photon selects the one that will take it most quickly to its goal, as though acting purposively. Photons, or quanta, create matter by structuring themselves, just as the brain—itself composed of a highly complex arrangement of the innumerable primordial light-entities—knows, remembers, and imagines by elaborate arrangements of light (i.e. electronic) impulses. Someday, we may seek to understand the universe by examining those ecstatic moments when our minds seem most clearly light and aligned with the light-based structure of the universe.

One of the most exciting new developments in this direction, (the interaction of science and mysticism) is the holographic universe theory of the Stanford brain researcher Karl Pribram.[27] While still highly speculative, this model of mind and universe appears to unite the frontiers of neurology and physics, while presenting a picture of the cosmos that makes sense of the fact that people have mystical experiences.

A holograph is a three dimensional picture created by reflecting light off a photographic plate containing a hologram or code, implanted by bringing together a laser beam and light reflected off the object onto the plate. A key characteristic of a hologram is that all parts of it contain the whole; if it is broken, the entire picture can be reproduced from any fragment.

Pribram's study first led him to the conclusion that the brain works by what is essentially a holographic process. It manufactures reality by creating holographic images within itself on the basis of frequencies that have no time or space or reality of their own. Memory, too, is made up of holograms, which explains why it seems to be dispersed through the brain, available to any part of it, rather than localized.

Then Pribram, following the thought of the physicist David Bohm and others, began reflecting on what sort of universe the holographic brain implies. The primary order of the cosmos—the "fine structures" or "quantified regularities" of Huxley—would not be actual space, time, or objects, but simply nondimensional waves prior to space, time, or matter. *The universe itself,* in other words, is a hologram, interpreted holographically by the brain.

This means the universe is not really made up of entities localized in space and time, this star here and that one there, this event now and that one a thousand years ago. Instead, just as in a photographic hologram, all of it is in every part, and the picture of the whole universe could be reproduced from any fragment of it—including the fragment of one's own brain.

The universe and its history or our own are simply images we are creating and stories we are telling ourselves from out of the holographic frequencies in our minds—in a holographic universe, there is no need to think of them coming from anywhere outside. In this model of the universe, we may note in passing, no theoretical objection exists to psychic phenomena such as clairvoyance (awareness of events far away), precognition (knowledge or vision of events prior to their happening), or retrocognition (perception of past events in present time). Near and far, past and future are all capable of being holographically reproduced from every fragment of space and time, if (so to speak) the light hits it right.

However, we generally use only a tiny bit of the universal hologram. The brain usually works as, in Henri Bergson's concept, a reducing valve. But a timeless, spaceless matrix of frequencies must exist from which we filter out what we use. This matrix would be, like the brain, a great hologram. Indeed, since it works by processes and is of a nature identical with our holographic minds, it could be thought of as itself a holographic mind, existing in its fullness in every fragment of the universe.

Unmistakably, this holographic universe is a picture of the universe very similar to that commonly experienced by mystics. Pribram has commented, as have other scientists and philosophers, on the almost uncanny parallel between the voidlike, mirrorlike, mindlike universe of modern physics and holographic theory, and that of ancient mystical visions like those of the Hwa-yen Sutra and of Plotinus. For both the scientists and mystics nothing really seems to exist except consciousness and waves; even time and space are contingent.

Yet those ancients could not have known about this model of the universe through the empirical and mathematical means of modern science. They intuited it. In other words, mystical consciousness may be a means of opening wider or even making infinite the reducing valve of the brain so one links up with most or all of the cosmic hologram in a flash of vision.

Another aspect of the relation of science to mysticism is the scientific study of meditative and mystical consciousness. An example of this study is biofeedback brain wave research, which works toward determining the complex EEG signatures of a number of states of consciousness. A British physicist has employed a device called the Mind Mirror, whose face presents twelve frequency ranges for each brain hemisphere and shows a continually changing pattern symbolizing the subject's mental state. This device makes easily visible what had previously been known: that people in meditation have a high production of alpha waves, the brain wave associated with calm, relaxation, and peace of mind; meditators also have a high symmetry between the two hemispheres. The Mind Mirror has also demonstrated a state called lucid awareness, in which the subject is active—talking, working, solving problems, even feeling emotion—yet does not lose alpha production or symmetry. It seems comparable to the sahaj or active yoga of Indic tradition. Use of the Mind Mirror and other brain wave biofeedback devices have reportedly enabled some people to develop facility in meditation and simple mental relaxation.[28]

None of these matters is the last word on the relation of mysticism to science. Some may turn out to be misleading. They are presented as examples of the sort of thinking and research that is going on, and as indicators that this will probably continue to be a lively field of exploration in the foreseeable future.

Meister Eckhart

We shall conclude our discussion of the intellectual expression of mysticism with a look at the sermons of the great mystical theologian Johannes Eckhart (c. 1260–1328), commonly called Meister Eckhart or the Master Eckhart. Rarely have the typical presuppositions and the psychological processes of the mystic been more clearly and boldly stated than by this medieval German Dominican friar. Never aspiring to be more than a preacher and condemned for some of his statements by the Pope, Eckhart did not shrink from probing the experiences of his soul to their uttermost limits of meaning and expounding that meaning.

The 28 sermons of Meister Eckhart, his most celebrated works, are mirrors of the inner movement of his self-awareness. They reach a climax of mystical radicalism and profundity in the last "Blessed Are the Poor." (It is presented as the reading selection at the end of this chapter.) It would be difficult to find any bit of prose that, in so short a compass, draws one as deeply into the dizzying intellectual paradoxes and the deep psychological realizations, both exciting and frightening, to which mysticism can lead the fearless soul. It takes us through the mature rediscovery of childhood, the conundrum of the god of ordinary piety versus the God above and beyond, the mysterious relation of God known and the God known only by unknowing.

In his writings, Eckhart presents four stages of the interaction between the soul and God: dissimilarity, similarity, identity, breakthrough. At the beginning, God is all and the individual is nothing; at the end, "the soul is above God." In the first stage, dissimilarity, the seeker realizes that he is nothing because God is everything, so totally different from his own nothingness. In the next stage (similarity), the person attaches himself to an image of God, such as the Father or the Son, which emerges in the soul. In the third (identity) comes the identity the mystic seems to seek: "the core of the soul and the core of God are one." But there is a final stage (breakthrough) when the mystic with his utter detachment abandons all things, even God, and lives seeking nothing, not even God. At this stage he breaks beyond God as God can be conceived, beyond the God of the Trinity or even explicit mystic unity, to the Godhead beyond God, as far beyond the known God as heaven is beyond earth.

But this is anticipating the climax of Eckhart's thought. It would be best to approach Sermon 28 more or less as Eckhart did. We shall first note a few important themes in earlier sermons.[29]

The first, a Christmas sermon, exphasizes that the real begetting of the eternal Son by the heavenly Father is in our hearts, a process silent and without beginning or end. For a mystic in the Neoplatonic tradition, as was Eckhart, the true spiritual realities are those quiet and out of time, yet deeper in us than even our own selves.

In a later sermon, Number 5, "The Love of God," we are told it is precisely from this deep point that true action comes, and it must come without calculation: "Do all you do, acting from the core of your soul, without a single 'Why.' . . . For if Life were questioned a thousand years and asked: 'Why live?' and if there were an answer, it could be no more than this: 'I live only to live!' " That response, reminding one of the immediacy of Zen, he expresses further in the next sermon, "The Kingdom of God Is at Hand." "Further," Eckhart affirms, "I say that if the soul is to know God, it must forget itself and lose (consciousness of) itself, for as long as it is self-aware and self-conscious, it will not see or be conscious of God. But when, for God's sake, it becomes unselfconscious and lets go of everything, it finds itself again in God, for knowing God, it therefore knows itself and everything else from which it has been cut asunder, in the divine perfection."

This is the first step: to know God by losing consciousness of one's self. There is a further step: to know God by losing consciousness of God. Thus far, though, Eckhart is simply concerned that one live out of the heart of one's being, where life can be spontaneous and unself-conscious. Such a life *is* one with God, for God himself is spontaneous and unself-conscious. Sermon 10 is entitled "God Laughs and Plays," and later, in Number 27, Eckhart proclaims, "God enjoys himself. His own inner enjoyment is such that it includes his enjoyment of all creatures not as creatures, but as God. His own inner enjoyment includes everything." For as Eckhart tells us in Number 25, "God Beyond Time!" "God is closer to the soul than the soul is to itself and therefore, God is in the soul's core—God and all the Godhead."

If an individual has meditated carefully on these themes—or better, let them work spontaneously in the self—this individual will be ready for the bombshells of Sermon 28, "Blessed Are the Poor."

Its basic theme is that to be poor in will or spirit means not seeking deliberately to satisfy God, as though one could *intentionally* do God's will if one were not in a state to do it *spontaneously.* This negation of will in spontaneity is the inner meaning of holy poverty, and the inner meaning of virtues is greater than their outer meaning. Not to will but to *be* is the important thing, and being without willing means acting out of one's being, naturally, rather than deliberately knowing God or doing his will. That is why like so many mystics Eckhart idealized the womb and infancy. At this time individuals do not have a God as a conceptualized deity whom they presume to know as another, and whose will they serve; instead they are simply a part of and with the God who *is,* the God above God. Within this divine being, a person was never born, nor shall ever die, but simply *is.*

A life *in* God is a life without God—few have stated the paradox that lies at the heart of radical mysticism more incisively than Eckhart. Others have tried, for it is a problem that all intellectual expressions of mysticism must sooner or later confront. For mysticism can give us a God so continuous with nature and the self that with a slight shift in our perspective, this God might disappear and leave us only nature and self. Yet the heights of mystical experience everywhere require that we be *free of* God as a restricting object badgering us with commandments and guilt and live with a God so great yet so near he can be enjoyed while forgotten, and served in the spirit of play.

The Brahman of Shankara's Vedanta and the Buddha-nature of Hwa-yen and Zen have much in common with Eckhart's Godhead above God: all must come out of similar experiences common to the serious practice of mysticism. We also think of Eckhart in reading the godless yet intensely religious (in a paradoxical sense) works of such writers as William Blake, Friedrich Nietzsche, and modern "Death of God" theologians like Thomas Altizer.

Mysticism and Religious Thought: Reading Selection

Here is the Sermon 28 of Meister Eckhart, "Blessed are the Poor."

Blessedness opened the mouth that spake wisdom and said: "Blessed are the poor in spirit, for theirs is the kingdom of heaven." All the angels and all the saints and all that were ever born must keep silence when the eternal wisdom of the Father speaks; for all the wisdom of angels and creatures is pure nothing, before the bottomless wisdom of God. And this wisdom has spoken and said that the poor are blessed.

Now, there are two kinds of poverty. One is external poverty and it is good, and much to be praised in people who take it upon themselves willingly, for the love of our Lord Jesus Christ, for he himself practiced it in the earthly realm. Of this poverty I shall say nothing more, for there is still another kind of poverty, an inward poverty, with reference to which, this saying of our Lord is to be understood: "Blessed are the poor in spirit, or of spirit."

Now, I pray you that you may be like this, so that you may understand this address; for, by the eternal truth, I tell you that if you haven't this truth of which we are speaking in yourselves, you cannot understand me.

Certain people have asked me what this poverty is. Let us answer that.

Bishop Albert says: "To be poor is to take no pleasure in anything God ever created," and that is well said. But we shall say it better and take "poverty" in a higher sense. He is a poor man who wants nothing, knows nothing, and has nothing. I shall speak of these three points.

In the first place, let us say that he is a poor man who wants nothing. Some people do not understand very well what this means. They are people who continue very properly in their penances and external practices of piety (popularly considered of great importance—may God pardon it!) and still they know very little of the divine truth. To all outward appearances, these people are to be called holy, but inwardly they are asses, for they understand not at all the true meaning of the divine reality. They say well that to be poor is to want nothing, but they mean by that, living so that one never gets his own way in anything, but rather so disposes himself as to follow the all-loving will of God. These persons do no evil in this, for they mean well, and we should praise them for that—may God keep them in his mercy!

I tell you the real truth, that these people are not poor, nor are they even like poor people. They pass for great in the eyes of people who know no better. Yet I say that they are asses, who understand the truth of the divine not at all. For their good intentions they may possibly receive the Kingdom of Heaven, but of this poverty, of which I shall now speak, they have no idea.

If I were asked, then, what it is to be a poor man who wants nothing, I shall answer and say: As long as a person keeps his own will, and thinks it his will to fulfill the all-loving will of God, he has not that poverty of which we are talking, for this person has a will with which he wants to satisfy the will of God, and that is not right. For if one wants to be truly poor, he must be as free from his creature will as when he had not yet been born. For, by the everlasting truth, as long as you will do God's will, and yearn for eternity and God, you are not really poor; for he is poor who wills nothing, knows nothing, and wants nothing.

Back in the Womb from which I came, I had no god and merely was, myself. I did not will or desire anything, for I was pure being, a knower of myself by divine truth. Then I wanted myself and nothing else. And what I wanted, I was and what I was, I wanted, and thus, I existed untrammeled by god or anything else. But when I parted from my free will and received my created being, then I had a god. For before there were creatures, God was not god, but, rather, he was what he was. When creatures came to be and took on creaturely being, then God was no longer God as he is in himself, but god as he is with creatures.

Now we say that God, in so far as he is only god, is not the highest goal of creation, nor is his fullness of being as great as that of the least of creatures, themselves in God. And if a flea could have the intelligence by which to search the eternal abyss of divine being, out of which it came, we shall say that god, together with all that god is, could not give fulfillment or satisfaction to the flea! Therefore, we pray that we may be rid of god, and taking the truth, break into eternity, where the highest angels and souls too, are like what I was in my primal existence, when I wanted what I was, and was what I wanted. Accordingly, a person ought to be poor in will, willing as little and wanting as little as when he did not exist. This is how a person is poor, who wills nothing.

Again, he is poor who knows nothing. We have sometimes said that man ought to live as if he did not live, neither for self, nor for the truth, nor for God. But to that point, we shall say something else and go further. The man who is to achieve this poverty shall live as having what was his when he did not live at all, neither his own, nor the truth, nor god. More: he shall be quit and empty of all knowledge, so that no knowledge of god exists in him; for when a man's existence is of God's eternal species, there is no other life in him: his life is himself. Therefore we say that a man ought to be empty of his own knowledge, as he was when he did not exist, and let God achieve what he will and be as untrammeled by humanness as he was when he came from God.

Now the question is raised: In what does happiness consist most of all? Certain authorities have said that it consists in loving. Others say that it consists in knowing and loving, and this is a better statement. But we say that it consists neither in knowledge nor in love, but in that there is something in the soul, from which both knowledge and love flow and which, like the agents of the soul, neither knows nor loves. To know this is to know what blessedness depends on. This something has no "before" or "after" and it waits for nothing that is yet to come, for it has nothing to gain or lose. Thus, when God acts in it, it is deprived of knowing that he has done so. What is more, it is the same kind of thing that, like God, can enjoy itself. Thus I say that man should be so disinterested and untrammeled that he does not know what God is doing in him. Thus only can a person possess that poverty.

The authorities say that God is a being, an intelligent being who knows everything. But I say that God is neither a being nor intelligent and he does not "know" either this or that. God is free of everything and therefore he is everything. He, then, who is to be poor in spirit must be poor of all his own knowledge, so that he knows nothing of God, or of himself. This is not to say that one may not desire to know and to see the way of God, but it is to say that he may thus be poor in his own knowledge.

In the third place, he is poor who has nothing. Many people have said that this is the consummation, that one should possess none of the corporeal goods of this world, and this may well be true in case one thus becomes poor voluntarily. But this is not what I mean.

Thus far I have said that he is poor who does not want to fulfill the will of god but who so lives that he is empty of his own will and the will of god, as much so as when he did not yet exist. We have said of this poverty that it is the highest poverty. Next, we said that he is poor who knows nothing of the action of god in himself. When a person is as empty of "knowledge" and "awareness" as God is innocent of all things, this is the purest poverty. But the third poverty is most inward and real and I shall now speak of it. It consists in that a man *has* nothing.

Now pay earnest attention to this! I have often said, and great authorities agree, that to be a proper abode for God and fit for God to act in, a man should also be free from all [his own] things and [his own] actions, both inwardly and outwardly. Now we shall say something else. If it is the case that a man is emptied of things, creatures, himself and god, and if still god could find a place in him to act, then we say: as long as that [place] exists, this man is not poor with the most intimate poverty. For God does not intend that man shall have a place reserved for *him* to work in, since true poverty of spirit requires that man shall be emptied of god and all his works, so that if God wants to act in the soul, he himself must be the place in which he acts—and that he would like to do. For if God once found a person as poor as this, he would take the responsibility of his own action and would himself be the *scene* of action, for God is one who acts within himself. It is here, in this poverty, that man regains the eternal being that once he was, now is, and evermore shall be.

There is the question of the words of St. Paul: "All that I am, I am by the grace of God," but our argument soars above grace, above intelligence, and above all desire. (How is it to be connected with what St. Paul says?) It is to be replied that what St. Paul says is true, not that this grace was in him, but the grace of God had produced in him a simple perfection of being and then the work of grace was done. When, then, grace had finished its work, Paul remained as he was.

Thus we say that a man should be so poor that he is not and has not a place for God to act in. To reserve a place would be to maintain distinctions. *Therefore I pray God that he may quit me of god,* for [his] unconditioned being is above god and all distinctions. It was here [in unconditioned being] that I was myself, wanted myself, and knew myself to be this person [here before you], and therefore, I am my own first cause, both of my eternal being and of my temporal being. To this end I was born, and by virtue of my birth being eternal, I shall never die. It is of the nature of this eternal birth that I *have been* eternally, that I *am* now, and *shall be* forever. What I am as a temporal creature is to die and come to nothingness, for it came whith time and so with time it will pass away. In my eternal birth, however, everything was begotten. I was my own first cause as well as the first cause of everything else. If I had willed it, neither I nor the world would have to come be! If I had not been, there would have been no god. There is, however, no need to understand this.

A great authority says: "His bursting forth is nobler than his efflux." When I flowed forth from God, creatures said: "He is a god!" This, however, did not make me blessed, for it indicates that I, too, am a creature. In bursting forth, however, when I shall be free within God's will and free, therefore of the will of god, and all his works, and even of god himself, then I shall rise above all creature kind, and I shall be neither god nor creature, but I shall be what I was once, now, and forevermore. I shall thus receive an impulse which shall raise me above the angels. With this impulse, I receive wealth so great that I could never again be satisfied with a god, or anything that is a god's nor with any divine activities, for in bursting forth I discover that God and I are One. Now I am what I was and I neither add to nor subtract from anything, for I am the unmoved Mover, that moves all things. Here, then, a god may find no "place" in man, for by his poverty the man achieves the being that was always his and shall remain his eternally. Here, too, God is identical with the spirit and that is the most imtimate poverty discoverable.

If anyone does not understand this discourse, let him not worry about that, for if he does not find this truth in himself he cannot understand what I have said—for it is a discovered truth which comes immediately from the heart of God. That we all may so live as to experience it eternally, may God help us! Amen.

Notes

[1]Paul Tillich, *Systematic Theology, I* (Chicago: University of Chicago Press, 1951), pp. 238–39.

[2]Mircea Eliade, "Methodological Remarks on the Study of Religious Symbolism," in *The History of Religions: Essays In Methodology*, eds. Mircea Eliade and Joseph M. Kitagawa (Chicago: University of Chicago Press, 1959), p. 98.

[3]Philip B. Yampolsky, trans., *The Zen Master Hakuin: Selected Writings* (New York: Columbia University Press, 1971), pp. 118–23.

[4]Swami Prabhavananda and Christopher Isherwood, transl., *Shankara's Crest-Jewel of Discrimination (Viveka Chudamani)*. New York: New American Library, 1970, pp. 110–12. Reprinted by permission of The Vedanta Society of Southern California. Copyright 1974 by The Vedanta Press, Hollywood.

[5]Sidney Spencer, *Mysticism in World Religion* (South Brunswick, N.Y.: A. S. Barnes & Co., Inc., 1963), p. 310. On ibn al-Arabi, see Annemarie Schimmel, *Mystical Dimensions of Islam* (Chapel Hill: The University of North Carolina Press, 1975); and Seyyed Hossein Nasr, *Three Muslim Sages* (Cambridge, Mass.: Harvard University Press, 1964), pp. 83–124

[6]See Garma C. C. Chang, *The Buddhist Teaching of Totality* (University Park: The Pennsylvania State University Press, 1971).

[7]Thomas Merton, *Seeds of Contemplation.* Copyright © 1949 by Our Lady of Gethsemani Monastery, pp. 20–21, 138–39. Reprinted by permission of New Directions Publishing Corporation and Anthony Clarke Books, England. Italics in original.

[8]See Winston L. King, *A Thousand Lives Away: Buddhism in Contemporary Burma* (Cambridge, Mass.: Harvard University Press, 1964), pp. 194–202, and the Appendix, "An Experience in Buddhist Meditation."

[9]William Johnston, S. J., ed., *The Cloud of Unknowing and The Book of Privy Counselling* (Garden City, N.Y.: Doubleday & Co., Inc. 1973), p. 103.

[10]See John Moffit, "Thomas Merton and the Anattā Doctrine," *Insight: A Journal of World Religions,* 2, no. 1 (Spring 1977), pp. 12–14.

[11]Johnston, *The Cloud,* p. 147.

[12]Swami Prabhavananda and Frederick Manchester, trans., *The Upanishads: Breath of the Eternal.* New York: Mentor Books. Copyright © 1948, 1957 by The Vedanta Society of Southern California, and reprinted by its permission. Pp. 123–24.

[13]Jeremiah 14: 2–10. From *The New English Bible.* © The Delegates of the Oxford University Press and The Syndics of the Cambridge University Press 1961, 1970. Reprinted by permission.

[14]Saint Teresa of Jesus, *The Interior Castle or the Mansions*, trans. by a Benedictine of Stanbrook; rev. by The Very Rev. Prior Zimmerman, O.C.D. (London: Thomas Baker, 1930).

[15]An accessible translation is by Swami Prabhavananda and Christopher Isherwood, *How to Know God: The Yoga Aphorisms of Patanjali* (Hollywood: The Vedanta Press, 1969).

[16]Erving Goffmann, *Asylums* (Chicago: Aldine Publishing Company 1961).

[17]I. B. Horner, trans., *The Book of the Discipline (Vinaya-Pitaka), Vol. 4 (Mahavagga)* (London: Luzac & Co., 1951).

[18]Abbot Justin McCann, ed. and trans., *The Rule of Saint Benedict* (London: Burns & Oates, 1952).

[19]Annemarie Schimmel, *Mystical Dimensions of Islam,* p. 101. See also Menahem Milson, *A Sufi Rule for Novices* (Cambridge, Mass.: Harvard University Press, 1975).

[20]W. Y. Evans-Wentz, ed., *Tibet's Great Yogi, Milarepa* (London: Oxford University Press, 1928).

[21]Seth and Ruth Leacock, *Spirits of the Deep: Drums, Mediums and Trance in a Brazilian City* (Garden City, N.Y.: Doubleday Natural History Press, 1972), pp. 120–21.

[22]J. M. Cohen, trans., *The Life of Saint Teresa.* Harmondsworth, England: Penguin Books, 1957). See also Helmut A. Hatzfeld, *Santa Teresa de Avila* (New York: Twayne Publishers, 1969).

[23]Cited in *Fabric of the Universe* by Denis Postle (New York: Crown Publishers, 1976), p. 189.

[24]Aldous Huxley, *Literature and Science* (New York: Harper and Row, Publishers, Inc., 1963), p. 8.

[25]See Fritjof Capra, *The Tao of Physics* (Boulder, Col.: Shambhala Press, 1975), p. 298.

[26]Arthur M. Young, *The Reflexive Universe* (New York: Delacorte Press, 1976).

[27]See Marilyn Ferguson, "Karl Pribram's Changing Reality," *Human Behavior,* 7, no. 5 (May 1978), pp. 28–33, for a nontechnical introduction.

[28]*Brain/Mind Bulletin,* 2, no. 20 (September 5, 1977).

[29]Citations are from Raymond B. Blakney, trans., *Meister Eckhart: A Modern Translation* (New York: Harper & Row Publishers, Inc., 1941).

Mysticism, Worship, and Technique

6

Symbolic Completion of Experience

The relation of mysticism to the formal worship of religious traditions, both public and private, is very complex. Many people have the idea that most mystical experience is encountered alone, apart from worship or technique, and represents a different genre of spirituality independent of the chapel.

But such an interpretation is not true. While it would be impossible to quantify the matter, it becomes obvious upon a moment's reflection that a substantial portion of mystical experience occurs within the context of group worship or of individual practice shaped by tradition. This concept is virtually assured by our definition of mysticism as experience realized in a religious context, in contrast to natural ecstasy.

It is through intentionally religious group and individual practice that we uphold the religious interpretation, even though spontaneous experience may sometimes be given a religious interpretation.

Thus, it was within the temple in Jerusalem that Isaiah saw the Lord "high and lifted up." Likewise, when a yogin like Milarepa practiced asceticism alone in the wilderness, his prior training an initiation by his guru or lama linked him to a collective tradition that gave religious meaning to his experiences.

These two examples are of individual experiences deeply affected in religious interpretation by the conditioning of traditions. Participation in group worship can in itself also stimulate heightened experience. In some instances, such as Confucian rites, a slow and sober activity lifts some participants to an almost mystical state. In others, like Sufi dervish dances, a far more vigorous practice has a comparable effect. In Roman Catholic mysticism centering on the Blessed Sacrament, it is perhaps not so much corporate worship as a visible or tangible manifestation of the Sacred derived from it, the consecreated bread and wine, that has transformative power.

Often worship that leads to mysticism has best flowered in small groups: prayer groups or Sufi orders or ashrams. This setting provides the support of others who accept the world view and the experience as meaningful, yet allows a degree of freedom and spontaneity. A group such as these can both impart techniques that induce experience and validate seemingly spontaneous experiences. But the relation of group tradition to the experience is different when we view the experience as induced by explicitly learned techniques, as in yoga. It also appears differently when it is thought to be spontaneous—even though culture often conditions this spontaneity, as in the conversion experiences of revivals or the journeys of novice shamans into the wilderness to meet their guardian spirits.

In this chapter the emphasis is not to be on the nature of the group but on worship and spiritual technique and their interaction with mysticism. We shall examine various styles of worship, initiation, and method such as yoga, dancing, singing, meditation, and Zen sitting.

The word technique is commonly used of practices like these related to mystical experience, but it would be misleading if it implies certain acts can produce such experience like an assembly line machine stamping out products. Mystical experience comes very subtly on its own or by divine grace and, as we have seen, always feeling spontaneous. All the mystical seeker can do is open himself or herself to the possibility of receiving it rightly, by stilling other thoughts and feelings and focusing attention on the divine. As the great mystical philosopher Plotinus said, we can only "fit ourselves for the vision, and then wait tranquilly for its appearance, as the eye waits on the rising of the sun."[1]

Nonetheless, the diverse spiritual traditions of the world have found that various postures and mental exercises are particularly conducive to this fitting and waiting. Moreover, since the style and language of the practice will be drawn from the larger spiritual tradition within which it is practiced, the particular technique will then have the effect of placing what mystical experience occurs within that context: Zen sitting puts its still joy within the Buddhist tradition whose model is the Buddha seated in similar pose on the night of his enlightenment; the Jesus Prayer of Eastern Orthodoxy puts its fruits within the context of the faith of he whose name it repeats. The technique helps one prepare and wait; it also helps give the interpretation and meaning that makes the experience religiously mystical and specific to a particular religion.

A key to our interpretation is Robert Bellah's comment that religious experience requires some symbol to "complete the experience,"[2] and probably to stimulate and communicate it as well. As we have seen, the zero experience of absolute mysticism requires symbol even as a flame requires impurities to give it the shape and color that make it visible. While the symbol might be only conceptual—an idea of God or of the Holy Spirit—it is not often that people hold ideas of high transcendence without giving them outward expression. Likewise, these expressions usually, consciously or unconsciously, acquire a routine. It is through reiteration that they become part of one's identity and culture—transformations that symbols of transcendence devoutly wish. While the symbol might seem purely sociological—Durkheim's *social effervescence* or *participation mystique*—in practice it is not likely to give a group cohesion without some collective gestures that recall and re-enact it.

Almost inevitably, something of the symbols and stimuli of desired mystical experience will be embedded in a form or worship or technique inseparable from the experience, including its ideological expression. Despite the fact the experience presents itself as self-validating, these practical forms will both induce it and provide its meaning through symbolic completion.

The relation of public tradition and private mystical experience is an intricate one, and to realize this is to realize one of the most important things about mysticism. Zero experience always has a context, and context of experience is never without a social aspect. The associated symbols completing the experience will interpret the social context, for they will link the experience to concepts, mental images, group affiliations—to language and culture in the broadest sense.

The linkage is obvious, but how important is it? That question raises a fundamental religious question, the sociological version of the old metaphysical question about the relation of the one and the many. Is religious experience induced by society, or is it something generated within the self, and is society only incidental or a vehicle of expression?

This question may never be adequately answered. It is, however, highly relevant as a background problem to our present concerns, since the nature of rite, worship, and socially learned techniques for mystical experience is of crucial importance to solving it. If we understood to what degree these techniques were indispensible to fostering religious experience and to perpetuating religious experiences from one generation to another, we would be closer to understanding whether religion is basically social or individual or so intractably both the question is wrongly put.

We can phrase the issue in contemporary terms by comparing two often discussed interpretations of rite. Emile Durkheim, who viewed individual religious experience as generated by society, perceived rite as the occasion when society "acts as itself."[3] In rite, society reinforces the symbolic messages that make religion within the individual, catching him/her up into society as something larger than the self. It is an experience that yields those feelings of wonder we then easily transfer to religious objects as convenient symbols of social and cosmic identity. The mystic, far from being a religious individualist, might in Durkehimian terms be one in whom a sociogenic reality has imposed itself most acutely. He is one who lives most in the world of *its* symbols and least in those grounded in his/her individualized ego.

The anthropologist Victor Turner, following (as we have seen) Gerardus van Gennep's study of initiation, points to the quality of rite that creates symbols of liminality or marginality as an existence outside the ordinary structures of society. These symbols adumbrate a state of *communitas* when all social contradictions to perfect human intercommunion will be reversed. Turner does not overlook the obvious ways a society reinforces its own reality through rite, but at the same time views rite as paradoxically a way society affords transcendence of its own usual structures.[4]

In any case, worship and technique offer a sharp focus of mind that suspends both wandering thoughts and critical consciousness, as well as a completed and interpretive symbol.

Formal Worship

One can understand the social character of the Hindu *bhajan* or bhaktic worship as an expression of devotionalism in its social context. In contemporary Madras, *bhajans* are often held by devotees in private homes on Saturday night. They consist mainly in singing hymns to Krishna and sometimes of performing a complete Krishna *puja* or devotional worship with offerings of music, food, fans, lamps, and incense. Frequently the marriage of Krishna and Radha is re-enacted by putting pictures or images of the two deities on a swing together and taking them in procession. As the devotion becomes intense late in the evening, dances may be done in a spirit of joy and release. The devotees are identifying with the gopis or milkmaids who were Krishna's eternal companions and whose only delight was to think of some new way to please him. The climax of the bhajan comes when the devotees roll on the floor and embrace, "taking the dust" of one another's feet, symbols of the sanctity of all God-loving devotees and of the equality of all who love the Lord, regardless of caste, age, sex, or wealth.[5]

In this devotion, we can see that the *bhajan* reinforces society in that it provides a powerful emotional attachment to traditional Hindu myths, deities, and styles of devotion. Yet it also is a socially approved occasion that transcends many structures in society, for in this occasion the ordinary barriers of caste, sex, and wealth—so important in Hindu society—are made to fall away. If, as it does frequently for many participants, the *bhajan* climaxes in ecstasy, we can see how the worship scenario both stimulated it and offered symbolic completion by presenting an interpretation: one is loving the delightful Lord, one is sharing the rapture of the God-intoxicated gopis.

Sufis of the Maulavi order also perform worship in which intense activity provides a climax. The great medieval mystic and poet Jalal al-din Rumi founded this order. Al-din Rumi said he did his best thinking and praying while spinning around; his followers are called by Westerners *whirling dervishes.* But their practice is more a dance than uncontrolled gyrations. Disciples form a circle around the shaykh. Chanting the *zikr* "Allah, Allah!"—they twirl round and round as they circle about the master, like planets revolving around the sun. Then suddenly, the master shouts "Hai Yar!" ("O Friend," a Sufi term for God), and all the dervishes stop suddenly. Some dervishes will be so overcome with religious fervor that they fall; others stand still until the music and chanting starts again.[6]

In this type of activity we can observe much the same process as in the previous examples. Both have reinforcement and transcendence of traditional society and both have group activity as stimulus and interpretive completion for individual experience. In particular, we here see the importance of the leader's role. Symbolically as well as psychologically, the shaykh is at the center of the circle. It was his charisma that has brought the group together; now it is a combination of his presence, and the fervor of the dance, that lifts many of the disciples to ecstasy.

But what are we to make of Zen monks? They meditate corporately, in identical posture, but each has his own subtle variation of the Zen technique. The purpose of each is to stop the ceaseless chatter of the *monkey mind,* the ordinary stream of consciousness that keeps us from knowing any deeper level of being. One monk may be shooting the monkey by counting breaths, another by concentrating on the posture, another by holding in mind the *koan* or riddle. A classic Zen text, the *Blue Cliff Records,* says that becoming absorbed in the sound of falling rain is an excellent way to settle the mind. It matters little what method one uses.

The mystical experience of Zen monks is a subtle combination of individualism and communalism so far as context is concerned. Each monk's technique will ordinarily be given him by the *roshi* or master in formal interview, and so is socially determined because it depends on this relationship. However, these interviews are a unique sort of dialogue in which the *roshi* seeks through probing questions—often nonsensical—and intuitive interpretation of the response to ascertain the monk's attainment. Thus, the personal variations of Zen are subject to the relation of the monk to the *roshi,* not solely to the monk's own predilections. If the master is sensitive, these variations should also be based on the individual's personality.

Another type of relationship between worship and mystical experience, the proximate stimulation of an experience that happened subsequently and by itself, can be seen in an episode in the life of St. Rose of Lima. Rose was a devout and ascetic young woman of Spanish-ruled Peru, who died in 1617. One day attendance at the public worship rite of mass led her to be so full of joy in the Lord she sang out, "O all ye green things of the Earth, bless ye the Lord!" and it seemed the trees themselves quivered and clashed their leaves together, making a resounding spiritual hymn to join in the saint's praise of the Creator.[7]

There is the matter of spontaneous ecstatic occurrences within worship itself. The Shakers, American Protestant and celibate communalists who flourished in the last century, experienced a period of unusual manifestations after 1837. Their worship had long consisted of drills, dances, and hymns of strange melody and rhythm, climaxed by extended periods of simple free offerings of praise and gifts. In this Era of the Manifestations, the gifts began to include messages from spirits, usually of Shaker founders or of figures from the Bible. Sometimes the spirits would give Shakers invisible baskets of flowers or fruit or plant a spiritual tree of life in the meeting room. Out of these experiences came a new form of Shaker art, quite other than their famous austere furniture and crafts. Shaker visionaries now made intricate tracery drawings of paradisal scenes and maps of heaven.[8]

We can compare these clear expressions of mystical experiences in the context of formal worship to that of another group also called Shakers, the Spiritual Baptists of Saint Vincent island in the West Indies. This black pentecostal church has a practice called *Mourning.* Mourning is "taking a spiritual journey" or "taking a pilgrim journey" or "going to a secret room." It consists of isolation of an individual believer for six to fourteen days or more, washing his or her feet in a basin of water with green leaves and a lighted candle coming out of the basin. Persons in spiritual isolation are given austere but adequate meals. During the period they pray, shout, and undertake their spiritual journeys which often include visions. These pilgrims draw symbols representing the stages of this journey on the floor of the isolation room. Successful mourners receive at the end a *crowning* rite, and are considered initiated into the Shaker elite.[9]

These examples indicate that while mystical experience is finally personal, and its most intimate and small-scale variables derive from the individual personality, it can be profoundly stimulated and affected by a corporate worship setting. Each Zen monk has his own *koan,* each Saint Vincent or American Shaker his or her own spiritual journey or picture of paradise. For each there is a space at the center where spontaneity and personality fine-tune the experience. But its meaning is influenced by worship and technique.

Marching and Dancing

Another category of activity also provides techniques that supply a visible sociological stimulus leading to ecstatic suspension of critical consciousness. This activity is dance and war interpreted as religious. Something of its effect can be garnered from the experience of simply playing a game on a field some Saturday afternoon. The material in this section is submitted to remind us that there are states akin to mysticism, or on its lower levels, far from subtle and sublime. They can be fervent, dark, or fierce.

Trance dance, for example, easily induces a suspension of ordinary awareness of space and time. The dancer undergoes physiological and psychological change through stylized and rhythmic movements, exertion and hyperventilation that modifies sensory experience. It intensifies but narrows the dancer's range of feeling and perception. At the same time, the dancer may more and more identify with the purpose and myth of the dance, so that he/she becomes the god, the story, the pure devotee, so far as range of consciousness is concerned. This alteration of consciousness may be interpreted as being lost in the love of God, as in the case of the Sufi whirling dervishes; or as possession by a god or spirit, as among the female zar dancers of East Africa or the mediums of Vodun and other Latin American spirit religions. Such elements as music, incense, heat, lights, setting, and sociology enhance the transformation of consciousness wrought by the dance and its interpretation.[10]

We can compare the feeling of calm and decorum induced by the slow dancelike Confucian rituals. The ancient philosopher Hsun-tzu spoke of their power to embellish joy and sorrow with appropriate expression yet contain the chaos of emotion by combining these dances with beauty, remembering, and longing. Ritual keeps human desires from leading to contention, yet enables them to be satisfied in a way that sustains charm and harmony.[11]

However, we do not only associate the mystical mood—particularly when combined with physical activity as a means of stimulating and expressing it—with the gentleness of a Saint Francis or the pacifism of Gandhi's *ahimsa.* We can also associate it with the grim work of the soldier and the intensity of the military crusade. In the Bhagavad-Gita, Krishna's responses to the battlefield queries of King Arjuna, at least on one level of interpretation, let us see this association. For those called to war, like that warrior-ruler, the zero state becomes unreserved participation in the great drama of God, a play with both its bright and fell scenes. Mysticism is not only a way out of that drama, but also a way toward full participation in it with sublime composure. Thus, in medieval Japan samurai found in Zen meditation a way to steel themselves for indifference to life and death,[12] and the Bhagavad-Gita teaches of *Karma yoga,* the way of liberation through egoless activity in the world.

The association of the zero experience with action—especially corporate action—can lend unity and power, indeed fanaticism, to religiously sanctioned military ventures. Such was the case in the sanguinary battles of the old Germanic berserkers, the Crusades, and the Muslim *jihad* or holy war.

The popular advocate of the first crusade was Peter the Hermit, one of a number of medieval wandering preachers who were on the boundaries of orthodoxy, thus sometimes suppressed, but were favorably received by the common people. As Pope Urban II in calling for the crusade at Clermont in 1095 had promised remission of sin to those who undertook it, so Peter the charismatic preacher called up a great army of the poor. Pressed by overpopulation and famine, intoxicated by the mystic's words, they saw themselves as an army of Christ for which all obstacles would be conquered by faith. Peter was small in stature and roughly dressed, but with unforgettable eyes and a transfixing glance. Rumor also said that he had a letter from Jesus Christ about the mission to Jerusalem. Peter's air of holiness was reportedly greater than that of anyone else in his day. Even the hairs of the donkey he always rode people seized as holy relics. He did not command his hearers to fight, but simply to walk armed by little more than faith for the Holy Land. Tens of thousands did. His army wound its painful way through Europe to Asia Minor, where the trained Muslim warriors massacred those who had survived the journey. The knights followed this crusade and took Jerusalem in 1099—slaughtering on the day of victory its entire population of Muslims and Jews, including women and children. Such atrocities seem to be a predictable culmination of mixing mystical militancy with the tension and dehumanization brought about by battle, seige, and fear.[13]

We can see the common root of trance-dance and the crusading army (of whatever faith) in the war dances of primitives. The fighting men of a tribe may dance with their spears—chanting, leaping, and thrusting—for hours or even days before finding strength to meet the enemy. They then advance against that foe continuing the same mechanical steps and songs. It is important their demeanor present an image of divine invincibility, for primitive combat, particularly by twentieth century standards, is relatively unbloody. More a psychological than a tactical exercise, the main hope of each force is to create such a vision of imposing terror as to cause the other to panic and run. But to do so, an army must itself feel imposing and terrifying. And if it must fight, its state of mind must strike and strike in a sort of tireless frenzy, without fear, as though possessed by savage gods. This altered consciousness is the task military dance, chant, and drum accomplishes. That altered consciousness would be mystical insofar as the experiencer actually found union with ultimate divine reality as he fought in the battle. One does not doubt that sacred warriors have often (though not always) felt such a divine partnership in the field.

Plato, fearing the power of music to arouse passion and betray rational judgment, forbade it in his ideal republic. From one point of view he did well, for if music can elevate the spirit, it can also blunt the sharp critical tools of the mind and call forth the dark side of human nature. Anyone will know this who has heard the raucous martial music of political rallies in modern totalitarian states or (as I have in Fiji) seen demonstrations of the dances in which primitives prepared themselves for headhunting forays.

But it is not really music, of course, that is to blame. Bach cannot be faulted for the effects of barbarous battle hymns; likewise not all meditative dance, nor even all marching (also practiced as religious rite by the peaceable Shakers), is the same as those turning human sensibilities to iron at the call of Mars. Yet the two are parts of one psychological continuum.

Private
Mystical Technique

Mircea Eliade has spoken of yoga as *interiorization of sacrifice*. The *tapas* or interior heat that gave spiritual power, so important to early yoga, was an inner version of the purifying sacrificial fire of Vedic ritual. More broadly, all private worship and spiritual technique is a miniaturization, with some variation, of the same tradition's public worship. Such a parallel is not surprising, for both adhere to the same social construction of reality; both address themselves to the same gods or forces.

The private practice, however, must be more potent and intense than the public if it is to fit one for genuine spiritual experience. It must through inherent intensity compensate for the absence of the group reinforcement of public religious occasions. The private technique must construct within the self an altar, a sacrifice, and a cloud of witnesses equal to the altars of the temples.

The question of whether public or private religion came first is unanswerable and perhaps pointless. However, the two support each other more often than not. Themes of one are recognizable in the other. But all private technique is not necessarily borrowed from public worship. All religions, in fact, have their special and self-perpetuating traditions regarding personal devotion. It might be prayers and rituals passed down within families; it might be the burden of popular prayer manuals and inspirational books; it might be the meatier practices of private meditation and devotion taught in seminaries and monastic retreats; it might be the special and initiatory transmissions of gurus, roshis, and shaykhs to disciples.

An interesting example of the interiorization process is the Hindu text of esoteric yoga, the *Shiva Samhita*. We should first note that pilgrimage and sacred rivers are among the more important themes of popular Hinduism. Important places of pilgrimage include Mount Kailas in Tibet, believed to be the abode of Shiva, and the place where the sacred Ganges, Yamuna, and Sarasvati rivers came together. (The Sarasvati was an invisible sacred stream said to flow underground.) Those who went on a pilgrimage to certain sites could obtain liberation from sin not only for themselves, but also for their ancestors. Finally, traditional Hindu cosmology made the mythical Mount Meru the center of the world.

All this is within and can be found in the *Shiva Samhita* as the adept explores his own subtle nature through the mystic arts. The yogic psychology upon which this medieval text is based tells us that three main channels of energy run up the torso: the *susumna* in the spinal column, and the *ida* and *pingala* on either side of it. The principal channel, the *susumna,* is identified with Mount Meru; aligned along it are the *chakras* or centers of psychic energy the yogin opens as he raises the *kundalini* or spiritual energy up the spine by yogic techniques. Within the body also, the book tells us, is the esoteric junction of the *triveni* or three rivers where the *ida, susumna,* and *pingala* meet. He who bathes in these waters by meditation is free from all sin and procures salvation for his ancestors; he knows heavenly felicity, even as he would in actual pilgrimage, but better. Whoever dies there—that is, dies in meditation—attains liberation.

Lastly, when the arising *kundalini* force reaches the summit of the skull, it is said to open the thousand-petal lotus upon an inner moon floating on an ocean of milk; this arousal brings great bliss and pours a sacred elixir into the inner Ganges. Above the moon is an inner peak of Mount Kailas where Shiva resides; that great yogic god is awakened to give not only rapture, but also cosmic consciousness.[14]

However fanciful this language sounds, we can notice two important points about it: an awareness that whatever is sacred outwardly is counterbalanced by an equally sacred—or more sacred—center within; and a sense that what is within if truly opened is infinite, containing all possible richness and all gods. This experience is the general one of mystics, yet the language by which they describe their inner realms is drawn from that pointing to the sacred in the worship of the outer temple.

Christian private mystical techniques also make pilgrimages, but because of the greater emphasis compared to Hinduism on the former faith's history, the sacred quest is often a journey in time as well as space. It may culminate in visualization visits to the scenes of the biblical scriptures.

Christian tradition, particularly Roman Catholic mystical theology, distinguishes between meditation and contemplation. Meditation is a practice of focusing attention by love and will on divine things in preparation for contemplation. It is the highest state of absorption into the life of God when all other psychological processes are suspended. Meditation, as inward pilgrimage to the world of sacred symbols, is the highest state of consciousness in which discrete content is present.

Thus, the notable seventeenth century spiritual writer Dom Augustine Baker tells us that we should prepare for meditation by taking points or images out of an appropriate book, then with the memory and understanding explore each until the soul draws from it "a reason or motive, by which the will may be inclined some way or other toward God." These reflections should produce acts of the will that improve life; also they should lead (as in, for example, representing to oneself a scene from the life of Christ) to rich feelings of tenderness, love, and devotion.[15]

Roman Catholic thought during the Counter-Reformation developed rather elaborate and often psychologically perceptive methods of meditation and contemplation. The school of Saint Ignatius, founder of the Jesuits, for example, presented these stages:

Remote Preparation: One must set the stage for specific meditative acts through a general life of generosity, mortification, purity of conscience, and awareness of God, as in many spiritual traditions.

Proximate Preparation: On the night before the meditation, one should assemble and reflect on the books to be studied and the fruits desired.

Immediate Preparation: Before starting, one makes an act (affirmation) of reflection and faith, and undertakes an "imaginative prelude" —imagining the scene to be meditated upon.

Body of Prayer: This consists of an exercise of memory, recalling the material; an exercise of intellect, endeavoring to understand its truth and meaning; and an exercise of the will. The term *will* here means a deliberate arousing of positive feelings about the subject of meditation. The meditator then makes resolutions concerning spiritual life.[16]

The use of imagination fired by will deserves a little discussion. Christian meditation requires imagination powerful enough to gather up and elevate all the senses toward the sacred Other. A long tradition exists concerning this elevation, with ultimate sources in Neoplatonism. Long before Ignatius of Loyola, Richard of Saint Victor (fl. twelfth century), a seminal spiritual writer, pointed out that the royal path to the contemplation of unseen things is the imagination, which he said runs like a servant linking inner and outer, reason and sense, bearing the gifts of one to the other.[17]

The senses involved, it should be noted, are not limited to inward seeing and hearing. In a striking passage in his *Spiritual Exercises,* Ignatius tells us that while the first task of the mediator is to see with the eyes of the imagination and the second to hear what they say, "the third is to smell and taste the infinite sweetness and delight of the Divinity" and the fourth is to feel with the touch, as inwardly to kiss and embrace where sacred persons have trod.[18]

Another traditional school of Counter-Reformation spirituality that should be mentioned is the Sulpician, established in the work of Cardinal Pierre de Bérulle (1575–1629) and J. J. Olier (1608–1657). It is quite Christ oriented. Remote, proximate, and immediate preparation in Sulpician meditation is comparable to the Ignatian. The immediate stage involves putting the self in the presence of God, uniting it with Jesus Christ, and invoking the Holy Spirit.

The body of the prayer has simplicity and beauty. It contains three parts: Jesus in the eyes (adoration and consideration), Jesus in the heart (conviction, reflection, and petition), and Jesus in the hands (resolutions and offering of self to the Holy Spirit). After these three stages comes thanksgiving, asking of pardon, and choosing one thought to be cultivated during the rest of the day.[19]

These techniques all follow generally the pattern of mystical experience we have outlined earlier: preparation, intensive climax, and afterglow. Clearly, the methods attempt by exercising the imagination to set the stage for mystical experience at the same time controlling its interpretation through controlling its images. Yet the same writers also recognize a far more formless and exalted state, to which meditation and any sort of discursive (that is, with specific content) prayer is preliminary. This more exalted state is, as we have seen, contemplation, and has been called a prolonged loving gaze upon God himself or, by the more bold, the unitive state, mystical marriage, or realization of the divine light. The practice of meditation can sometimes lead into contemplation. The wiser spiritual masters of the West advise that when this happens, the ordinary structure of meditation should be suspended and God allowed to lead the contemplative soul where he will. One can compare the process to the Sufi state of *fana* (falling away) or *samadhi* or *narodh* (cessation of consciousness) in Hinduism or Buddhism.

Techniqueless Technique

Finally, there is a very different sort of technique, or perhaps we should say antitechnique: the effortless or "walking" meditation of writers like Jiddu Krishnamurti and Barry Wood. Krishnamurti opposes any sort of technique, as he does all spiritual authority and tradition, believing that these only create tension between what the mind is and what one thinks it ought to be. This tension in turn builds up rigid patterns that imprison individuals and keep them from living in the present and the perpetual flux of true reality. Meditation, then, lets the mind be empty of things; yet allows it to be aware, seeing everything, including its own thoughts, clear of conditioning as it goes about ordinary life.[20]

This approach seems at first glance very much at odds with the traditional methods of East and West, whether yogic or Catholic. These traditional methods advocate strenuous exercise of will, concentration, and imagination; Krishnamurti believes all such exercises only forge the chains of mental prisons. He makes caustic remarks about the pointlessness of, for example, concentration. But Barry Wood, a perceptive though less well-known writer, points out that the abandonment of concept, purpose, structure, and the like which Krishnamurti requires is really no other than entering the "cloud of unknowing," "divine dark," "wayless abyss" (Ruysbroeck), or "emptiness" (Nagarjuna) of classic mysticism. For if these terms mean anything, the meaning would not be something impossibly "profound" or "far away," but something (being uncircumscribed) as much here at hand and in present time as anywhere else. That "something" goes by such mysterious names because nothing can be said about it. It is *"not an idea at all, but an experience* —and not a future experience, but our present experiencing."[21] The way to know it, the goal of all mysticism, is just to set aside all philosophies, theologies, codes, methods, presuppositions, and simply look at present experiencing. For the divine dark and all other mysteries are simply the ordinary world before our eyes, and ordinary daily life shorn of all ideas about it. But this methodless method is, of course, also a sort of method.

The Meaning of
Mystical Technique

What all these techniques have in common is a method, reinforced by social symbols and context, for attaining the mystical objective: to stop multiplicity of thought and provide an interpretation of the stoppage referring it to transcendence. Likewise, the technique expresses by its own language that it *is* a transcendent experience. In religion such expression is as important as the experience, or rather is inseparable from it. In Bellah's terms, what the technique says about the experience it induced is the experience's symbolic completion. Or, as Percival Lowell put it many years earlier in writing of certain rites of Japanese shamanism, "the means to the mystery is the mystery itself."

Whether the method is public or private, whether it suits temple or hermitage better, is less important than the idea of method itself. However, different methods work in different ways.

In some methods the combined tension and participation mystique of social pressure is a part of what makes it work—often a major part. In others the tension and concentration of solitude is a dominant feature. But the sovereign fact uniting both is the existence of a technique to allow a focusing of attention that stops the monkey mind and the critical consciousness. Even Krishnamurti's choiceless awareness only of the present is such a stoppage.

The technique may or may not be recognized as a technique by the practitioner. If it is learned, like yoga or ritual, the emphasis will be on its function and it will probably be acknowledged as method. But in Christian or Hindu devotionalism, devotees consider the critical mind necessary to recognize technique irrelevant, and perception is lost in its role as completing and interpreting symbol. The fact that it *shows* the experience is one of transcendence, as for example through the words of the fervent prayer and the kneeling posture, overshadows any awareness that these words and posture may also *induce* the experience.

The yogin is aware of the role of his practice of pranayama: breathing exercises designed to circulate the prana or vital force throughout the body and finally to purify the consciousness. He knows it evokes the experience of integration with the true self that climaxes the successful practice of yoga with meditation, even though his calling the force *prana* also links the experience interpretively with traditional esoteric anatomy and with an entire metaphysical world view.

The devotee fervently singing hymns of love toward the Lord may be less self-consciously aware that the activity stimulates as well as expresses the fire that burns within the heart. Of course some masters of devotional mysticism have been so aware. The great Christian spiritual writer Baron von Hugel once commented, in allegorical reference to this matter, "I kiss my child not only because I love him, but also in order to love him." But the words of the hymn, as they relate the overflowing feeling within the singer's breast, provide symbols of interpretation and transcendent reference for the feelings: they make them love for the eternal Lord.

What of spontaneous mystical experiences, such as those in nature, in which no evident technique, conscious or unconscious, was involved? Ralph W. Hood, Jr., through surveys of young people engaged in outdoor activities, found certain correlations with reported experiences of ecstasy or mysticism. He determined that these experiences tended to occur, not when a situation was stress-free, but when a situation the individual had anticipated would be low stress turned out to be stressful.[22] This is perhaps analoguous to the burst of joy, even ecstasy, we often feel in playing active sports. We usually anticipate an afternoon's play in terms of its being relaxing, low-stress. The game is semistructured, as were many of Hood's experiences. But within a game of tennis or baseball moments of high stress will occur: perhaps it is this subordinate stress, in a setting interpreted as relaxing, that triggers the spontaneous ecstasy.

Hood argues that the incongruity of anticipation and experience make an individual aware of limits and in so doing make transcendent experience available. The experience of limits, he rightly indicates, can be both negative and positive. When stress is more than one can handle, the reaction may be pathological or at best escapist. But in better circumstances it can induce the sort of experience that makes one believe the discovered limits can in fact be transcended, and so it leads to growth.

Hood's model need not be accepted as a full explanation of all spontaneous mystical experience for us to recognize its value not only in understanding the background of those experiences, but also for providing clues to how techniques for mystical experience work. For in all mystical method there seems to be an incongruity of anticipation and actuality in regard to stress and an experience of limits.

Physiological techniques, like yoga and Zen postures, with their rhythm or stability seem to promise only relaxation, yet prolonged stillness itself produces a certain tension as the body wants to move and the mind to wander. At the same time, it is an experience of limits: the stillness of Zen and the rhythm of yoga, together with its periods of quiet and breath control, are as close as one ordinarily comes (except in crisis situations) to being motionless while fully conscious. If Hood's representation is correct, the mind may transform stress into a flash of ecstasy. This ecstasy releases the tension and stops ordinary time and space perception so that the stress, perpetrated by incongruities within time and space, can be alleviated. This interpretation seems to fit with other observations that, in moments of extreme stress, time often ap-pears to slow down; one seems to be in slow-motion and to perceive the scene as it were from without, transcending it psychologically.

The techniques of rapid movement, such as trance-dance, may produce a comparable stress (the sense of incongruity with expectations and the sense of limits) as they reach the point of vertigo. However, vertigo, with its mind-numbing dizziness, is going too far and may change into the ecstatic flash just as one collapses.

The sense of reaching physical and psychological limits and hid-den incongruity is also a factor in mystical militancy. Marching to battle is a combination of corporateness and steady rhythm, relaxes dulling consciousness, a situation of emotional intensity—indeed, one that holds latent the danger of touching the ultimate limit, death.

It is easy to apply the same test to other techniques for inducing mystical experience: the focus on a single visual, audial, or mental object; the hard, fast psychological shifts of Zen (sitting alternating with walking) or of the Gurdjieff work; the combined reinforcement and tension of the presence of other people in a setting of public worship or group meditation.

In all these cases the technique—like some spontaneous situations —leads the individual to experience certain limits of physiological, emotional, and mental reality. It reverses the norms of everyday reality, forcing the body to act and feel in ways not requisite, nor even very useful, in everyday life. That creates both a stressful yet joyful sense of being able to transcend ordinary life. It may even create a "high" situa-tion, or at least the expectation of one, in its symbols and interpretation. It may also create tension by inducing expectations almost too full to be contained yet too good to be wished away.

Mystical techniques, however, cannot be understood in isolation from the society in which they are known and used. Their meaning is interrelated with the roles of the persons who use and teach them, with how they fit into society, and with what sort of groups they are asso-ciated. Is the mystic a leader or a recluse, a priest or a spiritual rebel, a warrior or a peacemaker? The answers will be immensely important for defining the mystic and his or her mysticism. This will be the subject of our next chapter.

Mysticism, Worship, and Technique: Reading Selection

I would like to present my own revised notes from a visit to a contemporary ceremonial magic performance. Ceremonial or ritual magic, it should first be explained, is very different from the sort of manipulative magic whose relation to mysticism is highly questionable. The leading purpose of ceremonial magic is, through potent rituals evoking a deity, to induce a mystical experience which becomes a nonrational encounter with ultimate divine reality.

The order performing the rite I attended was the Ordo Templi Astartes.* Like all serious groups, this order believes the ritual evocation of deities and the adherence to pagan seasonal festivals are spiritual paths leading to profound empathy both with nature and the unconscious. My narrative shows how intense ritual can lead to a "space at the center," which stimulates mystical experience and makes *communitas* possible within the group. Note also the capacity of members of this group for a split-level consciousness. They were unusually able to have a mystical experience and to observe themselves having the experience, even to analyze it, at the same time or shortly afterwards.

. . .

On May 6, 1977, I attended an evocation of Astarte, the ancient Canaanite goddess of love, performed by the Ordo Templi Astartes. The rite exemplified how the intensive ritual work in a close-knit group can arouse psychic energy leading to strong ecstatic or religious experience.

This affiliation of eight or ten persons generally does an hour or so of yoga asanas (postures) and pranayama (breathing exercises) before a magical operation in order to get into a light transic state. They then stare at jewels of the right color according to laws of correspondence for the deity to be evoked, in order to reach a calm and one-pointed state of mind. They next sit around a table bearing bright zodiacal and planetary signs and a candle of the proper hue. Holding hands, they engage in breathing exercises and spirtually absorb the rays of the candle, passing the power around by squeezing hands. Then, robed, they stand and silently enter the magical temple.

*Ordo Templi Astartes, P.O. Box 3341, Pasadena, Calif. 91103

Initial entry into this fane of wizardry is an overwhelming experience. On the floor I saw a large pentacle, or five-pointed star, laid in a circle. Just outside it were a wide mirror on a low stand and a desk uplifting a large ritual book. The many diagrams and esoteric ornaments were painted in brilliant luminiscent colors that glowed in the ultraviolet light.

The group first lit candles in the four cardinal directions. They chanted together a creedlike affirmation, which emphasized that magical evocation is done by power of will. The human will, they believe, can make itself sovereign over all entities cosmic and intrapsychic, for it expresses the divine essence of human beings. An invocation of the spiritual powers, more reverent in tone, was also said. After the initiates walked around the pentacle seven times chanting, they took their places.

The principal parts in the rite were those of the Receiver and Operator. The Receiver, a woman (since the deity was female), stood before the mirror with a candle in each hand. In her, it was believed, the goddess would manifest her personality and power. Also a glimpse might be caught of the passing glory in the mirror.

The Operator or Magus stood within the circle facing the Receiver. His function, supported by the concentrated energies of the entire group, was by the force of his will and his magical words to summon up Astarte into the woman's body and the mirror. Thus, he repeated over and over an invocation of Astarte in a chanting tone, his voice full of concentrated power. The emphasis was on his *command* to the ancient goddess in the name of Elohim (God).

Breaking the mood, he quietly asked the Receiver if Astarte was now there. She said in a low voice, "One more time." The Magus called out the invocation once more. The Receiver shook; the candles moved, making dim patterns in the mirror. Then suddenly the Receiver laughed, a lilting, sexual, musical laugh quite different from the woman's ordinary tone. At this point I myself felt a surge of tremendous tingling excitement.

The Operator addressed the now present goddess. I was introduced. Astarte said, through the lips of the Receiver, "I already know Robert Ellwood." She was asked petitions by others who came up to face her and touched her shoulder to receive power.

Someone inquired if she had an oracle—a divine message for the group or anyone in it. She said she would give one later to the right person, as it was private. To petitions she gave short answers, such as "You always have my blessing."

Finally the Magus asked the Receiver, "Is she still there?" The answer was yes, the goddess-presence was still strong, but she was leaving soon. Then followed a solemn dismissal of the visitant, an apology to her for the trouble, and a short rite of banishing, for which everyone knelt, as the Magus swung a sword to the four quarters.

Away from the temple, a critique succeeded the ritual. The Order keeps a magical log of all operations. Members of the group now submitted information for it from this experience. That was done in a generally critical, yet humorous and bantering tone. They joked even about the gods and the rituals—someone called Aphrodite "a flip goddess"—and recalled amusing incidents from other rites. It was very much like the "in group" jocularity of any religion, often found especially among seminarians. The members of the Order at this point gave an impression of being immensely alive, enjoying life, keyed up, and outgoing. The rite itself, the potent atmosphere of the temple and the transitory presence of divinity, had clearly induced a residual euphoria.

The Magus, also head of the Order, first asked about visual experience. No one had seen anything apart from the contact change in the personality of the Receiver, except for one person who saw a flashing glimpse of a woman other than the Receiver in the mirror. The Receiver delivered two or three messages she had gotten from the goddess but had felt it inappropriate to speak in the temple itself. For example, one member was told that she cried too much. The recipient of this admonition claimed she cried very little, but someone else commented that maybe it was not meant literally, that perhaps she cried too much internally.

From this discussion, and also from the asides in the temple itself, it was evident that the consciousness of members of the magical Order operated on two levels at the same time. On one hand, they were caught up in the presence of divinity; or the other, they, even the Operator and Receiver, maintained a critical distance from what was happening, being self-aware manipulators and observers of the performance. Yet the mystical experience was certainly real, however produced and interpreted. I myself have very, very seldom known such a powerful and unanticipated change of consciousness or bolt of ecstatic energy passing through me as I did at the climax of this rite.

Notes

[1]The *Enneads* in *Mysticism in World Religion* by Sidney Spencer (Gloucester, Mass.: Peter Smith, 1971), p. 167.

[2]Personal communication by Robert Bellah to Morris Augustine and Richard Kalish. Cited by Morris J. Augustine and Richard A. Kalish, in "Religion, Transcendence, and Appropriate Death," *The Journal of Transpersonal Psychology*, 7, 1 (1975), 7. See also

William J. Wainwright, "Interpretation, Description, and Mystical Consciousness," *Journal of the American Academy of Religion,* XLV, no. 3, Supplement (September 1977), 989–1010.

³Emile Durkheim, *The Elementary Forms of the Religious Life,* trans. Joseph Ward Swain (New York: Collier Books, 1961).

⁴Victor W. Turner, *The Ritual Process* (Chicago: Aldine Publishing Company), 1969.

⁵Milton Singer, "The Great Tradition of Hinduism in the City of Madras," in *Anthropology of Folk Religion,* ed. Charles Leslie (New York: Random House, Inc., 1960), pp. 119–21.

⁶John P. Brown, *The Darvishes* (1868; reprint ed., London: Frank Cass & Co., 1968), pp. 251–53.

⁷S. C. Hughson, *Athletes of God* (West Park, N.Y.: Holy Cross Press, 1950), p. 278.

⁸See Marguerite Fellows Melcher, *The Shaker Adventure* (Princeton: Princeton University Press, 1941), p. 217; and Edward Deming Andrews and Faith Andrews, *Fruits of the Shaker Tree of Life* (Stockbridge, Mass.: The Berkshire Traveller Press, 1975), pp. 220–21.

⁹Jeannette H. Henney, "Spirit-Possession Belief and Trance Behavior in Two Fundamentalist Groups in St. Vincent," in *Trance, Healing, and Hallucination: Three Field Studies in Religious Experience,* eds. Felicitas D. Goodman, Jeannette H. Henney, and Esther Pressel (New York: John Wiley & Sons, Inc., 1974), pp. 53–58.

¹⁰Erika Bourguignon, "Trance Dance," in *The Highest State of Consciousness,* John White, ed. (Garden City, N.Y.: Doubleday Anchor Books, 1972) pp. 331–43.

¹¹William T. de Bary, *Sources of Chinese Tradition* (New York: Columbia University Press, 1964), I, 108–10.

¹²See Huiren Li, "Some Notes on Mystical Militancy," *Insight: A Journal of World Religions,* 2, 1 (Spring 1977), 37–46.

¹³See Thomas Patrick Murphy, ed., *The Holy War* (Columbus: Ohio State University Press, 1976), and Edward Peters, *The First Crusade* (Philadelphia: University of Pennsylvania Press, 1971).

¹⁴Rai Bahadur Srisa Chandra Vidyarnava, trans., *Siva Samhita* in *The Sacred Books of the Hindus, Volume XV, Part 1* (Allahabad: Lalit Mohan Basu, 1942).

¹⁵F. Augustine Baker, *Holy Wisdom,* ed. the Right Reverend Abbot Sweeney (New York: Harper and Brothers, 1876), pp. 415–16.

¹⁶Cardinal Lercaro, *Methods of Mental Prayer,* trans. T. F. Lindsay (Westminster, Maryland: The Newman Press, 1957), p. 38.

¹⁷Richard of Saint-Victor, *Selected Writings on Contemplation,* trans. Clare Kirchberger (London: Faber and Faber, 1957), p. 91.

¹⁸Alexandre Brou, *Ignatian Methods of Prayer,* trans. William J. Young (Milwaukee: The Bruce Publishing Company, 1949), p. 146.

¹⁹Cardinal Lercaro. *Methods of Mental Prayer,* p. 107.

²⁰J. Krishnamurti, *Commentaries on Living* (London: Victor Gollancz, 1962).

²¹Barry Wood, *The Only Freedom* (Philadelphia: The Westminster Press, 1972), pp. 102–3.

²²Ralph W. Hood, Jr., "Eliciting Mystical States of Consciousness with Semistructured Nature Experiences," *Journal for the Scientific Study of Religion,* 16, 2 (1977), 155–63.

Mysticism and the Sociology of Religion

7

The Mystic and the Community

No mysticism is independent of community. Mystical experience is related to the environing community either directly (for those stimulated by group activity) or indirectly (those who seek private experience because of dissatisfaction with the religious community). At the least, according to our definitions, sociology is present in religious mysticism in a way it might not be with "raw" ecstasy, because what makes an experience religious is association with religious interpretive concepts derived ultimately from a socially transmitted language and world view. Whatever the biological source of ecstatic experience, the meaning we assign to it—whether we pass it off as a moment of vertigo, whether we call it "natural" or "sacred"—depends on a vocabulary derived from society.

Nonetheless, mysticism has an ambivalent relation to society. When we speak of meaning derived, through language and other symbols, from society, we speak of what "sociologists of knowledge" like Peter L. Berger and Thomas Luckmann call the *social construction of reality*. [1] Their point is that society and its world views are human products that eventually act back upon their producers. The process is a never-ending dialectical chain. Humans externalize or project what is within them. The experience in individuals of hunting becomes collectively a culture and science, with its gods and techniques, of hunting. The cultural objectification is then internalized in persons within the society to reinforce again the inward structures that were externalized.

Although Berger and Luckmann speak of the three moments of externalization, objectification, and internalization—it is not the intention to imply that culture or religion *begins* in subjectivity as an *a priori*. As there is no objective culture without externalization, so there could be no subjectivity without a coexistent culture to internalize. The process should rather be seen as a never-ending chain without a beginning nor an end. It is a process that is the nature of human life in society.

This position, cynics have commented, assumes that society pulls the biggest con game of all, making us believe the reality it constructs is the only reality. However, as Berger and Luckmann recognize, not everyone is equally "taken in." Nearly every society has its alienated individuals who march to a different drummer, as well as its true believers, who embrace the social vision with an untoward passion.

Very often the deviants and true believers associate their state of being different with mystical experience. A mystical experience has meant for them, even if interpreted in the language of their society, a special angle of perception or the transcendent that legitimates their special relationship to society. Mystical experience has such an inner ring of authenticity that it also authenticates whatever areas of life, indeed whatever life-styles, with which it is symbolically associated. When an individual's life is sufficiently different as to have only questionable social legitimation, this individual naturally craves a corresponding inner authentication. Mystical experience can answer to this need.

Although mystics may use the language of society because it is all they know, they likewise seem to break with socially constructed reality —or if they are orthodox mystic's they accept that construction in all its unambiguous purity. Being experientially concerned with ultimates, they are not content, as are most of us, to accept the social construction in a tacitly provisional way, as a working reality that allows an equally casual modicum of inner freedom.

A sociological definition of mysticism, to set alongside of philosophical and psychological definitions, is then possible. It would go something like this. An individual or group within society is mystical if it contrasts an ultimate transcendent reality to the society's concept of universal reality, or experiences the ultimate reality of the latter more directly than the ordinary member of society. The individual or group then requires the symbolic completion of that direct experience to be sociologically significant. That is, the mystic is one who believes that his experience puts him or her in a special relation to society and its reality and manifests this special relation through the symbol of special forms of interaction with society, forms that show the nature and meaning of the experience. He or she may become a sectarian or cultist, a monk or nun, or any other sort of special religious person. The mystic's sociological status, then, becomes in itself a symbol of the experience.

Every mystical experience—and every ecstatic experience of which we can have any knowledge—has some such sociological symbol. If it did not, we could know nothing of it. Even bare verbal communication is sociological, for it establishes a relation between persons that can bear manifold consequences and is part of the infinite network of interactions that make up a society. Thus, if we pursue its application with adequate care, our sociological definition of mysticism would be not only feasible but also sure. However, it would be necessary to discern the social ramifications of mystical experience that take only small-scale and ephemeral social expression, as well as those that take the form of major movements or institutions. We would also have to distinguish actual mystical social expressions from those that have only its appearance (e.g. the man who becomes a monk because his family dedicated him to the cloister as a child). Above all, since most human motives are mixed, we should be able the discern the sacred in the profane and the profane in the sacred.

In any case, the mystic will reflect his or her experience not just in his/her art and letters, but also in the group he/she joins or forms and in his/her subsequent relation to normative society. Whether authoritarian or egalitarian, whether emotive or repressive, whether celibate or connubial, whether structured or unstructured—his or her social relations will reflect in some way the subjective values the initial experience evoked. On their own scale the mystic will objectify and reify them as continuing symbols. Better yet, these relations will reflect what comes out of the subjectivity of the mystic in interaction with the value symbols of the society.

A final note: in practice the relation of mystical experience to groups and society is not as simple as it seems. The mystic may not simply have an experience alone and then draws a group around him or her to perpetuate its vision. Instead, very often people will be led to pre-existent groups in the hope of having an experience. Frequently, the mystic quest is not really so much a quest for self or God as a quest for community. We are social beings, and what we often want most to find is people who have found self and God, rather than self and God as such. We want a community offering that deep *communitas,* that inter-subjectivity, that goes with shared experience, interpretive values, and paradigms. Many will accept considerable authoritarianism in a religion so long as its language suggests *communitas* and talks of inwardness, freedom, and authenticity.

Mystical Groups

Groups based on the validity of mystical experience are intended both to legitimate and to stimulate this experience. These groups serve as sociological symbols completing the mystical experience.

Typically, these groups tend toward reproducing sociologically the zero experience of mysticism, plus giving it an interpretation. At the same time, they articulate the mystic's complex relation to society by providing vehicles and sub-traditions for its expression.

One way or another, all mystical groups express the intent of the traditional Western monastic counsels of perfection—poverty, chastity, and obedience—for they are concerned about the competition to the sociological stimulation and expression of mysticism likely to be lodged in possessions, sexuality, and self-will. They are also concerned about the ways all the latter militate against the ego-negation of the zero experience.

Mystical groups tend to move toward becoming total institutions (in the sense of Erving Goffman discussed in the preceding chapter), either practically as do monasteries or theoretically through the sovereign importance claimed for the group's work and world view. A prayer group may actually engage only a small percentage of its members' time, but they believe what it represents is the most important thing in their lives. They believe it ought to control all their values and significant actions. Here are some ways such mystical groups function.

1. Ideally, the group negates ego by reducing individual decision nearly to zero, thus approximating sociologically the zero experience.

The group does this either by making decisions for the individual, as in the case of those under religious obedience, or by presenting very strong values and paradigms that are internalized.

2. The group approximates mysticism's sense of being part of something infinite by enhancement of the participant. He or she is, in the group, part of something visibly larger than self whose ideal is *communitas,* in turn a symbol of the divine milieu.

3. The group provides a setting with favorable evaluation of mystical experience.

4. The group provides appropriate symbols and an intellectual tradition for the religious interpretation of unusual and ecstatic experience.

5. Insofar as some outlet is necessary for the ego and the ego-building drives, the group presents religious experience as the optimum occasion for it. Of course, in practice many members will find greater fulfillment in the administrative, scholarly, and economic life of the group or institution.

Mystical Groups
Supportive of Society

We shall now examine several types of mystical groups, some generally supportive of the environing society and its religion and some alienated from it. The first three types named can, in a broad sense, be thought of as supportive. This is a generalization to which we can think of many important historical exceptions and which indeed is rarely true except in a qualified sense. Any group that demarcates itself from society in life-style or ideology implies some degree of protest against that society. The implicit tension will be felt both by its members and by the nonmembers in the society.

Yet these groups are supportive of society in that they are derivative from the predominant religion of the culture. Most believers accept groups as normal and proper ways of practicing that religion in a particularly devout and experience-oriented way. Thus, these groups reinforce the religion. They provide the religion, in fact, with the indispensible validation of ongoing confirmation of its sacred realities.

These groups are:

1. *The group of devotees or disciples around a charismatic leader who is*

fundamentally an exemplary figure of the general tradition. Examples are the Buddha, Jesus, Francis, Sufi masters like al-din Rumi, and their disciples.

The charisma of the master derives not so much from episodic mystical experiences he has had as from his ability to symbolize the seamless union of the human and the transcendent. Such a union is the ultimate interpretation of mysticism. He may even be a *"saint by ascription,"* in Bharati's term, whose charisma lies in faultlessly and innocently playing the social role given the man of sanctity by his culture.

In any case, the charismatic mystic serves as a catalyst for the experiences of his disciples. The accounts of mysticism are full of disciples having confirmatory experiences while in the orbit of the master. Jesus's disciples cast out demons in his name and witnessed his transfiguration; those near the Buddha himself, found it easy to become *arhants* or fully liberated beings, an achievement that since the Enlightened One's entry into Nirvana has progressively become much more difficult.

The devotee or disciplic group is loose in formal organizational terms, though it involves intense commitment for an inner core. All five of the characteristics cited above are actually realized among the disciples because of the intense relation to the master validated by his charisma. There is considerable self-negation through obedience, and certainly the master offers a powerful religious symbol that authenticates the disciples' experiences and life-style. The master-disciple group, with its partial dissociation from society, provides an excellent climate for stimulating, as well as authenticating, mystical experience. It offers a combination of stress, in the separation from society and the high anticipatory exhilaration, and nonstress in the peace of acceptance by the master. There is, of course, the supreme stimulation of his presence and example, as well as of the techniques that he teaches. Finally, there is the mutual reinforcement in the spiritual outlook—and perhaps moderate competition for spititual prizes and the master's approbation —in the group of devotees itself. This reinforcement is supported by the community's image of the devotees as persons to whom mystical experience is daily bread.

The next two groups represent routinizations of the master-disciple group in ways fundamentally supportive of society.

2. *The monastic order or the religious commune.* The main variable between these two is celibacy versus marriage, though monastics are also more likely to have distinctive garb and more regulated a life. Both eschew personal property and submit their entire life to the institution.

One example of the monastic order is the Chinese Buddhist monastery, whose way of life in the first half of the twentieth century Holmes Welch has excellently described.[2] Most monks in these monasteries, predominantly in the Ch'an or Zen tradition, spent half the year in meditation and half devoting themselves chiefly to the more practical business of the order: organizing its economic life, caring for guests, training novices, performing services for lay patrons. All were up at 3 A.M., and meditators spent as much as ten hours a day in the meditation hall. The monasteries had exacting rules on how to dress, use the toilet, bathe, maintain continence, sit, eat, and receive strokes for infractions. Besides a hard disciplined life with little sleep, bland and barely adequate vegetarian food, and no privacy, a monk had to spend many hours a day focusing the mind on his *hua t'ou* (question on which to meditate) or rather using the *hua t'ou* to release him from the ordinary stream of consciousness. Were there rewards for such an austere and seemingly tedious life?

It appears that there were. Chinese monks seldom spoke about experiences of enlightenment; that was something very personal. Yet some have left autobiographies detailing experiences comparable to that of the American schoolteacher. Holmes Welch does not doubt that the monastic life of many was sustained by a joy comparable to hers, a joy the monastery with its simplicity and spiritual intention had actually encouraged and preserved. Welch tells of veterans of many decades of the monastic life who were called *lao-ts'an,* "old papayas." Utterly content, with the softly glowing beauty we sometimes see in elderly monks and nuns of the West, these old gentlemen of religion wandered from one famous cloister to another and at each longed for the hour of meditation.

Others, of course, were less successful. During the rigorous early stages of training, not a few novices fled, went mad, or sickened and died. Only those with a certain kind of mental equipment were able to abide the monastery or profit from it. The cloister, like all total institutions, is not for everyone. Indeed, if it were, its important "called out" quality would be meaningless. But there are those whom it enables to develop a peculiar human potential, one closely related to mysticism, to its fullest by becoming saints of rich inner peace and radiant holiness.

3. *The pious fraternity or prayer group.* These are intentional, spiritual groups within a dominant religious tradition that are not full-time institutions like monasteries, but seek to enhance individual spiritual and mystical life. Sometimes these groups are affiliated with monasteries. Holmes Welch tells us, for example, of devout Buddhist laymen who took some, but not all, of the traditional monastic vows at a temple. They would continue as householders and business or profes-

sional persons, but like the monks vowed not to take sentient life, drink alcohol, lie or steal. Such persons would usually maintain a relationship to the monastery in which they had taken the vows, receiving spiritual guidance from a wise monk and making frequent pilgrimages to it. Often this group and other groups of lay devotees who had not formally taken vows formed societies in the towns and cities where they lived. Here they met to practice devotions and to study and propagate Buddhism.[3]

Religious fraternities and prayer groups, of course, do not have to be Buddhist or associated with monasteries. In American Christianity countless charismatic groups, prayer groups, and devotional guilds have comparable functions. They are groups within or parallel to the normative religious organizations (e.g., parishes, churches, temples) and adhere to the church's doctrines, but are interested in practicing the religion with a view to special personal commitment, experience, and spiritual development. They are voluntary even for people who are members of the normative organizations, but for this very reason are likely to be much more stimulative of religious experience. They bring together people who can easily communicate their high evaluation of religious experience. Not all, of course, are directly concerned with mystical experience in the strict sense. But we can hardly deny that in many devotional groups, frequently comprised of ordinary people, strong religious feeling easily interpreted as the "presence of God" or "movement of the Spirit" arises: an encounter with ultimate divine reality in a direct nonrational way.

I have visited Protestant and Roman Catholic prayer groups related to the "charismatic" movement, which has endeavored to recover such gifts of the early Christian church as healing and speaking in tongues. The intense manner in which all, not just the leadership, participated evidenced the seriousness and outside-the-institution character of the group. I heard testimonials, prayers, and contributions to Bible study from the humblest persons present. As the sessions moved to mutual intercession and the laying on of hands for healing, I felt the group dealt with personal needs and sustained an atmosphere that permitted belief in the power of God to meet them. Finally, when *glossalalia* or "tongues" came, I sensed an opportunity to attain release of inner power that had probably long been blocked. However, in the long run these groups only reinforce the dominance of Catholic and Protestant Christianity in the society rather than undermine it. This type of spititual life is not a new thing in the annals of mysticism. For example, Teresa of Avila, already mentioned, would sometimes meet with her nuns in the courtyard of the convent where they would sing spiritual songs and pass into deep holy joy and ecstasy.

Emergent Groups

Two remaining examples are of groups that are usually also master-disciple relationships and their routinizations, but in which the interaction of the group to the society tilts in the direction of alienation. This means the source of the group's authentication is divergent from the society's. Its members see themselves as instruments of a protest against society on behalf on transcendence. They thus set up an alternative life-style or social order, in which the symbols of demarcation between the group and the society are clear. Mystical experience can often be important to such groups, for it can provide that authentication independent of the society and its normative religion that alternative groups need.

This sytle of religious life that sees itself chiefly in contrast to its spiritual environment I will call *emergent religion.* It has roots in the same spiritual soil, of course, but is like a mutant plant breaking through the brush to contrast with the surrounding vegetation. Dictionary definitions of the word *emergent* suggest several salient characteristics of this sort of religion. As an adjective, *emergent* defines something arising out of a fluid, suddenly appearing, coming as a natural or logical outcome of a situation; or it is something appearing as novel in a process of evolution. As a noun, the word indicates something that stands out, like a tree above the forest.

These definitions apply quite well to the counterpart of established religion. New spiritual movements emerge out of the fluid sea of popular religion, perhaps suddenly, perhaps in response to situations that impel change such as wars, conquest, or new cultural contacts, or perhaps as an inevitable result of a process of development. Like a new volcanic island looming up through the surface of the sea, emergent religion is likely to appear strange and novel, yet it still has deep and longstanding sources in the same ground as that underlying its environment.

We can distinguish two basic kinds of emergent religion. They may be called *intensive* and *expansive* religion. This pair corresponds with what some sociologists of religion have called respectively *sect* and *cult,* but those terms no longer seem to have appropriate connotations.

Intensive emergent religious groups withdraw from society in favor of a more intense and rigorous commitment to major symbols of the established religion. Within American Christianity, they would be groups like the Amish and Jehovah's Witnesses; within Judaism, extreme Hasidic groups.

Expansive emergent religion, on the other hand, withdraws from society in order to realize a more broadly based experience than normative religion. It seeks to combine elements of the established faith with new ideas and teachings from science, far-away places, and inner visions. In America, examples would be movements such as Spiritualism and various meditation and devotional activities brought in from India or Japan.

As an example of mysticism in intensive groups, we may look at aspects of the uprising of the Anabaptists in Munster, Germany, in the early 1530s. This period was indeed a time of stress. The Black Death had passed through the region in 1529, the price of rye tripled, Germany was in upheaval over the Lutheran Reformation, and a Catholic prince-bishop ruled Munster with a regime out of touch with current economic and social realities. During this period Melchior Hoffmann, a visionary and true successor of the itinerant prophets of the Middle Ages, came to Munster. He preached the imminent Second Coming of Christ.

Hoffmann had not long before joined the Anabaptists or "Rebaptizers." They were a radical Protestant group, indirectly related to modern Baptists, who believed in baptism only after adult conversion and in following the New Testament literally. With him came Anabaptist refugees who had been expelled from neighboring states. Their presence and Hoffmann's preaching incited a mass frenzy in the town that led to the Anabaptist conversion of a large part of the population, the overthrow of the old regime, and the attempt to establish in its place a millenarian utopia.

Signs and wonders shook the town of Munster; ex-nuns saw apocalyptic visions in the streets, which threw them to the ground in frenzy. New and more militant leadership replaced Hoffmann. They threw out the "Godless ones" and established for the remaining saints a society of "all things in common." But soon enough the New Jerusalem of Munster ended in horrible tragedy: utopia quickly turned into a reign of terror by fanatics within, and to carnage and starvation imposed by beseiging armies from without.[4]

In this account we see direct revelation by direct vision in the context of an intensive group of Anabaptists. This intensive group then spreads to the entire city, in other words the state becomes the sect. The development of this sect has three interrelated stages.

Initially, the visions of Hoffmann and his following provided a way of handling the intolerable tensions of the present by transcending those evils, interpreting them as part of a world that was passing away. Second, we see the mass conversions and ecstatic phenomena of the ordinary people of the city. After their former lords had been disposed of, they establish themselves as a community striving for *communitas,* as a people with a deeply shared experience and interrelation that set them apart from the ungodly world outside and gave them a special destiny. Third, the new leaders of this new community—who in their religious fanaticism turned out to be far more ruthless than the old—used their own visionary experience, deemed as shared and so validated by all the saints, to legitimate their authority. That authority, in the circumstances, had to have an immediate and subjectively supported charisma since it was obviously lacking the support of tradition.

Most intensive groups, of course, do not possess nor seek political power. But within their orbits they do strive to be total, since consistency is important to them; so much so it motivated the original break with the world and its compromises. Also, as at Munster, subjective religious experience tends to support the group's coherence and to sustain the authority of its leadership, because they seek coherence of inner and outer and tend to disdain the mere outer forms of religious structure and tradition. But because mysticism does not always sit well with the desire for consistency and the scriptural legalism that intensive groups wish to obtain—and also is a result of mysticism's break from normative religion—we often see a latent tension between mysticism and the intensive group. This group accepts and desires—ever requires—the mystical experience that supports its claims, but vehemently castigates such experiences contrary to its beliefs. It finds it necessary to expel such contrary experiences, figuratively or actually, for they threaten its legitimacy as surely as mysticism with consistent symbols affirms it.

Expansive emergent groups, on the other hand, do not so much use mysticism as a means of upholding a consistency-based truth, as make it a symbol of an expansion of consciousness that may run ahead of certain social definitions, at least, of consistency. To these people, mysticism is a vehicle of quest; if the attitudes toward it are somewhat more structured in most groups than they like to believe, the mobility from group to group of a great many followers of expansive religion more than compensates.

An example, roughly contemporary with the Munster sectarians, to represent expansive emergent religion is the Rosicrucian enlightenment.[5] The term *Rosicrucian* (from "Rosy Cross") has not been found in use before the early seventeenth century, but many scholars believe the style of life and spirituality it represents is based on that of the great physician and occult philosopher Paracelsus (1493–1541). That style is the way of the wanderer who believes he possesses, or is believed to possess, wisdom giving him mastery of alchemy, control over nature, and near immortality. Like a shaman within civilization, the Paracelsean and Rosicrucian person moved through this world seeing much but having few attachments, unless to a band of disciples or colleagues. Here are some lines from a curious nineteenth-century book about the Rosicrucians and their way of life.

> They speak of all mankind as infinitely beneath them; their pride is beyond idea, although they are most humble and quiet in exterior. They glory in poverty, and declare that it is the state ordered for them; and this though they boast universal riches. They decline all human affections, or submit to them as advisable escapes only—appearance of loving obligations, which are assumed for convenient acceptance, or for passing in a world which is composed of them, or of their supposal. They mingle most gracefully in the society of women, with hearts wholly incapable of softness in this direction; while they criticize them with pity or contempt in their own minds as altogether another order of beings from men. They are most simple and deferential in their exterior; and yet the self-value which fills their hearts ceases its self-glorying expansion only with the boundless skies. Up to a certain point, they are the sincerest people in the world; but rock is soft to their impenetrability afterwards. In comparison with the hermetic adepts, monarchs are poor, and their greatest accumulations are contemptible. By the side of the sages, the most learned are mere dolts and blockheads. They make no movement towards fame, because they abnegate and disdain it. If they become famous, it is in spite of themselves: they seek no honours, because there can be no gratification in honours to such people. Their greatest wish is to steal unnoticed and unchallenged through the world, and to amuse themselves with the world because they are in it, and because they find it about them. Thus, towards mankind they are negative; towards everything else, positive; self-contained, self-illuminated, self-everything; but always prepared (nay, enjoined) to do good, wherever possible or safe.[6]

Whether these personages, exalted but not wholly attractive, actually existed is problematic; we have much literature about them and their lore, but little if any that is verifiable about their history. Nonetheless, a genre of writing broadly called *Rosicrucian* patrols the borderlines of magic, alchemy, mysticism, and early modern science. This writing had an appreciable role in the development of science, and more or less ephemeral orders of Rosicrucians have sprung up over the last three and a half centuries. More important for our purposes, the style and goal has influenced and epitomized a type of mysticism important both in the East (where it is represented by the Taoist adept and legends of Taoist immortals or Indian *siddhas*) and West. Although very different from sectarian mysticism, it also represents a mystical alienation from society and normative religion.

Yet alienation is never so pure as to be without sociological meaning, however much that may have been the objective of the Rosicrucian. We find in the passage above that the Rosicrucian's ideal is an inner reality, enhanced by wisdom and mystical adeptship, so splendid he can live independent of society. But he discovers such an attainment is not entirely possible. First, he must have an attitude toward society. This attitude is a humanly understandable mixture of disdain and rather conditional desire to do good with his superlative abilities. Second, he finds that society has attitudes toward him: the majority feels puzzlement or malicious misunderstanding; a minority has an eager desire to contact him, adulate him, and identify with him. They find something in their own subjectivity resonates with what he represents.

Third, the Rosicrucian is not without sociological links on his own level. There always hovers about him a vague idea that he is not entirely alone, but belongs to an ultrasecret order; that he occasionally meets confreres and superiors. Moreover, somewhere sometime he had a master who initiated him into the fraternity. The text that began the Rosicrucian furor in Europe, the *Fama Fraternatis* of 1614, tells of the travels of the archetypal founder of the modern order, Christian Rosencreutz. (Both he and the order are undoubtedly fictional rather than historical realities.) Rosencreutz traveled to Damascus and Fez, where he learned much secret wisdom, and then returned to Europe to establish his order. It was comprised of eight unmarried men, who were to wear no distinctive garb, but vowed to heal the sick gratis, meet together once a year, and each select a successor to himself in the brotherhood.[7] Even if fictional, here is a sociological model. It often happens that the social expression of expansive religion is more theoretical than real, for to the expansive mystic inner reality and independence from society are the ultimate realities. However, sometimes it does form close and long-lasting organizations.

An example of both sides is Zen in America. This classic Chinese and Japanese form of Buddhism, which we have already looked at in the case of the American schoolteacher and in the Chinese monastery, has had two rather different meanings in America. In novels like Jack Kerouac's *The Dharma Bums* and Pirsig's *Zen and the Art of Motorcycle Maintenance* (both considerably autobiographical), Zen seems to indicate primarily a footloose, unstructured life-style in which wandering and experiencing both veils and facilitates a spiritual quest. It is a quest that must take place outside the walls of normative society and religion; it is much attuned to poetic consciousness; and it seeks absolute freedom and oneness with the universe—the goals of the Zen masters of old.

The other style of American Zen is that of the several formal Zen centers, such as the one where the American schoolteacher underwent *sesshin.* They are generally communal and have a highly structured spiritual practice under the guidance of a *roshi* or master. In all respects feasible, they emulate the life of a Chinese or Japanese monastery.

Yet both are expansive rather than sectarian religion. Like Rosencreutz on his journey, they represent the assimilating of wisdom from far away, rather than an intensification of the domestic faith. The object of their mysticism is a kind of inner freedom—a space at the center—rather than reinforcement of traditional or charismatic authority, although that may in fact occur in regard to, say, Buddhism or the *roshi.* Yet the sociology of these groups indicates that the idea of alienation expressed through individual quest is not absent and makes them part of an expansive process for the majority of people who experience them.

It is instructive to compare the composition of the Chinese Buddhist devotional groups of which Holmes Welch spoke and American Zen centers. The former, representing the conventional religion of that society, drew middle-aged, middle-class people who were clearly trying to round off their life with a more spiritual dimension, but were not at all rebels. Some had been Christians—in the China of that period, a foreign and somewhat daring faith—but turned to the solace of the more familiar way as they grew older.

However, in America, it is the Zen Centers—and comparable Eastern or unconventional movements—that draw adventurous seekers, often young and unsettled. Many of them move easily from one movement to another, but enjoy the camaraderie as well as the spiritual gifts of each as they sample it. They tend to see life as a series of experiences, rather than an occasion for a single commitment. Mysticism, with its exaltation of inward experience and its self-validating rather than social reinforcement, fits well with that mood. Zen centers, meditation movements, and the like, in America, offer a contrast and an opportunity for the expansive style. Because they purvey mysticism and are sufficiently foreign, they do not seem oppressively demanding of commitment or social conformity.[8]

Leadership and Mysticism

It should be apparent by now that the relationship of leader and followers is extremely important in the sociology of mysticism. Time and again, one finds the social context of mystical experience to be a tightly knit society or even community composed of a guru or master and disciples. The paternal authoritarianism, or even nondirective charisma, of the master seems to reduce areas of decision-making tension, while stimulating through example the virtue of mysticism. The reinforcement of the disciples no doubt stimulates and validates mystic experience for the leader himself, particularly when it enables him to attain a socially recognized role.

An example would be the modern Hindu mystic Ramana Maharshi, mentioned earlier. As a teenager, the death of his brother led him to think seriously about the large issues of human identity. Ramana left home to take up the life of a mystic hermit. When he was only twenty, he was a radiantly spiritual youth who lived in a cave. Children liked him and would play around the young meditator. Gradually people who wanted to be near him—whether disciples, lay devotees, or relatives—moved into his vicinity, and there appeared an ashram.

The Hindu ashram or spiritual settlement is informal by monastic standards. It includes serious disciples, visitors, relatives, and hangers-on, not to mention troupes of monkeys and herds of cows. Yet it is an intentional community centered around a holy man. He gives instructions; in the early years of his ashram, Ramana practiced silence, but occasionally wrote out what he wished. In these spiritual settlements meals and work are usually communal, and silence is kept for times of meditation. Because heavy administrative work is not the holy man's vocation, it is handled by an emergent leadership within his inner circle of disciples.

This sort of charismatic and—insofar as it is exercised—authoritarian leadership seems best to induce frequent and spontaneous mystical experience in disciples. The annals of Ramana's ashram in south India are full of persons from all over the world, of many backgrounds and stations, who found the master's presence and the ambiance of his ashram gave a very special peace and self-knowledge.[9] The Buddha during his days on earth, though his style was peripatetic, seems to have had a comparable relation of charismatic authority to the disciples. Among them rich mystical experience was an everyday occurrence.

Informal yet vital groups like these, however, find it difficult to manage the crisis of the second generation, the crisis following the death of the master. Many disappear, their work done. Others become routinized as monastic orders, denominations, and sects, the *viva voce* authority of the founder replaced by scripture or constitution, the charisma that spoke for itself superseded by ballots and laws. As we have seen, routinization by no means excludes further mystical experience. Yet just as the movement tends now to lose its springtime hope for a new spiritual order, its expectation of inward or outward miracles daily, so the spiritual life becomes less spontaneous and more a gradual, programmatic development under guidance and by the book. Often it is taught that attainment is harder now since the original glory has departed and times have degenerated. Today Buddhists less frequently become arhants than in the time the Enlightened One's disciples. Yet in compensation, routinization makes something of the tradition available to segments of society before untouched. It makes it possible for aging and conservative businessmen, like some of the Chinese gentlemen who became lay Buddhist devotees, to set foot on the mystic's path, though they would not likely leave all to become enthusiastic disciples of a movement in its first generation. It makes possible also the full integration of the spiritual experience with culture; the full wonder discovered within can then be expressed not only in philosophy, but also in art and music.

The Role
of the Mystic
in Society

As we have indicated, the relation of mystics and mystical groups to the community varies immensely. Many mystics have existed in communion with the normative religion of the society, and indeed have given it formal affirmation. This was the case even when tension existed with the institutions of the religion in which the mystic was most immediately involved. John of the Cross was quite loyal to the Catholic faith despite antagonism, and at one point even imprisonment, from his order because of the saint's zeal to reform it.

The German Protestant mystic Jacob Boehme (1575–1624) had an important mystical experience in 1600, and subsequently wrote his youthful work *The Aurora,* offering a mystical philosophy based on a dialectical process. (In yes and no shall all things consist, he said, and one must pass through the center of hell to rebirth.) But the local Lutheran pastor did not consider such high thinking appropriate to a shoemaker, and persuaded the town council to condemn Boehme and forbid him from writing further. Yet despite some years of silence, Boehme's inner fires prevented him from holding his pen in check forever. Clerics then raised the populace against him, and the mystic was forced to flee to a friendly castle. Nevertheless, he never claimed to be other than Christian and Lutheran, and at the end was judged orthodox enough to receive deathbed communion.

Why such paradoxical tensions between organized religion and those whom one might suppose would be its most exemplary representatives? Religion has basically two roles: to support the normative values of society and to provide moments of ecstasy and transcendence. The "ordinary" religionist, whether lay or professional, is likely to accept the support of normative values role unquestioningly and to have ecstasy well subordinated as a reward for living a moral life in conformance with the normative values. One receives communion only if one is morally impeccable or has made a good confession. But mystics are likely to experience the two roles of religion as at cross-purposes because of their overwhelming interest in the second. They may not reject the first; it simply holds little interest for them. This will set them apart in the eyes of others. They will consider mystics religious in an unbalanced way, enjoying the raptures of faith, but not contributing their part to its upholding of family and community stability.

Thus, even in a religion that gives no endorsement to celibacy, the mystic may find marriage a problem. Islam values marriage highly and has no formal place for spiritual celibacy. But Martin Lings, in his excellent study of the modern Muslim saint Shaikh Ahmad al-'Alawi, tells that as a very pious young man al-'Alawi was married and divorced several times, basically because in his zeal for religious practice he had no time nor interest for family matters. Eventually he established a celibate household of disciples in Algeria not too different from the Hindu ashram. As pilgrims began coming from far and near to be in the presence of this holy man, he became a pillar of Islamic religion in a broader sense, despite his difficulty with one or two of its values as they apply to ordinary folk.[10]

This was not an unlikely outcome. Regardless of severe tensions with them at some periods, society often uses mystics to validate the normative religion and so, sometimes ironically, the normative values and structures of society. Saint Rose of Lima, whose ecstasy after receiving communion we have already cited, endured a ten-year struggle with her parents who wanted her to marry. Her call to religion finally prevailed; she practiced extreme asceticism in a hut where she lived at the back of her family's garden, sleeping on broken glass and the like. After her early death, she was canonized, and eventually became patron saint of all the Americas.

Even if persecuted, the mystic may uphold society by serving as a model for the fruitlessness of alienation, for suffering nonresistance, and the religious sublimation of discontent. Francis of Assisi was certainly aware of the social evils of his day. Yet rather than directly break with church and state, he kissed the sores of lepers, ate garbage with the extreme poor, and went unarmed to visit the sultan when others bore the crusader's sword. At the same time, he promoted devotionalism with a new sense of feeling and love. All this won Francis both powerful enemies and friends, the friends partly because they preferred his way to that of out-and-out rebels like the "heretical" Waldensians and Cathars. Francis's actions were reformist in the long run, but when they occurred, they consolidated and validated the ultimate authority of the normative religion.

On the other hand, the mystic may be the articulator of alienation, which in turn becomes political protest. This can be the case even when the mystic seems thoroughly orthodox, just as it is when she or he is heretical, and religious and secular rebellion flow together. The Chinese Buddhist monk Mao Tzu-yuan (1086–1166) is an alleged founder of the White Lotus religion, for many centuries a popular eschatological form of Buddhism associated with subversion and peasant protest in China. Mao, as a young monk, reached enlightenment while in meditation when he heard a crow's call. He later became a master of Pure Land, and the later books of that school regard him as a standard teacher.

But the books of other schools, such as T'ien T'ai and Ch'an, depict Mao as a heretic who established the White Lotus sect, which practiced immortality and stirred up the masses. Later, in times of trouble the White Lotus movement established its own armies and founded ephemeral theocratic kingdoms in rebellious provinces.

We cannot here sort out the historical puzzle of the two divergent images of Mao. The matter has been well discussed by Daniel L. Overmyer.[11] We can point to the mystic's access to transcendence and his endeavor to talk about it (for Mao was certainly a popularizer of Pure Land Buddhism), but all religions can have different social meanings to different people in different situations. Mao may well have founded a group that became the sect (or rather sects) going by the White Lotus name, but these movements found themselves in different relations to society in various times. They were briefly favored, for example, under the Yüan dynasty, but were rebels under both the following Ming and Ch'ing houses. It is more usual, no doubt, to see a group move from a marginal to an established position—from sect to denomination—but the White Lotus example, like that of the Old Believers in Russia, shows it can move in the other direction.

The group, charismatic or routinized, which the mystic forms may also have political impact by providing a model of a different order of society, even a model of the *communitas* that is the political ideal. An illustration of this impact is The Church on Earth by the Prophet Simon Kimbangu, an African Christian church centered in Zaire. Kimbangu (1889–1951), first converted by Baptist missionaries, was a mystic, healer, and prophet. He became a subject of legend in his own lifetime. Several variants are told, for example, of a story that as a child he fainted and fell into a hole, where a man "neither black nor white" appeared with a Bible in his hand and said, "This is a good book. You must read it and proclaim its contents." After his conversion and baptism in 1915, Kimbangu became a lay evangelist and performed numerous miraculous healings. Many compared Kimbangu's ministry to that of Jesus Christ, and he did nothing to discourage the rapidly spreading idea that his seat at N'Kamba was the location of a new Pentecost and home of a new prophet sent to bring Christ to the blacks. But the Belgian colonial government, fearing political overtones in the movement, completed the drama by arresting Kimbangu, sentencing him to death, and persecuting the movement. The King of Belgium, however, commuted Kimbangu's sentence to life imprisonment. The prophet spent the rest of his life behind bars as a living martyr to his followers. In its continuing church life, the Kimbanguist church has consistently emphasized ecstatic and mystical experience; before Sunday worship, devout members spend the entire night in prayer in small groups, and such phenomena as visions and speaking in tongues are not unknown.[12]

The relation of mysticism to political goals and models is complex: a paradoxical mix of reactionary rhetoric, practical conservatism, sectarian idealism, and utopian vision. All these strands can be found in Kimbanguism.

Reactionary rhetoric is evidenced in the initial emphasis that the ministry of the prophet was a replay of the New Testament; its wondrous healings and biblical teaching meant a return of an idealized moment in the remote past. Not only was it a recalling of the Palestine of Jesus, but it was—in the context of disturbing social change in colonial Belgian Congo—a recalling of traditional African ideas about the charismatic prophet. Kimbangu used many symbols, down to the great staff he carried, of the traditional priest and ruler.

This movement also, due to its intense concern with inner life, was conservative when compared to surrounding society. It showed high morality by both African and Christian standards. However, it talked mostly of personal rather than social reform. During its persecution, it did not strike in return, accepting Kimbangu's living martyrdom as a divine sign, and teaching pacifism and nonretaliation. At the time of Congolese independence, despite its clear nativist credentials, the church rejected the temptation to seek close alignment with the new government, but continued to disdain political involvement. This meant that its social leaven, while present, has worked indirectly, and that by not being an immediate agent for change, the church by default has had a short-term conservative impact.

Yet it has also displayed sectarian idealism, viewing itself as a divine family, a new chosen people. The church now has a hierarchical organization under the prophet's three sons, suggesting that those who enter the church become members of his spiritual household. N'Kamba, where the founder lived and ministered, has become a New Jerusalem, a holy and ideal city. All these tokens show something other than sheer conservatism going on; rather, behind a facade of indifference to the things of this world, the forms and institutions of a new world order, validated by the prophet's rapport with transcendence, are gestating. They are not without force even now.

For a fourth characteristic of the mystical movement's relation to society is the movement's enactment of utopian vision. The faith of Kimbangu has spread through Africa as a movement transcending class, tribe, and nation and has had its part in the evolution of modern African consciousness. The church has been a modernizing agency through its development of extensive social services: hospitals, educational institutions, youth centers, agricultural cooperatives. Such works as these, of course, are forces for change that belie any apparent indifference to the social order.

Where the emphasis falls in a movement and whether the central symbol is imported or indigenous will depend on many circumstances. But most mystical movements center on a charismatic person and will have something of all four of these characteristics in the symbols of their relation to society in general.

Mystical Experience and Ethics

Mysticism should influence how those who know its experiences make value-decisions and handle interpersonal relations. But the way in which mystical experience affects those areas of life, like its relation to the social and political order, is a complex one, comprising several factors in paradoxical relationship.

Initially, mystical experience and fascination with its possibility, may lead to introversion and a sort of ego-centricity that talk of loss of ego in the One does not entirely obliterate. Self-consciousness, some-times acute and painful, is often characteristic of the budding mystic. It inhibits the rich interpersonal life and social concern one would associate with a full ethical life, even though the individual may be scrupulously moral by the standards of his religion. More than one celibate saint has been devout and upright, yet seems from the record to have been pathologically unable to interact with persons of the opposite sex.

Yet as mystical experience deepens, the individual becomes caught up in another order of reality, another world, which has different para-digms for human affairs than the ordinary. Citizenship in another realm becomes a felt experience, and so behavior as a subject of that order is more than a facade. It is a mandatory articulation to an individual of who he or she is—a deadly serious matter. The self-validating experi-ence creates a thorough awareness of self and a paradigm of its ideal nature that is now inescapable, for it is not merely formal but *known.* This knowledge of self gives the more mature mystic, like Saint Francis and Charles Finney (who became a leading abolitionist) a courage that sometimes seems superhuman in standing against evils appearing as a pervasive and deep-rooted as society itself.

Also, we must consider the shattering psychological and even physiological hammer blows of powerful mystical experience. It can leave one weak, but weak in a gentle and ethically significant way, like the Ancient Mariner who, after his ordeal, could only say softly, "He prayeth best, who loveth best, all things both great and small." The experience itself tends to efface ego, but as we have seen, this efface-ment can be a sense of oneness with all things expressed in love. It can also be a sense of a larger identity, even a divine identity, that gives the individual a feeling of tremendous importance. At its best this efface-ment can translate into a call to work great good in the world.

Finally, adumbrating the topic of the next chapter, we must recall that nearly all interpretations of the mystic path, Eastern and Western, make a highly disciplined and moral life a basic condition of spiritual life. Until an individual has set the house of his or her way of life in order, this individual cannot expect more than chaotic results from prayer and meditation. The mystic path and its several expressions, then, are great forces for ethical life in societies where they have many disciples.

Mystical experience, joined as it is with religious interpretation, will not leave an individual ethically the same as was before. It batters down the ego to leave only hypersensitivity, or purpose, or marvellous emptiness, or love.

Mysticism and the Sociology of Religion: Reading Selection

The following passage, from an important book about the life of slaves on southern plantations before the Civil War, clearly illustrates the role of ecstatic and mystical experience for these people in terms of their particular sociological situation. Note particularly the author's conclusions, which point out the communal meaning of the most personal emotionalism in this situation, and the way in which even the most chaotic religious ecstasy can be part of finding, rather than losing, an identity. While the deeply felt religious experience of these blacks was probably not always mystical according to our definition, it must have been frequently so interpreted insofar as these repressed and mostly uneducated people could put it into words. This excerpt will bring home to American readers in a particularly poignant way the powerful social meaning, whether as protest or accommodation or both, which mystical and cognate religious experience can have, and how groups can evoke it.

On the plantations and farms the slaves met for services apart from the whites whenever they could. Weekly services on Sunday evenings were common. Where masters were indulgent, additional meetings might take place during the week, and where they were not, they might take place anyway. Masters and overseers often accepted the Sunday meetings but not the others, for the slaves would stay up much of the night praying, singing, and dancing. The next day being a workday, the meetings were bad for business.

The slaves' religious meetings would be held in secret when their masters forbade all such; or when their masters forbade all except Sunday meetings; or when rumors of rebellion or disaffection led even indulgent masters to forbid them so as to protect the people from trigger-happy patrollers; or when the slaves wanted to make sure that no white would hear them. Only during insurrection scares or tense moments occasioned by political turmoil could the laws against such meetings be enforced. Too many planters did not want them enforced. They regarded their slaves as peaceful, respected their religious sensibilities, and considered such inter-

From *Roll, Jordan, Roll: The World The Slaves Made,* by Eugene D. Genovese. Copyright © 1972, 1974 by Eugene D. Genovese. Reprinted by permission of Pantheon Books, a Division of Random House, Inc., pp. 236–39. Explanatory notes omitted.

ference dangerous to plantation morale and productivity. Others agreed that the slaves presented no threat of rising and did not care about their meetings. Had the slaves been less determined, the regime probably would have been far more stringent; but so long as they avoided conspiracies and accepted harsh punishment as the price of getting caught by patrols, they raised the price of suppression much too high to make it seem worthwhile to planters with steady nerves.

When the meetings had to be held in secret, the slaves confronted a security problem. They would announce the event by such devices as that of singing "Steal Away to Jesus" at work. To protect the meeting itself, they had an infallible method. They would turn over a pot "to catch the sound" and keep it in the cabin or immediate area of the woods. Almost infallible: "Of course, sometimes they might happen to slip up on them on suspicion."[a] George P. Rawick suggest that the practice of turning over a pot probably had African origins, and John F. Szwed links it to rituals designed to sanctify the ground. The slaves' belief in its efficacy gave them additional confidence to brave the risks, and their success in avoiding detection led some whites to think that there might just be something to the pot technique.[b]

The desire of the slaves for religious privacy took a limited as well as a general form. Eliza Frances Andrews went down to the plantation praise-house after dinner one night to hear the slaves sing. "At their 'praise meetings,' " she commented, "they go through all sorts of motions in connection with their songs, but they won't give way to their wildest gesticulations or engage in their sacred dances before white people for fear of being laughed at."[c] But the slaves had no objection to pleasing curious whites when they expected an appreciative response. They took enormous pride in their singing and in the depth of their religious expression. They resisted being laughed at, but they responded to expressions of respect. Gus Feaster, an ex-slave from Union County, South Carolina, proudly told of such instances:

At night when the meeting done busted till next day was when the darkies really did have they freedom of spirit. As the wagon be creeping along in the late hours of moonlight, the darkies would raise a tune. Then the air soon be filled with the sweetest tune as us rid on home and sung all the old hymns that us loved. It was always some big black nigger with a deep bass voice like a frog that'd start up the tune. Then the other mens jine in, followed up by the fine little voices of the gals and the cracked voices of the old womens and the grannies. When us reach near the big house us soften down to a deep hum that the missus like!

aFisk University, *Unwritten History of Slavery*, p. 87.
bRawick, *Sundown to Sunup* pp. 41 ff.; John F. Szwed in personal correspondence. Also, Rawick, ed., *Indiana Narr., VI* (2), 98.
cE. F. Andrews, *War-Time Journal of a Georgia Girl*, Feb. 12, 1865 (p. 89).

Sometimes she hist up the window and tell us sing "Swing Low, Sweet Chariot" for her and the visiting guests. That all us want to hear. Us open up, and the niggers near the big house that hadn't been to church would wake up and come out to the cabin door and jine in the refrain. From that we'd swing on into all the old spirituals that us love so well and that us knowed how to sing. Missus often 'low that her darkies could sing with heaven's inspiration.[d]

This pride, this self-respect, this astonishing confidence in their own spiritual quality, explain the slaves' willingness to spend so much of their day of leisure at prayer meetings. Often they would hear the white preacher or the master himself on Sunday morning, but the "real meetin' " and the "real preachin' " came later, among themselves. Richard Carruthers, an ex-slave from Texas, explained another feature of the concern with prayer. "Us niggers," he said, "used to have a prayin' ground down in the hollow and some time we come out of the field, between eleven and twelve at night, scorchin' and burnin' up with nothin' to eat, and we wants to ask the good Lord to have mercy."[e]

The meetings gave the slaves strength derived from direct communion with God and each other. When not monitored, they allowed the message of promised deliverance to be heard. If the slaves had received false information or had been misled by the whites, they provided an opportunity for correction, as when the white preachers led them in prayers for the Confederacy, and their black preachers, in secret session, led them in prayers for the Union. But above all, the meetings provided a sense of autonomy—of constituting not merely a community unto themselves but a community with leaders of their own choice.

The slaves' religious frenzy startled white onlookers, although few ever saw it fully unleashed. The more austere masters tried to curb it but usually had little success. Emoline Glasgow of South Carolina had a Methodist master who took one of his slaves to church and determined to keep him in line by bribery if necessary. He offered to give the slave a new pair of boots if he behaved himself. All went well until about the middle of the service, when the slave let go: "Boots or no boots, I gwine to shout today."[f] The slaves took their letting-go seriously and condemned those who simulated emotion. When the Catholic priests forbade shouting in Louisiana, Catherine Cornelius spoke for the slaves in insisting that "the angels shout in heaven" and in doggedly proclaiming "The Lawd said you gotta shout if you want to be saved. That's in the Bible." Sincerity meant everything. Emma Fraser, an ex-slave from South Carolina, talked about her singing in church in the way that others talked about shouting. "But ef

[d]Botkin, ed., Lay My Burden Down, p. 146.
[e]Yetman, ed., Life Under the "Peculiar Institution," p. 13 (testimony of Lucretia Alexander of Arkansas).
[f]Rawick, ed., S. C. Narr., II (2), 135.

I sing an' it doan move me any, den dat a sin on de Holy Ghost; I be 'tell a lie on de Lord.''[9] The frenzy, as W. E. B. Du Bois called it, brought the slaves together in a special kind of communion, which brought out the most individual expressions and yet disciplined the collective. The people protected each other against the excesses of their release and encouraged each other to shed inhibitions. Everyone responded according to his own spirit but ended in a spiritual union with everyone else.

Possession appeared much less often among the slaves of the Old South than among those of Saint-Domingue or Brazil, where the practice of Vodûn and the rites of the African cults ran high. Yet ecstatic seizures, however defined, appeared frequently and submit to differing interpretations. Critics have recognized in them a form of hysteria, and Frantz Fanon even speaks of a kind of madness. Roger Bastide has suggested that they are vehicles by which repressed personalities surface in symbolic form. Many anthropologists, however, have remained skeptical of psychoanalytic explanations and have pointed out that no genuine schizophrenic could possibly adjust to the firm system of control that the rituals demand. No matter how wild and disorderly they look to the uninitiated, they are in fact tightly controlled; certain things must be done and others not done. They thus require, according to Alfred Métraux, social, not psychological, explanation. Yet, schizophrenia aside, a psychoanalytic explanation is compatible with a social one. The question may be left for experts, if any. Two things are clear. First, the slaves' wildest emotionalism, even when it passed into actual possession, formed part of a system of collective behavior, which the slaves themselves controlled. The slaves may have been driven wild with ecstasy when dancing during their services, but never so wild that their feet would cross without evoking sharp rebuke. And second, the slaves' behavior brought out a determination to assert their power and the freedom of their spirit, for, as Max Weber says, ecstasy may become an instrument of salvation of self-deification.[h]

Notes

[1]Peter L. Berger and Thomas Luckmann, *The Social Construction of Reality* (Garden City, N.Y.: Doubleday and Co., Inc., 1966).

[2]Holmes Welch, *The Practice of Chinese Buddhism 1900–1950* (Cambridge, Mass.: Harvard University Press, 1967).

[3]Welch, *Practice of Chinese Buddhism,* pp. 383.

[9]Saxon *et al., Gumbo Ya-Ya,* p. 242; Rawick, ed., *S. C. Narr.* II (2), 87.
[h]Max Weber, *The Sociology of Religion* (trans. Ephraim Fischoffs; Boston, 1964) p. 157.

⁴Norman Cohn, *The Pursuit of the Millenium* (New York: Oxford University Press, 1970) pp. 257.

⁵Frances Yates, *The Rosicrucian Enlightenment* (London: Routledge & Kegan Paul, 1972).

⁶Hargrave Jennings, *The Rosicrucians,* 4th ed. (New York: Arno Press, Inc., 1976), pp. 30–31.

⁷Yates, *Rosicrucian Enlightenment,* pp. 238–51.

⁸On Zen in America and these two expressions of it, see my *Alternative Altars: Unconventional and Eastern Spirituality in America* (Chicago: University of Chicago Press, 1979).

⁹See Arthur Osborne, *Ramana Maharshi* (London: Rider and Company, 1954).

¹⁰Martin Lings, *A Sufi Saint of the Twentieth Century* (Berkeley and Los Angeles: University of California Press, 1961).

¹¹Daniel L. Overmyer, *Folk Buddhism Religion: Dissenting Sects in Late Traditional China* (Cambridge, Mass.: Harvard University Press, 1976).

¹²Marie-Louise Martin, *Kimbangu: An African Prophet and his Church,* trans. D. M. Moore (Grand Rapids, Mich.: Wm. B. Eerdmans Publishing Company, 1975).

The
Mystic
Path

8

The Problem
of the Way
of Ascent

One aspect of the expression of mysticism encompasses all three of the Wachian forms and is so important it requires a separate chapter. Widespread in the great mystical traditions of the world is the concept (and experience) of a paradigmatic path the mystic may follow in his or her spiritual development. It is a great course with marked stages, leading the mystic from first awakening to an ultimate unitive state. We have alluded to the mystic path before; now it is time to examine its traditional nature and the issues raised by this concept.

Evelyn Underhill in her monumental work *Mysticism* presents a summary of the "classic" mystic path.[1] She bases her presentation on traditional Catholic mystical theology derived from the writings of such writers as Teresa of Ávila, John of the Cross, and Dom Augustine Baker. She lists five stages, and they will be basic to our discussion.

1. *Awakening or Conversion.* This stage is the beginning experience of the joys of the spiritual life; here its riches of feeling and insight may be chaotic and unbalanced, yet in some they are enough to stimulate a desire to deepen and stabilize them.

2. *Self-knowledge or Purgation.* When that desire is acted upon, the incipient mystic will first need to purge his/her life of all that is contrary to the quest through discipline and morality. Concurrently, the seeker inwardly becomes aware of the vast distance between the self and the ultimate, however much the awakening experiences may have given brief, sporadic, but powerful contacts with its reality.

3. *Illumination.* As time goes on, the seeker may be rewarded by various happy experiences of prayer, contemplation, sense of divine presence, and advancement. It is a good state, and for some it may be enough, but it is not true union with the divine.

4. *Surrender or the Dark Night of the Soul.* Before the seeker realizes union he or she experiences a second and profounder purgation. It involves subtle but deep withdrawal from attachment to the senses, inner darkness and dryness, all leading to a total giving up of all in the ego that separates the mystic from God.

5. *Union.* This stage is the true end of the mystic path. Union with God is usually not characterized by ecstasies and raptures. These may never be so intense as in first awakening and may be very common in the illuminative stage. Instead this stage is marked by a calm, steady, radiant peace suffused with quiet joy. This state is compatible with an active life for good, and indeed is the inner reality that has animated the great saints in their labors.

This is the outline of the path. As Underhill rightly acknowledges, mystics are very diverse and a schema like this should be regarded only as a summary of the experience of many, though not all, who attain mystic fulfillment. Some become great souls by living very well the spiritual life of only one of the steps. Some seem to skip a stage entirely, or seem to live two or more at the same time, experiencing, say, illumination and the Dark Night intermittently rather than sequentially. Some are under the guidance of a spiritual tradition or director who more or less deliberately leads the seeker through stages like these; others seem to discover and undergo them spontaneously and unwittingly. Yet for all that, the outline of the path appears to make sense of much that is uncovered in exploring the phenomena of mysticism.

How would the idea of the mystic path affect our discussion in this book so far? We have presented a scattering of experiences interpreted by the experiencers as direct, immediate encounter with ultimate reality. But it is evident they could be placed along the path at different points. Many of them, including perhaps such powerful and influential awakenings as those of Finney and Bucke, are really just initial conversions from the perspective of the path, not to be made absolute but regarded as messages saying there is more than ordinary reality. Some phenomena of mysticism, such as the rules of the monks and the asceticism of Saint Rose of Lima, assist the purgative stages. The joy of the shouting slaves and the ecstasy of the magical evocation and much else may be at the illuminative stage. Far fewer of those we have met in this general survey have passed on to the Dark Night of the Soul, but we have cited its classic exponent, Saint John of the Cross, and the anguished progress of the Zen monk Hakuin. The unitive state radiates out of the pages of the Upanishads, the final joys of Saint Teresa, and possibly (we would have to know more about her subsequent life to be certain) the Zen breakthrough of the American schoolteacher.

All these experiences are mystical, both by our definition and the equally broad definitions of Evelyn Underhill: mysticism is the intensive form of the essential human religious experience and "the expression of the innate tendency of the human spirit towards complete harmony with the transcendental order."[2] But while many may be called, through the experience of "awakening" encounters, with ultimate reality, few may reach the complete harmony of union with it.

Some forms of elementary experience may, by its own nature, be incapable of leading one to ultimate union. Spiritual openings like the possession trances of Maria José or the fervor of the crusader that are exploited for particular ends of healing or war are very likely not to lead past ultimate surrender to ultimate union, but will probably be kept just at a level adequate to meet those ends. The experiencer's intention and concept of the spiritual world is not prepared to carry him or her further —though we cannot say this positively, for once an individual has engaged the transcendent order, unexpected change of motive and perception can occur.

Magic and occultism also usually falls short of the absolute self-negation necessary to the highest stages. They may be ways of perpetuating in a studied, "scientific" way the intense but almost inevitably self-centered, feeling-centered experience of beginners in the spiritual life. Yet the case of magic and occultism is tricky, and these words— like mysticism itself—have been applied to a wide gamut of teachings and practices, from the grossly superstitious and selfish to the fairly sublime. Evelyn Underhill states that magic wants to get; mysticism wants to give. Yet, as she intimates in a well-informed chapter on magic and occultism (she was once herself briefly a member of an occult order), the more mature of magical and occultist traditions are concerned with more than just "getting" in the crude sense; they are spiritual techniques and their initiations and degrees parallel the mystical stages. Nonetheless, most magicians and occultists, whether Western wizards or the siddhas of India, would probably agree there is a difference. The magician wants an acquisition of power, experience, or even immortality; the mystic wants ultimate emptiness, possessing nothing yet possessing all things. But it should not be forgotten that this divergence may not occur until fairly well along in the path. Most beginners—indeed many well along in the purgative or illuminative stages—may believe only love motivates them. But without realizing it they may also be attached to the power and joy their spiritual state yields, and to the blissful eternity they believe it will give them. In this respect the magicians and occultists are simply more honest, though more self-limited also.

Nonetheless, I do not hesitate to say I favor Underhill's model of the mystical path. I would urge that the spiritual adventurer, like Shakespeare's Prospero, abjure "this rough magic," and end instead with an ordinary life plenteous in compassion and forgiveness. Surrendering the calling up of spirits, the manipulation of other's lives even (as he thinks) for their own good, and the quest for "higher" knowledge and conditions of awareness, as did the wizard of *The Tempest,* he or she should set foot on the great path, different in language but comparable in most traditions, leading through mystic death to ultimate union.

Yet problems remain in integrating the mystic path into the study of mysticism and religion. Our position has generally been to define mystical experiences and their relation to the forms of religious expression on grounds of self-interpretation; to use criteria from this path, and especially to define or grade mysticism in terms of surrender of union, would require a reading of implicit motive and subjective state in others that goes beyond phenomenology and is risky psychology. Moreover, it would mean distorting the meaning of intense religious experience to many who have known its riches. Charles Finney's conversion, for example, may have been only an awakening from the outlook of the path, but to him it was important and all-fulfilling, the whole of the path collapsed into one hour of right relationship with the one Mediator.

There is, in other words, an important religious point of view that acknowledges religious experience of the mystical sort, but discounts the value of the mystical path. It holds that right relations with God should not be made dependent upon such an inward progression. The path idea, it admonishes, makes mysticism too much a human accomplishment rather than a fruit of simple faith that can be well-grounded in one such evening as Finney's. It also argues the mystical path's schematic quality is not really true to the complexity of human nature and experience.

This position is commonly found among Protestant Christians and Pure Land Buddhists. It was well stated by Martin Luther when he said we are "always sinners, always justified" and that redemption is by God's grace received in us through faith. In other words, no path or practice carries us to a state where we are qualitatively in a different relation, wrought by an acquired holiness, to God than that of any human sinner. This humbling realization was eloquently sung by George Herbert:

> Profaneness in my head,
> Defects and darkness in my breast,
> A noise of passions ringing me for dead
> Unto a place where is no rest:
> Poor priest, thus am I drest.

> Only another head
> I have, another heart and breast,
> Another musick, making live, not dead,
> Without whom I could have no rest:
> In him I am well drest.

It could be persuasively argued that this realization is what is discovered in the Dark Night of the Soul, that the mystic and the Reformation divine who truly know their loves and needs will not end far apart. Yet certain theologians, such as Emil Brunner, have deeply mistrusted the mystic path. They believe it attempted to "anticipate God's grace" by outlining roads toward gifts that God wishes to give freely in his own time, without regard for the merits and states of believers.

Underlying this viewpoint is an awareness of the complexity of inner life which, at least in the case of Luther, was very painfully acquired. It is awareness that even the most sanctified find—or manifest without apparent self-knowledge of it—unworthy traits and feelings. The more a mystic searches inwardly, the more he or she may be aware that self-centeredness is not so much extirpated as redirected even in sainthood. The mystic also knows human nature is rooted in biological nature that no culture can wholly change. It is best, as well as most candid, we are told, to lay aside the model of a path to a sanctity (whether called unitive or something else) that pretends to more than the human state can bear, in favor of simple faith and grace in the context of ordinary life.

However, the concept of a path remains important to mysticism. At least as presented by Evelyn Underhill, its tentative and outline nature is so emphasized, and individual differences are so much brought out, that we would be very naive indeed to think of it as a check list by which we judge mystics according to how they conform to its contours. Although the illustrative material in connection with the stages is helpful in understanding mysticism, what the pattern finally says is simply that there is a dynamic with a direction—toward union—in the serious spiritual life. However, while common motifs may appear, no two advances toward union are the same.

This idea in itself is important for understanding mysticism. Whether we agree with the mystical path concept or not, it is important to most mystical traditions in the world and some understanding of it is necessary for understanding these traditions. Therefore, we shall now discuss the path on the basis of the five stages summarized by Underhill.

Awakening to Infinity

People start on the mystical path through an immense diversity of gates. To be sure, there is never uniformity in mysticism, but as souls approach unity, a certain convergence occurs. The beginnings, then, are the most varied of all. Some, like Bucke, have an apparently sudden and spontaneous experience. Some may be stirred by a natural sign, like the Buddist monk Mao-Tzu-Yuan whose thirst for enlightenment was aroused by hearing the cry of a crow in the middle of the night. For others it may be just the natural outgrowth of a devout life, in which the transition from ordinary piety to mysticism is so gradual that no particular moment can be assigned to it.

On still other occasions, the awakening may be in the context of ordinary religious practice. Saint Catherine of Genoa, when 26 and depressed from an unhappy marriage, was suddenly caught up in an overflowing experience of divine love and her own inadequacy while making her confession to a saintly priest.[3]

In some instances the awakening may have elements of supernatural call. The archaic shaman, as we have seen, may receive his initial call through voices in his head regarded as gods or spirits. In an delapidated church Saint Francis of Assisi was early in his career told by Jesus through the painted lips of a crucifix to repair his church. The modern Hindu mystic Satya Sai Baba reported visions of gods moving across the sky from early childhood.

Sometimes the awakening may be essentially a sad discovery of the sin and misery of the self and the world. Chariot rides stimulated the Buddha's quest for enlightenment. On these rides he saw four things: an aged man, a dying man, a corpse, and a monk. The first three taught him that all life, however pleasant-seeming, ends in the apparent futility of old age, sickness, and death. He knew he could no longer live for any other end than finding a way to have a liberated life in the face of these ancient enemies. The fourth sight, the holy man, suggested the ideal of a life dedicated to that end.

His actual mystical experiences apparently did not take root until after this awakening to the human condition. His great enlightenment came six years later. In other instances, too, we find—as we have observed before—even initial mystical experiences may be intentionally sought rather than unexpected. Charles Finney and the American schoolteacher had vowed to persevere in prayer or meditation until they slaked their intellectual and spiritual thirst; many mystics were already monks or nuns and in principle engaged in the religious venture when the mystic awakening deepened their pursuit.

The awakening is not the end of the quest. However the awakening comes, it is only an opening of the door, perhaps only the slightest opening. Yet it may seem so powerful to the experiencer that he or she is likely to think it has penetrated to the very heart of God or is a final revelation of truth. While the possibility cannot be totally excluded that a beginner might have such a rare and sudden grace, it is far more probable that the novice has fallen into the common temptation of absolutizing awakening encounters with transcendence. For these experiences can be very intense, but are also likely to be partial, one-sided, and inchoate. If the experiencer remains only on their level, the spiritual life is apt to stay orientated toward emotionalism, revelations, partial truth (since no experience however intense can communicate everything about the divine), and egocentric preoccupation with the seeker's own feelings. This egocentric preoccupation is virtually inevitable when whole new areas of feeling the experiencer did not know were possible suddenly open up, but it is a preoccupation at odds with the calm peace of supreme mysticism. Finally, beginning experiences will probably come and go with jagged rhythm of their own, leaving the recipient bouncing between rapturous elation and the depths of emptiness and despair when he or she feels the new-found grace has departed. The awakened mystic does, however, now know that a larger universe of reality and experience exists than ever before. But he or she must deepen and stabilize the relationship with it; otherwise the seeker might leave the spiritual life in cynicism and disappointment, or continue on an immature level of religion virtually as inadequate as none.

Preparation

The five stages of the mystic path enumerated by Evelyn Underhill are by no means absolute. Some authorities have presented a simpler pattern. Saint Isaac the Syrian, who has deeply influenced the Christian mysticism of the Eastern Orthodox Church, named only three: penitence, purification, and perfection.[4] The ancient yoga of Patanjali, with its eight limbs, embraces more entities. All outlines, however, include an insistence that a serious spiritual endeavor must embrace preparation of an individual's morals and life-style. This endeavor is fundamental to the process of deepening and stabilizing the transcendent encounters broached by the awakenings.

The real point of this step is that an individual's life must be consistent with the spiritual quest and supportive of it. The self-emptying required in high prayer and meditation will scarcely be meaningful or fruitful if otherwise a person's life centers around possessions, power, and ego. The calm of advanced illumination and union can hardly comport with a life generally chaotic, emotional, and subject to whim or fancy. In many cases it is emphasized that for the engaged mystic this preparation must go beyond the level of morality acceptable in ordinary religionists. The first two steps of the Yoga Sutras of Patanjali, for example, are Yama, abstention from evil-doing, and Niyama, observances of good. Yama enjoins avoidance of harming others, falsehood, theft, incontinence, and greed; Niyama commends purity, contentment, mortification, study, and devotion. In general these are, of course, profitable to all, but for the yogin, nonharm generally means vegetarianism, and nontheft and mortification mean a life of great austerity and outward poverty, perhaps of dependence upon alms.

In the same way, the Buddha's eightfold path—right views, right intentions, right speech, right conduct, right livelihood, right effort, right mindfulness, and right concentration—is really a series of preparatory moral steps leading up to the last. The Buddhist monastic rule includes (1) not taking life, (2) not taking what is not given, (3) not indulging in sexual misconduct, (4) not lying, (5) not drinking liquor, (6) not eating after noon, (7) not watching dancing, singing, and shows, (8) not adorning oneself with garlands, perfumes, and ointments, (9) not sleeping in a high bed, and (10) not receiving gold and silver. Very devout Buddhist laymen will sometimes undertake the first five. But more characteristic of the lay ideal are the four unlimited virtues: unlimited friendliness, unlimited compassion, unlimited sympathetic joy, unlimited evenmindedness. A person who exhibited these virtues would surely be a very great saint. In the same way, in Catholic Christianity monks and nuns undertake the "counsels of perfection"—poverty, chastity, and obedience. Monks and nuns are especially, though not exclusively, concerned with the higher reaches of the spiritual life and those mystical states not meant for everyone. The laity, on the other hand, can win salvation by faithful adherence to the ordinary rules of morality and the precepts of the church.

It is usually emphasized, however, that the edifice of the spiritual life should be built on the foundation of faithful practice of the routine observations of the religion. At least after the great philosopher al-Ghazzali emphasized the importance of harmonizing mysticism and orthodox practice, Sufi mysticism in Islam was based on the Five Pillars of Islam demanded of all Muslims: the confession of God as God and Muhammad as his envoy, prayer five times a day, the fast of the month of Ramadan, the giving of alms, the pilgrimage at least once in a lifetime to Mecca. The mystic does not abrogate these ordinances, but marks them on a deeper level than those merely concerned with outward conformity: for him, the prostrations in prayer are not just gestures, but inward acts of self-abnegation before the all-seeing omniscient God veiled by the world of appearances.

Some mystics, of course, have viewed matters differently. In early Sufism there was an antinomian strain. It rejoiced in affirmations of the unity of the ecstatic with the divine Friend and the liberation that this identity with the source of law afforded from its slavish observance. But in time wiser heads prevailed. Within Hinduism and Buddhism, the "short path" of Tantrism has sometimes seemed to demand only the virtue of absolute obedience to one's guru, and to call for demonstration of this obedience by the reversal of all other values through doing outrageous commanded acts that contravene ordinary morality. Teachers such as Milarepa, Marpa, and Nāropa tell of themselves, or their pupils, being ordered to build houses and destroy them, attack a wedding procession and violate the bride, eat excrement, commit robberies, and the like as a part of horrendous but immensely powerful initiations.

The Taoist *feng-liu* were likewise innocent of ordinary morality and exalters of impulse.

For the most part, though, mysticism has not consisted of such colorful and shocking exceptions to moral norms. Instead, the mystic's has been a way of perfection observing with exactness the ordinary values of religion. In the West particularly, this stage is spoken of as purgative or pentitential. It stresses that this is precisely the time when the mystic emphasizes the "law", when he or she fervently accepts its disciplinary and humbling function. While there have also been antinomian movements in Europe, in general Judaism and Christianity, like Islam, have sought to curb the ego through morality rather than by the paradoxical purgation of license.

Purgation, penitence, and perfection—these terms have all been used to describe the preparatory state, depending on whether the emphasis is on removing what is unsatisfactory in the experiencer's previous life, or compensating for it according to the laws of a moral order, or thinking positively on the unconditioned sublimity of the new life. Different as the emphasis is, all of them—as does mystic lawlessness—represent the reversal of ordinary life that is the key to the mystic door. And just as the way of life is reversed, so the laws of cause and effect, of gain and loss, are marvellously superseded. The Gospels speak of those who give up family and lands for the sake of the Kingdom and receive back a hundredfold; the *Yoga Sutras* of Patanjali relate that those who observe the *yama* of abstention from theft will find that all the wealth of the world will flow toward them. Whether these gains are to be understood materially or spiritually, the point is that the purgative stage of moral perfection opens up a realm of vastly transfigured value, and so is far from merely negative. That transvalued world, whose gleaming was seen in the awakening stage and whose door is now propped open at least a bit, is now to be explored more thoroughly.

Illumination

This midstream stage in the spiritual life is a highly varied one and so replete with its own little progresses in prayer and insight that Evelyn Underhill speaks of it as a way within the Way. Yet it has its distinctive meaning. The illuminative phase is the happy fulfillment of the promise of prayer, meditation, and sense of the divine presence as we ordinarily understand them—even if they fall short of a quality of union scarce perceiveable until the individual is well along.

In the illuminative stage, rapturous and ecstatic experiences may be frequent. The experience of Saint Rose of Lima, cited earlier, wherein the trees themselves seemed to bow and clap and the birds to sing, at dawn in praise of their Creator, we may take to typify it. Whatever form it takes, a rich awareness of God in the world and the soul marks this state. The universe seems divinely alive, and the inner self is continually aware of the divine voice and of the reality of prayer or meditation as direct unmediated encounter with the ultimate. It is the stage when prayers seem answered, either inwardly or outwardly, when God seems very real—the Divine Bridegroom is a common image among Christian mystics—and the earth itself seems luminous with unearthly light.

In yoga, it would be the stage after the seeker has established a life according to abstentions and observances. The seeker must also set up a devotion to God in some *ishvara* or saviour form, while the practice of *asana* and *pranayama* (postures and breathing) deepens his or her meditative life. In Buddhism, it would correspond to the second of four stages reaching *samadhi*—supreme unitive meditation—recently outlined by the Dalai Lama.[5] The first is the stage of aquiring concentration. The second is one of intermittant concentration, in which distractions come and go. However, this stage is a time of considerable joy and ecstasy invoked by the coming and going of concentration. It does, however, fall short of the quieter but more perfect uninterrupted concentration in which all barriers have been overcome. The *Visudhimagga*, the classic Theravada Buddhist text on meditation compiled by Buddhaghosa in the fifth century A.D., likewise speaks of a *pseudonirvana* in the middle stages of *vipassana* or realization of nirvana by analysis. It is characterized by brilliant illuminations, rapturous and devotional feelings, vigor and clear perception. But also there is a subtle attachment to these feelings.[6]

Sufi paths delineate a comparable stage. Generally, it has two parts: based on effort and God's grace. However, continual interplay echoes between them. An individual starts with conversion and purgative efforts to control his or her lower nature and establish appropriate self-discipline. But when a detached state is well-wrought, the gifts of God's grace begin to flow. The first states of grace bring awareness of God's nearness and allow self-forgetfulness in the thought of the Beloved but are less than falling away into union. They appear to correspond to illumination.

In the Christian West, the illuminative stage has hardly been better treated than by Saint Teresa of Avila; it seems to embrace the second and third stages described in her *Life*. These begin with the first reliable breakthroughs of the supernatural and proceed through a period rich in vision and ecstasy. In this period the flowers planted at the beginning now burst open into bloom, to use the saint's metaphor. The culmination in the third stage of illumination is the prayer of quiet. This culmination is really a unitive contemplation and falls short of the full union of the fourth stage only in that God "appears to allow the faculties to be conscious of and to enjoy the great work that He is doing. Sometimes—indeed very often—the will being in union, the soul is aware of it and sees that it is rejoicing in its captivity."[7] It is, like so much that Saint Teresa describes, a subtle state. All that keeps it from being complete union is that enough of an ego awareness remains to appreciate the wonderful work that God is doing.[8] Few go beyond this stage.

Yet in that very appreciation, in all the joys of illumination, lie exquisite dangers that inhibit the soul in ways it scarcely yet realizes— dangers that can carry seeds of spiritual disaster. An individual can become attached to spiritual experiences as pleasures, as interesting foci around which to build his or her ego, possibly as marks of superiority or special power. Even in the best cases—and there have been very saintly people who have never left the illuminative state—the time and energy devoted to the inner life, valuable as it is, tends to create a division between inner and outer, between devotion and work in the world, as separate set-apart things, even as the most perfect union between self and God is not yet realized.

The Night Passage

To move from illumination to the unitive state requires a second purgation, deeper and more delicate than the preliminary abstinences and observances, to clear away subtle spiritual attachment and egotism. It is the *pratyahara* stage of yoga, the withdrawal from the gross physical senses after a good foundation of *yama, niyama, asana,* and *pranayama* to develop the inner senses and prepare to plunge into the depths of *raja yoga* leading through concentration and meditation to *samadhi.* In the West, such authorities as Saint John of the Cross and Madame Guyon describe it as a period of chaos and deprivation, a stagnation of the spiritual life in which God seems hidden, the old feelings and graces are gone, and one is left to wander as on a desert at midnight without a compass. At the same time, just as night desert air is clean and chill, a certain sense of God's presence may remain, keeping the soul from falling into utter despair. Yet it is a cool presence that emphasizes God's utter purity and makes the slightest fault, the slightest grain of egotism remaining in the mystic, seem immense. The seeker sees, with cleansed eyes unbedazzled by sunny transports and answered prayers, how far he or she has come and how far there is to go.

Yet the value of this transit is not always clear except in hindsight. The mystics stress it as a time of disharmony, of emotional confusion and apparent relapse, when the patterns of a lifetime of grace are uprooted. Doubtless some have lost faith entirely in this stage, and some have gone mad; we generally hear only from those who have managed to make the other shore. But the individual does not direct his or her apprehension in this stage toward the goal so much as toward a sense of being adrift in midstream with no line and no one to help. Saint John of the Cross wrote, "The greatest affliction of the sorrowful soul in this state, is the thought that God has abandoned it, of which it has no doubt; that he has cast it away in darkness as an abominable thing . . . the shadow of death and the pains and torments of hell are most acutely felt, that is, the sense of being without God."[9]

Yet there also comes a desire to escape. The *Visudhimagga* has, after the pseudonirvana stage, a stage obviously cognate to the Dark Night of the Soul. During this period the ecstasies of the former state fade away and the chief experience is one of the empty weariness of all conditioned reality, however subtle and seemingly spiritual. This realization produces effects of oppression, fear, and pain that rack the meditator's being. It leads him or her to desire to leap free of all the forms of thought involved in the wheel of individual existence. The meditator is now ready for the great supreme insight.[10]

We see, then, that the ultimate meaning of the Night Passage is positive. That meaning is contained in the words surrender and love. The Dark Night is, ideally, a process in which all shreds of ego are surrendered in love to the Ultimate that no hindrance to union with it may remain.

Supreme Union

The supreme goal of mysticism has been described in many ways. But all emphasize that it is an ineffable state in which the seeker realizes ultimate transformation, unconditioned freedom, and a sense of perfect integration of self with Ultimate Reality.

The yogic tradition speaks of it as *nirvikalpa samadhi,* a *samadhi* out of which a person does not return, for it is continuous and absolute, in contrast to *savikalpa samadhi,* intermittent unitive meditation. The difference is that between a bucket emptied once and for all into the ocean, so that its waters would be irretrievable, and a pail simply dipped into the broader sea and then withdrawn again. The Upanishads in many places speak of it as a contemplative discovery that atman, the innermost self, is Brahman, God—that "thou art that." In the Mandukya Upanishad it is also a fourth state of consciousness that integrates into one and goes beyond the other three: waking, dreaming, and sleeping without dreams.

For Plotinus, the great Neoplatonist philosopher in the West and intellectual father of much of Christian, Jewish, and Muslim mysticism, the dominant images are of oneness and vision. It cannot be better put than in his own words:

> When the Soul turns away from visible things and makes itself as beautiful as possible and becomes like the One; (the manner of preparation and adornment is known to those who practice it;) and seeing the One suddenly appearing in itself, for there is nothing between, nor are they any longer two, but one; for you cannot distinguish between them, while the vision lasts; it is that union of which the union of earthly lovers, who wish to blend their being with each other, is a copy.

In words that anticipate Saint Teresa's enjoyment in the unitive state without discrete knowledge of what is being enjoyed, the Greek goes on to say:

> The Soul is no longer conscious of the body, and cannot tell whether it is a man or a living being or anything real at all . . . after having sought the One, it finds itself in its presence, it goes to meet it and contemplates it instead of itself. What itself is when it gazes, it has no leisure to see.[11]

The same motif of contemplative vision easily correlates with the theme of supernatural light. According to the Hesychast mystic Saint Gregory Palamas, whose Greek Orthodox school developed Neoplatonism in a Christianized direction, it is through light—the divine energies —that God communicates himself insofar as he can be known to the mystic. This uncreated, supernatural light, of which physical light is only a pale hint, is sometimes called the Light of Tabor, referring to the radiance seen by the disciples in Christ at the Transfiguration. This light gives a certain knowledge—*gnosis*—which in turn elevates the seeker to mystical union with what is known, or, in the bold but profound term of the Eastern Christian mystics, to deification.[12]

For others, also in the Neoplatonic tradition, this Light is so strangely bright some describe it as dark and trackless, at least in comparison with the false lights and stifling clarity of the ordinary world. Thus, the great Flemish mystic Jan van Ruysbroeck (1293–1381) could say:

> If the spirit would see God with God in this Divine Light without means . . . he must have lost himself in a Waylessness and in a Darkness, in which all contemplative men wander in fruition and wherein they never again can find themselves in a creaturely way. In the abyss of this darkness, in which the loving spirit has died to itself, there begin the manifestation of God and eternal life.[13]

While the ideas are not identical, they remind us of the Buddhist Nirvana, also defined negatively except when the image of rising light is used. Nirvana is where there is no "this world" or "world beyond, no moon or sun, no coming nor standing nor going; it is unborn, uncompounded, deathless, and the end of all suffering." The seeker attains it in the perfect equilibrium of nonpartiality and nonattachment to even the subtlest supports, even the idea of God itself as something to be grasped.

Yet at the same time, spiritual masters emphasize that love is the *sine qua non* of the unitive state. It is a tracklessness in which the individual goes with empty, nonclinging hands because he or she has surrendered the self in love to the Infinite. Before tasting Nirvana, the Buddhist streamwinner will have attained unlimited compassion. This compassion is the supreme virtue that is the necessary ethical expression of a true understanding of egolessness, the dependent co-origination of all things, and nonattachment. *The Cloud of Unknowing* tells us that love is the way and the end of the journey past knowledge in which it seeks to guide us. Ruysbroeck informs us that the contemplative lost in the Waylessness and Darkness must "inwardly cleave to God, with adhering intention and love, even as a burning and glowing fire which can never more be quenched. As long as he feels himself to be in this state, he is able to contemplate."

Saint John of the Cross, supreme singer of mystic love and union, begins the commentaries of his *Spiritual Canticle* by speaking of the soul, desiring to be united with its divine Spouse, setting "forth her love's anxieties, reproaching Him for His absence, the more so because, being wounded by her love, for the which she has abandoned all things, yea even herself, she has still to suffer the absence of her Beloved and is not yet loosed from her mortal flesh that she may be able to have fruition of Him in the glory of eternity."[14] Yet at the end of the same book, full of an exquisite understanding of the nuances of love human and divine, we find that the divine Lover too is wounded by love of the soul, but he is able to draw the soul to Himself because her love-wound has isolated her inwardly from all else in anticipation of the Bridegroom's coming. For lovers like most to be together and isolated from all other society. In much the same vein, some mystics have spoken of an experience of spiritual nuptials or marriage to the divine Lover.[15]

What these and many other verbal symbols of the unitive life indicate is its unconditional quality, its achievement of the mystic's ultimate transformation, and its freedom endowed with power.

The ocean of light, the waylessness, the landmark-free realm of the Divine Dark or of Nirvana—all indicate that the experience is of unconditioned reality, from out of which the experiencer now speaks as a person immersed in it. Indeed, he or she is in it and it is in him or her; the two have become one. This is the ultimate transformation of the individual, for it (ideally speaking) crosses the most unimaginable barrier we face, that between the finite and the unlimited, the conditioned and the unconditioned. In unitive consciousness, we are one with the other side.

This transit gives the mystic an equally unimaginable freedom. Many are the accounts of those who, isolated by preoccupation with the aching wound of love, have upon the consummation of that love returned to the world with serenity and power to spread love. Saint Catherine of Siena was for three years a recluse full of austerities, but upon her mystic marriage left her cell to greet her family and then enter on an active career in which she deeply influenced the politics of Europe. The individual truly caught up in divine union can undertake an active life with innocence and confidence, or this exalted spirit can remain in relative retirement, but serve as a spiritual magnet to the world.

The return of the mystic to the world, then, is an important possibility in the paradigm of the spiritual path. It is vividly portrayed in the East in the famous Zen oxherding pictures, a series of allegorical paintings illustrating the path through Zen enlightenment. After the novice achieves mastery, indicated by his finding and taming an ox, he experiences Nirvana—the void, a single white round circle. After this stage we find him back on a road, approaching the gates of a city "with bliss-bearing hands," but so joyous and unself-conscious that he tarries to laugh, dance, and play with children on the way. For him even the highway and the entrance to the city are framed by the "gateless gate." He needs no map or compass, because love calls him with equal visibility in every direction, and he has only to choose between one joy and another.

Unitive Philosophy

As we have indicated, the spiritual path with these five stages may be as much an ideal paradigm as a concrete psychological reality. Many very devout people have had other experiences; many traditional spiritual authorities, such as those of the Eastern Orthodox Church, leave out elements such as the Dark Night of the Soul in its Western form and otherwise modify it. Yet if any feature of this path is universal among religious traditions with an idea of a mystic way, it is that it begins with purgative discipline and ends with a unitive state or its equivalent. The grand course finishes in ultimate transformation, immersion in unconditioned reality, and full freedom.

However we interpret the unitive state and its joy, the accounts of that condition and the human ideal it represents have given rise to certain philosophical perspectives. They endeavor to articulate a world in which the unitive state is the highest and most cognitive human condition, the one in which people most see and know what really is. These philosophies describe in metaphysical and analytic terms a universe in which the mystic's infinite One is the basis of all that is and the realms of multiplicity are delusive—and the One can be found by searching the roots of consciousness.

This outlook is what Margaret Lewis Furse has called mysticism as a world view. As she rightly points out, philosophy that embodies the mystical world view is not the same as mystical experience and is not necessarily based on first-hand mystical experience. In the West, most mystical philosophy can be traced back to Plotinus; it may, then, be derived from mystical experiences nearly two thousand years old, and even that master claimed to have had only two or three experiences of the highest, most unitive sort. Nor have we direct evidence that so marvellous an exponent of the mystical world view as Meister Eckhart had deep mystical experiences, however splendidly he presents the metaphysics and the deep and radical freedom of the unitive state.

Furse summarizes the most common propositions of the mystical world view in these terms.

Reality is a One beyond all apparent separateness, and this One is ultimately indescribable. But the self has an innate kinship with the One—the soul or divine spark is really a pure reflector or concentrate of this reality—and so has an intuitive knowledge of it, which can be developed. All true morality is in harmony with the One, and a person can gain deeper knowledge and experience of it by ascetic discipline. Perceptively, Furse shows that the mystic seems first to be discontinuous with environment reality, for much sets him or her apart, but this seeming isolation is for the sake of a more ultimate continuity.[16]

What of the philosophical meaning of mystical language. Is it only a mass of words about that which cannot be spoken? Frederick Streng has reminded us that the great Mahayana Buddhist text, the *Perfection of Wisdom in Eight Thousand Lines,* speaks of three functions that words have to a bodhisattva, who is supremely one in the unitive state. They are to explain, to evoke a feeling of joy, and to cleanse thought.[17] It need hardly be necessary to interpret to the perceptive reader, who has followed us thus far, how the words of mysticism, whether of philosophy or experience or the path, all serve at least one of those functions, though now one and now another.

Notes

[1]Evelyn Underhill, *Mysticism* (London: Methuen & Co., 1911), pp. 203–7.

[2]Underhill, *Mysticism,* p. x.

[3]Underhill, *Mysticism,* pp. 219–20.

[4]Vladimir Lossky, *The Mystical Theology of the Eastern Church* (London: James Clarke, 1957), p. 204.

[5]The Fourteenth Dalai Lama, *An Introduction to Buddhism* (New Delhi, India: Tibet House), 1965.

[6]Daniel Goleman, *The Varieties of the Meditative Experience* (New York: E. P. Dutton & Co., Inc., 1977), pp. 27–28.

[7]*The Life of Saint Teresa,* trans. J. M. Cohen (Harmondsworth, England: Penguin Books, 1957), p. 118.

[8]*The Life of Saint Teresa,* p. 122.

[9]Saint John of the Cross, *The Dark Night of the Soul,* trans. David Lewis (London: T. Baker, 1908), pp. 84–85.

[10]Goleman, *Varieties of the Meditative Experience,* pp. 28–30.

[11]W. R. Inge, *The Philosophy of Plotinus* (London: Longmans, Green, and Co., 1918), II, 134.

[12]Lossky, *Mystical Theology of the Eastern Church,* p. 220.

[13]Jan van Ruysbroeck, *The Adornment of the Spiritual Marriage,* trans. C. A. Wynschenck (London: J. M. Dent & Sons, 1916), pp. 169–70.

[14]Saint John of the Cross, *Spiritual Canticle,* trans. E. Allison Peers (Garden City, N.Y.: Image Books, 1961), p. 49.

[15]Saint John of the Cross, *Spiritual Canticle,* p. 454.

[16]Margaret Lewis Furse, "Mysticism: Classic Modern Interpreters and their Premise of Continuity," *Anglican Theological Review,* LX: 2 (April 1978), 180–93.

[17]Frederick J. Streng, "Language and Mystical Awareness," in *Mysticism and Philosophical Analysis,* ed. Steven T. Katz (New York: Oxford University Press, 1978), p. 154.

Postscript: Mysticism and the Future of Religion

9

What is the meaning of mysticism, not only for the religious past, but for the present and future of religion? This query is intimately bound up with a search for the ultimate source and value of self-validating ecstatic experience realized in a religious context. Some would say that mysticism, like ritual, is part of a lingering archaic, even reptilian, mode of mental activity that evolution is gradually replacing with more rational and situational ways of responding to the universe. Others would see in mysticism the spark of authentic nonsensory cognition that actualizes our cosmic identity and foretells inner or outer evolution by making us, for a moment, what we were ultimately meant to be.

Sorting out this quandary is not just a simple matter of choosing A or B, for as we have tried to show, mysticism is not just ecstatic experience, however cognitive. Instead mysticism is this experience plus interpretation, an interpretation fired by associations and feelings evoked by the experience but drawn from the setting.

The real transitions involving mysticism in the foreseeable future will probably not be in psycho-biological evolution, but in social evolution as it affects the interpretation of mystical ecstasy. Biology changes very slowly, but society, language, and religious symbol systems change rapidly. This means, as it has in the past, that mystical experience will not so much be the future of religion as it will energize and validate those changes that social evolution is bringing about. The intrinsic nature of mysticism, of course, has its own ways of influencing religious structures and behavior, as we have seen. But other forces usually affect these factors, which in turn influence the interpretation of mystical experience.

For this reason we must receive with considerable caution the common ideas that if religion became more mystical and less dogmatic it would be better, and that mysticism is the true spiritual core of all religion. While a valid case can be argued for some of the assumptions underlying these propositions, they are highly ambiguous unless we take setting into account. Depending upon setting, what people regard as mystical experience can as well release the demons of war and hate in the name of a spiritual cause. For the self-validating nature of mysticism is a two-edged sword: it might enable the wondrous experience of transcedence, yet validate the separation of its associations from the control of reason. Therein comes the dark side of mysticism. Those who release self-validating experiences from the supervision of reason and social control neglect these controls to the peril of all. The danger may, strictly speaking, lie not in the flash of ecstasy but in the feelings and symbols associated with it. In practice, however, often little separation of the two occurs. The self-validating experience easily becomes the false romanticism of exalting feelings as cognitive and guides to action over reason or tradition. One then is likely to evoke the mood of the Nazi madness or of solipsist fanaticism of Charles Manson.

Idealization of the role of mysticism in society should also be tempered by an understanding of the conservative impact of mysticism in practice. Except when coupled with radical movements of a revolutionary type, mysticism easily works as counterproductive to social change. This is true even in ostensibly radical sectarianisms. In the long run it tends to reinforce orthodoxy or to make sectarianisms into orthodoxies, as the normative religion incorporates mystics as validating saints, as it did Sufis and Franciscans. A great interest in mysticism in a society inevitably focuses energies on subjectivity that otherwise might have been used to effect desired outward changes. This inward focusing obtains whether the mysticism is among the upper and middle classes, who are mostly likely to go for voguish sorts of self-realization, or among oppressed classes, who find in mystical movements distraction from their condition and strength to endure. Yet none of this is inevitably true; when mystical experience energizes strong and mature personalities moved by compassion and determination, like Catherine of Siena or Gandhi, great societies and the course of history can be changed.

Moreover, mysticism can finally be the only guarantor of any future to religion, because it points to the one undeniable empirical fact in religion, that people report having experiences of ultimacy now as much as ever. Without denying there are sound philosophical and social reasons for religious affirmations apart from subjective experience, we suppose that given all the alternatives to a religious world view now available, it is hard to conceive of religion persisting without continual mystical experience on the part of some.

This is not to say that religion will necessarily become *more* mystical, whatever that would mean precisely, but that insofar as it perseveres, the mystical element will be present and will point to the continuity of religion in all times and places.

Yet this statement is paradoxical, as all statements about mysticism seem to be in the end. For we must not overlook a theme that has surfaced from time to time in this study: the perhaps unexpected but frequent tendency of mysticism to lead finally to a secularization of religion. In writers like Eckhart, Woods, and the Zen masters we have noted that pursuit of the mystical experience of oneness and transcendence can lead to a loss of distinction between sacred and profane, between the religious world of God as ordinarily understood and the world that simply "is." Thus, for the mystic the natural world can become divine, and the "religious" realm withers away. Does this mean, then, that mysticism is really the enemy of religion and that, if it were more and more to flourish, it would not continue to validate religion but would undermine it?

The answer is simple: it would do both, for it has always done both, and we do not see any reason to think it will be different in the future. Mysticism, as the basic empirical and experiential fact of religion, both supports and undercuts religion (at least in its doctrinal, liturgical, and institutional forms). This dual operation is a major factor keeping religion in a continual state of tension and flux—however ironical that may seem to those seeking their opposites in mysticism.

The end of the mystic quest may be the validation by experience of religious reality. It may also be not merely the raptures of prayer or the exaltations of contemplation, but (as with Eckhart) the final attainment of an ordinary life without "God" as an Other or even as a concept.

We might ask then, Why bother? What is the point of mysticism at all? Why not just live an ordinary life?

The celebrated Zen teacher D. T. Suzuki once told before an audience the story of the old Chinese master, Ch'ing-yuan, who said that before he studied Zen, he saw mountains as mountains and waters as waters. When he had made some progress, he no longer saw mountains as mountains and waters as waters. But when he got to the very heart of Zen, he again saw mountains as mountains and waters as waters. A questioner then asked what was the difference between the first and second seeing of mountains as mountains and waters as waters. No difference at all, Suzuki said, except the second time the master was walking a little bit off the ground.

Even if mysticism runs beyond ordinary religion to place an ordinary "unreligious" life a little bit off the ground, the tension it creates for religion can facilitate the perseverence of religion. In the end, we conclude, mysticism and religion are uneasy but inseparable colleagues who, like the mirrors of Fa Tsang's hall, reflect each other.

Index